A
Dream
COME TRUE

A *Dream* COME TRUE

JAMES RYLE

CREATION HOUSE
BOOKS ABOUT SPIRIT-LED LIVING
ORLANDO, FLORIDA

Creation House
Strang Communications Company
600 Rinehart Road
Lake Mary, FL 32746

Belinda, you are my most cherished dream. Anna, David, Jonathan and Rachel — may your dreams exceed the reach of your father's, and may you bring even greater glory to Christ and His kingdom in all you say and do.

Beloved friends who call me Pastor — may the world come to know the love you have for the Lord Jesus, the faith you have in His Word, the zeal you have for worship, the affection you have for the body of Christ at large, and the passion you have for saving souls and redeeming lives. You are an exemplary congregation, worthy of reproduction around the world!

Bill Snell, Walt Roberson, Greg Fitch — Champions to the core; faithful to the call. I love you.

Bill and Lyndi, Randy and Holly, Gary and Carrie, Dale and Liz — did you ever know that you're my heroes? You're everything I wished I could be. I can fly higher than an eagle. For you are the wind beneath my wings.[1]

To the gifted staff at Creation House — Wow! What a difference your input made in the outcome of this project. Tom and Deborah — ask Steve for a raise!

Dear Reader, thank you for giving me a chance to help Jesus become your dream come true! I hope to see you in heaven.

C O N T E N T S

t is my delight to offer a brief introduction on behalf of James Ryle. This man of God has been a wonderful blessing to my family and our community. I know James as a pastor, confidant, mentor and friend. He's also a fairly decent golfer.

Our relationship developed as the result of a remarkable dream that James shared with me prior to the 1989 college football season while I was head coach at the University of Colorado. The dream foretold that our team, the Colorado Buffaloes, would have a golden season resulting in being ranked number one in the nation and that I, as head coach, would be given the Coach of the Year honors at the season's conclusion. Knowing that James had very little exposure to college football and was hardly versed to be making such predictions, I was personally more than a little dubious. Still, his innocent exuberance and seemingly undauntable faith buoyed my own secret hopes that such a thing would happen. After all, what football coach wouldn't like to believe that such a dream might come true?

As amazing as it may seem, the dream did come true! After our first game of the season, a victory over the Texas Longhorns, the Denver Post ran a story with the following headline: "CU Buffs Have Golden Season Debut." James and I both were stunned to read the words he had seen in a dream actually printed in the newspaper. Little did either of us know what God had in store.

The season unfolded and gave us more than our share of thrills as we watched with wonder how God seemed to be proving the dream true with each successive game. A deep bond of brotherhood was forged between James and me in those joyful moments of seeing the hand of the Lord bless us. A favorite scripture came to summarize our feelings over that wonderful season: "All that we have accomplished you have done for us" (Is. 26:12, NIV). The season concluded with a rousing victory over Iowa State, followed by a special edition publication titled "The Golden Season." Our team was ranked #1, and I was honored with the NCAA Coach of the Year award.

That unforgettable season did much to turn my heart toward God with greater sensitivity to hearing His voice. If God would speak in a dream about a football season, what other more pressing matters might He address if we would only listen? The vision for Promise Keepers became more believable to me as a result of learning to regard the thoughts and impressions which come into our lives from God. I knew that God was blessing my life, and that it had to be for something far more important than football. He wanted me to be a man of integrity in my walk with God, with my family and with my church, and to encourage other men to do the same.

Since 1989 I have gained much admiration for the grace of God given to my pastor. He is truly an extraordinary communicator. Whether it be from the pulpit on Sunday morning, an adjoining seat on an airplane en route to an away game, over breakfast before a game, speaking to the coaches and team in chapel services, or lying prostrate side by side in prayerful worship — invariably, James will have some fascinating bit of insight about the Lord or the Scripture that captures our hearts with a greater love for Jesus. You will find your own heart stirred to a deeper commitment to God as you read what he has written.

James Ryle is vulnerable, unpretentious, loving, generous, courageous, faithful and coachable. I admire him greatly for these things. Yet the most valuable gift by which I personally have benefited has been the godly counsel that James has given me at crucial times in my life. No matter how difficult a situation may have been, James has always been able to pinpoint the exact spiritual principle or biblical example which was profoundly relevant to the need. I have become a better man of God by following his counsel.

This is why I am eager for you to read this book. James brings his unique, God-given ability for explaining truth and applies it to the mysterious and often misunderstood subject of dreams and visions. The results are inspiring for believer and non-believer alike! I commend this book to you with complete confidence that Almighty God will stir your heart with faith to believe that your dreams can come true whenever they are focused on Jesus Christ.

Bill McCartney
Boulder, Colorado, February 1995

*"Your young men will see
truth from God in visions
and your old men will know
about the truth from God
through their dreams. "*

Acts 2:17
A Translator's Handbook on the Acts of the Apostles
by Barclay M. Newman and Eugene A. Nida

I t was about three o'clock in the morning. I lay in my bed for a little while thinking about what I had just dreamed. It was too fascinating to forget and too real to dismiss. I quietly got out of bed and went into my study to seek the Lord for an answer. As I read the Bible during those early morning hours, the Holy Spirit caused my heart to soar with excitement over what I discovered. Little did I know that it was but the beginning of a remarkable journey with Jesus into the world of dreams and visions.

Having traversed its wondrous terrain for some time now, with trusted Bible firmly in hand and the blessed Holy Spirit guiding each step along the way, I offer my findings to you with calm assurance that you will be inspired to dream as never before. I am equally certain that the Lord will help you understand some of the mysteries that have puzzled your sleep and preoccupied your waking hours.

My confidence is not self-generated, nor merely experience-based. It derives its boldness from the promises of Scripture. The Lord in faithfulness will fulfill His Word upon which so many have placed their faith — "It shall come to pass in the last days, says God, that I will pour out of My Spirit upon all flesh; your sons and daughters shall prophesy, your young men will see visions, your old men shall dream dreams."[1]

This is a verse with attitude. There is an emphatic and indisputable finality in those two little words: "says God." Peter, speaking under the inspiration of the Holy Spirit on the day of Pentecost, added those two words to Joel's text to make a point which God wants us to note. The argument thereby is removed beyond the bantering opinions of man. Dreams and visions are part of the package of our life in the Spirit, *says God.* Dreams and visions, along with prophesy, will inundate the church in the last days, *says God.* Old and young, male and female, rich and poor, fat and thin, big and small, short and tall, one and all, shall dream dreams and see visions by the ministry of the Holy Spirit for the purpose of affirming God's holy Word and exalting His only Son, Jesus, *says God!* Do you see what I mean? *Attitude.*

A Consensus of Commentary

D.D. Whedon, a respected commentator, turned his talents upon the text of Acts 2:17 and wrote, "After a long withdrawal of miracle and sign, the Baptist's birth was announced by a vision of Zechariah's. Our Savior's birth was heralded by the dreams of Joseph, the vision of Mary, and that of the shepherds. Simeon, Agabus, the Apocalyptist, and others prophesied. All these were in essence concentrated in the Spirit's power bestowed at Pentecost."[2] Of this *power* Matthew Henry said, "Both your young men and your old men shall see visions, and dream dreams, and in them receive divine revelations, to be communicated to the church."[3] The Greek verb which is translated "shall prophesy" signifies not merely to foretell future events but to communicate truth in general under a divine inspiration.

Simon J. Kistemaker, in his exposition of the Acts of the Apostles, said:

God reveals Himself in prophecy, in visions, and in dreams, as the Scriptures repeatedly testify. With the outpouring of the Holy Spirit, all believers, without distinction of gender, age, and social status, receive the wisdom and ability to know God.[4]

Another scholar wrote:

Prophesy, visions, and dreams; the three principal forms assumed by the influences of the Spirit under the old covenant, are exalted in character and united as a whole, when, under the new covenant, the Holy Spirit enters into the heart, and dwells in it.[5]

The great Martin Luther, commenting upon Peter's quote from Joel, expressed his view of dreams and visions with masterful eloquence.

For what are all other gifts, however numerous they may be, in comparison with this gift, when the Spirit of God Himself, the eternal God, descends into our hearts, yea, into our bodies, and dwells in us, governs, guides, and leads us? Thus, with respect to this declaration of the prophet, prophecy, visions and dreams are, in truth, one precious gift, namely, the knowledge of God through Christ, which the Holy Ghost enkindles through the word of the Gospel, and converts into a flame of fire.[6]

Finally, Everett Ferguson noted:

Although early Christianity rejected the profession of divination by dreams as magical meddling in the spirit world, the signifying potential of dreams was affirmed both in scriptural text and in personal experience. Early Christians shared in a widespread cultural attitude toward dreams, an attitude rooted in classical antiquity, that remained virtually unchanged for hundreds of years. Despite the few who scoffed at the attribution of meaning to dreams, or saw demonic agitation at work in them, the majority of writers in late antiquity agreed with

Tertullian's famous dictum that dreams [and visions] were a major source of insight about the divine world.[7]

The Purpose of This Book

There is something about dreams and visions that holds a peculiar fascination with all people. Even the fact that you now hold this book in hand, preparing yourself to explore its pages, gives some indication of your own curiosity in the subject. You are not alone. Virtually *everybody* has at least one dream or vision they can recall rather vividly. It may be a puzzle waiting to be solved, a promise waiting to be realized, or a premonition waiting to happen. The fact that dreams and visions are at the same time both common and yet so unusual could be the reason why we are so eager to find out more about them.

Morton Kelsey conducted a ten-year study on dreams and visions that changed his life.

> I discovered that my dreams were wiser than my well-tuned rational mind and that they gave me warnings when I was in danger. They also described in symbols the disastrous situations in which I found myself. These strange messengers of the night offered suggestions on how to find my way out of my lostness.
>
> When I followed these symbolic suggestions, much of the darkness lifted, and my situation no longer seemed hopeless. Many of my psychological and physical symptoms of distress disappeared. In addition to all this, I found a very personal Being at the heart of reality who cared for me; my theological dry bones were covered with sinew and flesh. And then, as I continued to listen to my dreams, *I experienced the risen Christ in a way that I had not thought possible.*[8]

Of course some have dismissed dreams and visions as being nothing more than a self-induced fantasy. This attitude reveals both the arrogance and the ignorance of those who hold to it. To think that dreams and visions have no meaning or relevance is impertinent in light of both biblical and church history.

Down Through the Ages

From the moment God appeared to Abraham in a vision to the revelation of Jesus Christ to John on the Isle of Patmos, dreams and visions have factored highly in the development of our faith. This being true, how eager then should the serious student of the Word be to recover the richness of biblical insights given on this oft-neglected spiritual blessing. The purpose of this book is to provide biblical teaching on the subject of dreams and visions so as to restore within the heart of all believers a value for this neglected gift of God.

The Bible, the experiences of the early church, the deeper experiences of renowned Christians through the ages and the almost universal interest in dreams and visions today — all these join together to make a strong appeal to our hearts and minds. There *is* more to dreams and visions that we perhaps have thought. It's time we gave them their due and listened to see if God is reaching out to us through them.

On a More Personal Note

Winston Churchill said, "Writing a book is an adventure. To begin with it is a toy and an amusement. Then it becomes a master, and then a tyrant. And just when you have reconciled yourself to your servitude — you kill the monster and fling him to the public!" By this you can appreciate the task undertaken to place this volume in your hands. I'm *glad* that you have it; yea, ecstatic!

As for this book, it is born of study, experience and opportunity. *Study,* in that I have devoted several years of my life to the spiritual quest of showing myself approved unto God as a workman that needs not be ashamed; one who rightfully handles the Word of truth. *Experience,* in that I myself have had many significant dreams and visions from the Lord which have proved helpful and true over the years. And *opportunity,* in that now, more than ever, a book on this subject could be of great benefit to the church as we press ever onward in these last days unto the great and final day of the Lord.

I humbly and happily, therefore, offer my findings on the topic of dreams and visions into the great library of history. Perhaps this volume may be found of good use in the hands of my peers as well as those who will follow after me in the days to come. For should the

Lord tarry, then the days ahead will surely be filled with even more signs and wonders than those which are behind us or at present. Sons and daughters will dream as never before. Visionaries will speak as the oracles of God. And the infallible Word of God will be magnified by the power of the Holy Spirit.

My Prayer

O God, let those who know Your voice and who love Your Word speak, and may this work stand in defense of their faith against a swarming company of wicked men who would strip from Christendom all vestige of power and revelation! May the nay-sayers find themselves silenced by the simple wisdom with which You have graced this work. May the sooth-sayers find themselves exposed by its light. May the gain-sayers find themselves out of business by its success. And may the yea-sayers be fully empowered by its inspiration!

O Lord, may it be that an anointing will abide upon this work so that those who read it are not simply held with interest for the moment, but are inspired with faith for the day in which they live and the night in which they sleep. May You be pleased to use this book to bless the dreamers in Your kingdom with higher vision and truer insight into Your holy Word than ever before. May this book bring all who read it to the Bible, that the Bible might bring all men unto You through Jesus Christ our Lord.

May this book terrify the devil, stupefy the rebellious, mystify the world, pacify the critics, ratify the covenant, edify the church, magnify the Word, and glorify the Lord! Amen.

Pastor James Ryle
Boulder, Colorado January 1995

MIDNIGHT IN A CARPENTER'S SHOP

Mary looked unusually radiant as she came walking toward Joseph. His heart leapt within him at the sight of his bride-to-be. She seemed to him to be more full of life than ever before. "Joseph, my beloved, I have something I must tell you," Mary said. Joseph smiled broadly and gave her his undivided attention, captivated by the light in her eyes. In the following few moments as he listened carefully to his love, his world came crashing down like the walls of Jericho. Mary was pregnant, and Joseph was *not* the father!

Joseph's heart was broken, and his mind raced with a hundred questions. "Who *is* the father? How could Mary have done such a thing? What will I tell my friends? What will the family have to say? What is to become of our marriage plans?" It's true that Mary had said something about an angel, but Joseph didn't really hear much after she told him she was with child. Everything went kind of foggy at that point.

He left Mary and wandered off into the night, trying to sort out his options. The hard choice, according to the Law, would be to stone Mary for her unfaithfulness or, at the very least, put her to an open shame before her family and friends by denouncing her as an adulteress. Joseph's anger may have driven him to such measures had not his love for Mary been so strong.

He was an honorable man and thought of a quiet, private settlement beyond the public eye, keeping Mary from scandal. Still, the more he tried to work through his feelings, the greater became his overwhelming sense of despair. It was a night he thought would never end.

Like many men do when faced with problems, Joseph made his way to his workshop to tinker on some of his projects. He fumbled around with a couple of wooden beams, a hammer and three large nails — but he couldn't think of any use for them, so he set them aside for a later day. He shuffled aimlessly about the carpenter shop, whittling away the time, torn between sorrow and rage. The candle burned low, and the corner cot beckoned to him. Joseph curled under the blanket, sighed once or twice, and closed his eyes. It didn't take much; they were almost swollen shut from crying.

Whether it was the fatigue of a hard day's work or the emotional drain of such disturbing news, or perhaps a numbing blend of both, Joseph found it difficult to get any sleep. He would doze off for a moment, only to be startled awake by the night noise that visits all of our homes: the creaking walls, the drip of water, the brush of tree branches, the incessant tingling of wind chimes or the bark of a neighbor's stupid dog.

Sometime in the early morning hours, when an eerie stillness settled upon the city, Joseph finally drifted into a deep sleep. It was then that the angel of the Lord visited him in a dream and said, "Joseph son of David, do not be afraid to take Mary home as your wife, because what is conceived in her is from the Holy Spirit. She will give birth to a son, and you are to give him the name Jesus, because he will save his people from their sins."[1]

Joseph woke up from the dream and walked into history. He followed the angel's instructions explicitly, and he was happy to do so, for he truly loved Mary. And he, most privileged of all men, was the one who first spoke the blessed name of Jesus.

Jesus. His name was revealed in a dream, and knowing Him is a dream come true.

What the Prophets Did Not Know

Do you realize how amazing this is? Think of all the prophets who exerted every ounce of spiritual insight they possessed, attempting to look into the future so as to uncover the Redeemer's name.[2] They had been able to accurately foretell many significant facts about Him — the specific tribe to which He would belong (Judah), the exact family line through which He would be born (David), even the actual place of His birth (Bethlehem). They also had a good sense about what He would do once He came (preach the gospel to the poor, etc.) — but *none* of them knew His name.

Isaiah gave it the best shot of all the prophets: "For unto us a child is born, unto us a son is given: and the government shall be upon his shoulder: and his name shall be called Wonderful, Counselor, The mighty God, The everlasting Father, The Prince of Peace" (Is. 9:6). Close, *really* close, but not exact. Isaiah knew that the Savior would be born of a virgin, but even he couldn't discern His name.

How fascinating that a Jewish carpenter woke up from a dream one day and said, "His name shall be called Jesus." Joseph had no credentials that qualified him as a prophet. To our knowledge Joseph wrote no books, preached no sermons, made no significant contribution that would in any way cause us to give him more than a passing thought — and yet, for two thousand years, people all over the world have united in praise of the name that was revealed to Joseph in a dream. The name of Jesus! Every time you say His name, you validate the fact that God speaks in dreams.

Dreams and the Birth of Jesus

As it turns out, Joseph was quite the dreamer. No less than four times we are told that Joseph dreamed:

- Take Mary and name the child Jesus (Matt. 1:20-21)
- Flee to Egypt with Mary and the child (Matt. 2:13-15)
- Return to the land of Israel (Matt. 2:19-21)
- Dwell in the town of Nazareth (Matt. 2:22-23)

Joseph followed the instructions given to him by the angel in each of the dreams. In so doing he not only preserved the life of the child Jesus, but he also fulfilled long-standing prophecies concerning the Christ.

In addition to the four dreams given to Joseph, Matthew also tells us that God warned the Magi in a dream that they should not return to Herod.[3] They, like Joseph, obeyed the dream, and Jesus was kept from the wicked ruler. Thank God that Joseph and the wise men did not regard their dreams as nonsense!

And Thus the New Testament Begins

The interest of the Bible student in the subject of dreams and visions is immediately stirred in the opening pages of the New Testament. The Gospel of Matthew records five supernatural dreams which God gave to men, providing them guidance into His will. This is a fact that is often passed over in commentaries.

The inclusion of dreams at the introduction of the gospel, along with the account of Pilate's wife at the time of the crucifixion, are enigmatic, a mystery to teachers and students alike. Nowhere else in the New Testament is the subject of dreams or visions spoken of with any sense of authority. We are not taught by Jesus, nor the apostles, any particular precept concerning dreams or visions.

Nevertheless, provided throughout the historical record of the New Testament and Old Testament alike, are several notable examples of God guiding people through dreams and visions. The enigma is this: the Bible doesn't teach about dreams and visions in any systematic manner, yet by giving many significant examples, it validates their existence and use by God as a means of communicating to man.

J. M. Lower wrote, "The use of dreams and visions in the Bible seems consistent with the manifest nature of God. Throughout the Scriptures, God is declared as revealing Himself and making His ways known through chosen men."[4] However, we must realize that no special sacredness or significance is ascribed by the Scriptures to dreams in general. No class or variety of dreams is recommended by the Bible for our scrutiny that we may through this or that method of interpretation seek guidance from them for our lives.

But someone might ask, "If dreams and visions are so important, shouldn't the Bible say more about them?" James Hastings makes an excellent point on this question.

> The superstitious attitude characteristic of the whole hea-
> then world, which regards *all* dreams as omens and seeks
> to utilize them for purposes of divination, receives no
> support whatever from the biblical writers. Yet, dreams
> are a recognized mode of divine communication, and
> dream-revelations may be presumed therefore to have
> occurred throughout the whole history of revelation,
> even though comparatively few are actually recorded.[5]

The Bible merely affirms that God has on certain, specific occasions, in making His will known to man, chosen to approach them
through the medium of their night-visions, and has through these
warned them of danger, awakened them to a sense of wrongdoing,
communicated to them His will, or made known His purposes. And
so we are told in a matter-of-fact manner, without any qualifying
remarks, that the angel of the Lord appeared unto Joseph in a dream.
It happened.

The Angel of the Lord

If you read again the story of Jesus' birth you will notice that the
angel of the Lord makes no less than four startling appearances:
First to Zechariah as he is standing before the altar of incense in the
temple; next to Mary in her humble dwelling; then to Joseph in a
dream; and finally to the shepherds in the field keeping watch over
their flocks by night. Of these four appearances, only one happened
in a dream. Why?

Why didn't the angel appear to Joseph like he did to everybody
else? It could seem to us that Joseph may have been cheated a bit. I
mean, wouldn't it be better to actually see an angel standing right in
front of you, telling you plainly what God wanted you to know,
rather than merely having a dream? A dream can be doubted and
dismissed, but an angel standing before you with the majesty of
heaven beaming from his countenance and the authority of God
issuing from his lips — well, let's just say you're not likely to roll
over and go back to sleep!

Why did the angel of the Lord visit Joseph in a dream? So many
of us wake up from a dream, scratch our heads, shrug our shoulders

and say something like, "Man, that was sure weird," and then go on with our day as planned. Men and women of average good sense, in Bible times as well as today, generally regard dreams as typical of that which is fleeting and unreliable. "Like a dream he flies away, no more to be found, banished like a vision of the night."[6] And, "Their present life is only a dream! They will awaken to the truth as one awakens from a dream of things that never really were!"[7]

The vanity and deceptiveness of dreams is proverbial. Solomon wrote, "Dreaming instead of doing is foolishness, and there is ruin in a flood of empty words; fear God instead."[8] "The hungry man may dream that he eats, but his soul continues empty; the thirsty man may dream that he drinks, but he remains faint."[9] The following saying from the Apocrypha sums up the modern view in a sentence: "Whoso regardeth dreams is like him that catcheth at a shadow, and followeth after the wind."[10] Indeed, many have spent their lives chasing after dreams and never catching them. And so asks the poet Wordsworth, "Whither is fled the visionary gleam? Where is it now, the glory and the dream?"[11]

Since dreams are so unreliable, wouldn't it have been better if the angel had just appeared to Joseph and told him the news? Why do it in a dream? We need only to look at the three times the angel did appear, and there we find a possible answer.

How Do I Know It's True?

In the temple Zechariah was startled and filled with doubt, exasperating Gabriel with his intolerable unbelief: "How can I be sure of this?"

"I am Gabriel!" the angel protested. "I stand in the very presence of God. It was he who sent me to you with this good news!"[12] Did Zechariah really think that Gabriel would actually stand in the holy place and tell a lie? Gabriel was flabbergasted! Angels are often astonished at the incredible dullness of sinful man.

Mary, in her home, was frightened and filled with confusion, and the angel had to patiently explain to her how God would do the impossible. This differed significantly from the incident with Zechariah. He and his wife, Elizabeth, had long been asking for a child and were being given the answer to their prayers, but Mary was a virgin. She had honest misgivings about the angel's announcement and was rightly deserving of some explanation. The angel answered, "The Holy Spirit will come upon you, and the power of the Most High will overshadow you. So the holy one to be born will be called the Son of God."[13]

The shepherds in the fields were terrified and filled with astonishment, having to be consoled before they could be directed to seek for the child in Bethlehem. "Fear not: for, behold, I bring you good tidings of great joy, which shall be to all people. For unto you is born this day in the city of David a Savior, which is Christ the Lord. And this shall be a sign unto you; Ye shall find the babe wrapped in swaddling clothes, lying in a manger."[14]

In each instance the angel was initially distracted from his mission by having to overcome the human resistance to his presence through unbelief, confusion or fear. But when the angel came to Joseph in a dream, Joseph had no response whatsoever! There's not much you can do in a dream, other than *have* it. The angel appeared in the dream, delivered the message and left without his feathers ruffled. No hassle, no fear, no doubts and no arguments from Joseph. *Hmmm.* Maybe the Lord speaks to us in dreams and visions in order to bypass our natural disposition to debate the things of God!

Concerning this angelic message to Joseph, Edersheim writes,

> The fact that such an announcement came to Joseph in a dream would dispose him all the more readily to receive it. There were among the Jews three things that were popularly regarded as signs of divine favor: 'A good king, a good year, and a good dream.' In fact, so general was the belief in the significance of dreams that it gave rise to a popular saying, 'If any one sleeps seven days without dreaming (or rather remembering his dreams for interpretation), call him wicked — as one not remembered by God.[15]

Augustine and the Question of Dreams

Augustine responded to a question asked by his dear friend, Nebridius, concerning the means whereby heavenly powers revealed things through dreams during sleep.

> The question is a great one, and, as your own prudence

must convince you, would require, in order to its being satisfactorily answered, not a mere letter, but a full oral discussion or a whole treatise. I shall try, however, knowing as I do your talents, to throw out a few germs of thought which may shed light on this question, in order that you may either complete the exhaustive treatment of the subject by your own efforts, or at least not despair of the possibility of this important matter being investigated with satisfactory results.[16]

Clearly Augustine did not consider that dreams and visions were inconsequential — mere mental fancies to be dismissed as having no relevance to a life of faith and holiness. Rather, he regarded them with measured reverence, emphasizing the importance of handling their discussion with patience, wisdom and care. Should we not follow his example and do the same?

Charles Spurgeon, in a sermon about a dream he had, said,

We must take care that we do not neglect heavenly monitions through fear of being considered visionary; we must not be staggered even by the dread of being styled fanatical, or out of our minds. For to stifle a thought from God is no small sin.[17]

God's Neglected Gift

Dreams and visions fill the pages of Scripture and are generously strewn throughout church history. But for the past few hundred years very little serious attention has been given to this subject at all. It seems that dreams and visions have become God's neglected gift! In 1968 Morton T. Kelsey, former professor at Notre Dame and an Episcopal clergyman, wrote a ground-breaking book on dreams titled *God, Dreams and Revelation*. In it he said, "Finding a Christian today who pays attention to dreams is unusual."[18] That was almost thirty years ago, and there has been little change from then until now. Why is so little said about something that is so vital and enriching to a life of faith?

Our Western world-view is prohibitive to much of what occurs outside the realm of science and reason. Yet, inasmuch as dreams and visions do in fact occur, science has been pressed to offer its opinion on the subject. This is rather surprising given the fact that science cannot adequately even tell us what sleeping is. How then can it explain dreams?

Dreams are generally regarded as psychological, emotional, stress-related activities of the mind that occur during sleep. Dreams are merely one of the ways that the nervous system reacts to physical stimuli. Dreams are the rehashing of yesterday's forgotten experiences. Some say that dreaming is a meaningless occurrence, while others see dreams as the key to unlocking the secrets of the human personality. On and on it goes.

These are typical of the comments to be found among the sundry scientific explanations for the existence of dreaming. Yet never in the scientific view are dreams deemed to be spiritual. Never would it be allowed by science that God is the author of the dream. Certainly not. Nor are we ever encouraged by science and reason to seek religious meanings to the dreams that we do have.

While we might expect science to be so predictably detached from something so potentially divine, it is astounding to find that so many within the church are equally indifferent to the purposes of God in dreams and visions. Many Christians today seem to think that the idea of God speaking to them in a dream is ludicrous. Have we as Christians in today's world become so fashioned by it that we prefer reason over faith, mind power over spiritual wisdom, the opinion of man over the teachings of Scripture? God forbid!

How tragic and absurd that we limit our faith within the borders of our own power and perceptions. Tragic because of what we relinquish by rejecting the spiritual work of God accomplished through dreams, and absurd because of the overwhelming body of evidence both in the Scriptures as well as throughout history testifying to the significant role dreams and visions have played in the lives of truly great men and women.

A Powerful Influence

As we will see, some dreams are nonsense and should be discarded as such. However, we deprive ourselves and many others of God's blessings when we ignorantly dismiss a dream that may contain significant insight from the Lord. It is an undeniable fact of history that powerful influences have occasionally occurred in the lives of men and women while they were dreaming, affecting their conduct and their destiny.

Charles Spurgeon, while preaching *A Young Man's Vision*, said, "How much good in this world would have been lost if good men had quenched the first half-fashioned thoughts which have flitted before them [in dreams and visions]!"[19]

James Hastings provides a comprehensive and compelling overview showing some of the things that have happened in the lives of ordinary people through their having experienced extraordinary dreams:

> Jurists have in their dreams prepared briefs of which they have been only too glad to avail themselves in their waking hours; statesmen have in their dreams obtained their best insight into policy; lecturers have elaborated their discourses; mathematicians solved their most puzzling problems; authors composed their most admired productions; artists worked out their most inspired motives.
>
> It was in a dream that Reinhold worked out his table of categories. Condorcet informs us that he often completed his imperfect calculations in his dreams. The story of the origin of Coleridge's *Kubla Khan* is well known. The part played by dreams in the conversion of John Bunyan, and John Newton (more about this in chapter eight), are renowned instances of a phenomenon illustrated copiously from every age of the church experience.[20]

A Muslim Is Saved by Jesus — in a Dream!

There are many reports coming out the Middle East of God moving powerfully among the Muslims through dreams and visions of Jesus Christ.

In February 1995 our church hosted a missions emphasis night, and we heard a stirring account of what God is doing among the Shiite Muslims of southern Lebanon. Carl Mederas, a missionary whom we support along with several other churches, reported that the Lord has not only opened the doors for the gospel, but also the hearts of many men and women.

One man fell to his knees in the street and began crying aloud that

Jesus had saved him. Carl spoke with the man and heard his amazing story. A week earlier the man had dreamed that he was bound in chains like a mummy, and was forsaken at the bottom of a deep pit. As he looked up he saw the hands of a man pulling him up out of the pit.

The man wondered within himself at the meaning of the dream until he heard Carl preaching that Jesus had come to lift us out of the pit of sin and break the chains of bondage. That's when the man fell to his knees and began praising Christ openly in the midst of his village. Jesus had shown this man that He was his Savior and his God.[21] For this dear man, as well as for the countless disciples throughout history, knowing Jesus is a dream come true!

A Strategy for Evangelism

Dr. Bill Bright, the founding father of Campus Crusade for Christ International, once said,

> If we could but show the world that being committed to Christ is no tame, humdrum, sheltered monotony, but indeed the greatest adventure the human spirit could ever know — the world, standing now outside looking askance at Christianity, would come crowding in to pay allegiance to Christ. We could expect the greatest revival since Pentecost.[22]

The past thirty years have proven that these were not merely the exuberant boastings of a young Christian zealot, but rather the prophetic forecast of a godly visionary. Dr. Bright infused his organization with an uncompromising commitment to Jesus Christ and staffed his ministry with young men and women who were aggressively gracious in their witnessing for the Lord. The roll call of heaven will surely bear record of the achievements these champions have wrought for God's kingdom!

Bill Bright is an unassuming man of humble heart and average appearance. He frankly admits to being a rather ordinary fellow. One might wonder, then, how it was that he came by having such extraordinary faith and courage to dare something so impossible as taking the college campuses and universities of the world for the cause of Christ. What exactly was it that set his heart on fire?

The Fellowship of the Burning Heart

In 1947 Bill Bright was at Forest Home Christian Conference Center with Dr. Henrietta Mears, whom Billy Graham has called the greatest Christian woman of the twentieth century. They were joined by William Evans, Jr., for a time of fellowship in one of the cabins. Little did these three friends know what God was about to do to them as they talked about their love for Jesus. I had the privilege of interviewing Dr. Bright for this story and relate to you in his own words what happened all those years ago.

> It was a wonderful time of fellowship. We were simply continuing our conversation when suddenly the Holy Spirit came upon us in a sovereign act. I didn't even know who the Holy Spirit was; I only knew I was overwhelmed with His presence. We dropped down on our knees worshipping Him and praising Him. At that moment a young, struggling Presbyterian pastor entered the room. No one spoke to him, but God touched him, and he too experienced an empowering transformation.[23]
>
> Right there in that room God the Holy Spirit enveloped all of us. We were ecstatic, we practically jumped up and down. It was a life-changing experience for all of us. That night God gave us what I call a vision of expendability. We each determined that we would be expendable the rest of our lives to the Lord. We then wrote out what we called the Fellowship of the Burning Heart, calling on men and women to be expendable for Jesus Christ.

Thus the seed of faith was sown in the heart of Bill Bright. How could he have known that it would grow into a worldwide ministry? The following night Bill preached to several hundred college students gathered at the Hollywood Presbyterian church, where he himself had received Christ three years earlier. As he gave the invitation to these students to become expendable to Christ, they all leapt to their feet. Bill went up and down the coast from San Diego to Seattle, preaching the gospel to students, and the response was always the same. God was moving in his ministry with power that exceeded all previous human efforts. A short time later the Lord would speak to Bill once again in a heavenly vision.

A Slave of Jesus Christ

As we continued talking, Bill told me this story.

On a Sunday afternoon in the spring of 1951, God impressed in me to sign a contract to become a slave of Jesus. A couple of nights later while I was studying for my final exams in seminary, the Holy Spirit came upon me again, like He did at Forest Home. There was a young man in my room who didn't know what was happening to me. I liken it to when Paul was met by Jesus and the people around him didn't know what was happening.

I tried to explain it to my friend, but he never comprehended what I was experiencing. I realize now that God didn't mean it for him, He meant it for me. I was overwhelmed with the presence of God and the vision that God gave me for the world. I was so energized that, even though it was after midnight, I suggested to my bewildered roommate that he and I go running! Looking back on it makes me chuckle a bit; it was such a crazy thing to do. But I was so filled with power I felt I had to let out some steam.

I asked Dr. Bright if he would elaborate the details of the vision God gave him. My love and respect for this man of God soared when I heard his response, "Frankly," he said, "I couldn't even talk about it for years. Even at times now I can't talk about it." At this moment in our conversation the Lord's presence became evident upon Bill and his voice trembled as he continued.

The vision God gave me is something deep in my spirit that you can't describe. The best I can tell you is that even though the Campus Crusade staff now numbers thirteen thousand full-time employees, and over one hundred thousand trained volunteers, and we have helped to present the gospel to over five hundred million people around the world — the best is yet to come! We have yet to fulfill what God showed me that night.

In a sense, what He said to me was like broad strokes on a large artist's canvas — the mountains, the hills, the streams and the trees are all there at a single glance. As we have followed Him through the years He has filled in the details of the painting so that I can see, as it were, the very feathers of the birds in flight.

When I asked Dr. Bright if God had ever spoken to him in dreams, he replied,

I have walked with the Lord now almost fifty years and I don't ever remember having a dream, but I've discovered that dreams come from the Lord day and night and can be experienced in different ways — some while you are asleep, and some with your eyes open, wide awake.

I've heard the Lord, not in dreams specifically, but He speaks very clearly to me. I have never heard His audible voice, but there have been countless divine moments that the Lord has spoken to me. I have been accused of being a man of great faith, but really I am just a very ordinary person — a slave of Jesus. He created the heavens and the earth, and there is nothing too big for Him. When He finds anyone who has yielded himself — totally, completely and irrevocably — anyone whom He can trust, He will impart to them great things.[24]

Dr. Bright concluded our conversation with testimony of a word the Lord spoke to him near the end of a forty-day fast.

America and much of the world will, before the end of the year 2000, experience a great spiritual awakening. This divine visit of the Holy Spirit from heaven will kindle the greatest spiritual harvest in the history of the church.[25]

Dreams and visions will play a part in this coming revival.

The Inescapable Phenomenon of Dreams and Visions

One scholar writes,

31

Dreams have always played an important part in the literature and religion of all peoples. They have furnished mythologies; they have been the sources of systems of necromancy; they have become both the source and the explanation of otherwise inexplicable acts of Providence. Growing out of them we have a theory of nightmares and demonology. They have become the working material of the prophet, both biblical and pagan. Medieval civilization is not without its lasting effects of dreams, and modern civilization still clings with something of reverence to the unsolved mystery of certain dreams.

While we have almost emerged from anything like a slavish adherence to a superstitious belief in dreams, we still must admit the possibility of the profound significance of dreams in the impressions they make upon the subject. That dreams have been and are a valuable means of shaping men's thoughts and careers cannot be denied, and as such, have played an important part in the social and moral life of individuals and of society.[26]

The Reverend John Farrar wrote in 1889,

Dreams have excited much interest among persons of all classes, in consequence of their prevalence; and perhaps it would be difficult, if not impossible, to find a person who has not had more or less of this experience."[27]

Even Aristotle was forced to admit, "The fact that all or most men suppose some significance in dreams constitutes a ground for believing that the supposition is based upon experience."[28] There is simply no way around it. Dreams happen, and *sometimes* God is pleased to make Himself known to man through the phenomenon of dreaming.

The Question We Must Ask

Why would God speak to man through dreams? Man is the crown of God's creation, gifted by our Creator with intelligence, elevated by our Sovereign above beasts of the field and other lower things. It seems so beneath God to mask His will in the riddles of night visions, and to chance His holy purposes on the fleeting whims of such fanciful images as occur in our dreams. Why would He do such a thing?

The fact is that in *any* revelation which God makes to man, He stoops infinitely. God's thoughts are not our thoughts, and His ways are not our ways. As high as the heavens are above the earth, so are His thoughts above our own. The clothing of His messages in the forms of human conception and language involves great condescension on His part — however the message may come. The question, therefore, we ought always to ask is not, "Why would God speak to man through dreams and visions," but rather, "What is man, that thou art mindful of him? and the son of man, that thou visitest him!"[29]

God visits man! Oh, say it again and never lose the wonder of it! Praise God we are not left to ourselves, fallen creatures that we are. Thanks be to God that salvation does not require anything of us other than faith, which God is pleased to provide. He visits us; He speaks to us; He loves us! Thus are we the envy of angels and animals alike. We are not creatures of earth alone, nor are we creatures of the celestial realm. We are sons and daughters of God Almighty through our Lord Jesus Christ, and as such we shall dream dreams and see visions! Longfellow captured a glimpse of this in his *Psalm of Life*:

Tell me not in mournful numbers,
    Life is but an empty dream!
For the soul is dead that slumbers,
    And things are not what they may seem.

Life is real! Life is earnest!
    And the grave is not the goal;
Dust thou art, to dust returnest,
    Was not spoken to the soul.[30]

Conclusion

Since dreams were so evident at the birth of Christ, would it not seem reasonable that dreams would continue after He was born? We know for a fact that dreams and visions factored highly in the life of the early church. The book of Acts gives at least nine examples confirming this, and we will look closely at these in the coming pages. We also know that several church fathers from the Ante-Nicene and Post-Nicene period had profound experiences with God through dreams and visions. History stands unaltered in its testimony to these things, as we will amply demonstrate.

We know, too, that many significant men and women in the church today have themselves experienced what has proven to be guidance from God through a dream or a vision. All this begs for an answer to the question: Why are dreams and visions so easily dismissed as having nothing to offer us today? Why do we regard those who dream as though they are deluded or, worse yet, diabolic? How is it that we have neglected something that has played such a vital role throughout the rich history of God's dealings with mankind?

William Alexander summed it up most succinctly when he wrote:

> Of all the subjects upon which the mind of man has speculated, there is perhaps none more perplexing than that of dreaming. But whatever may be the difficulties attending the subject, we know that it has formed a channel through which the Lord was pleased in former times to reveal His character and dispensations to His people.[31]

It now remains for us to discover if He continues to do so unto this day. If so, what should our attitude be toward dreams and dreamers? How should we regard those things reportedly seen in dreams and visions? What means are available to determine if the dream is indeed the voice of God, or merely last night's pizza?!

And what whall we say to the poetic question of Wordsworth, "Whither is fled the visionary gleam? Where is it now, the glory and the dream?" Well, in the case of Joseph, the dream is alive and well and His glory is increasing ever brighter with each successive generation! And through the ages, men and women who have sought after Jesus Christ have found Him to be *a dream come true*.

Why Bother With
Dreams and Visions?

The youthful evangelist, fresh out of seminary, was eager to convert the old sinner. No one had been able to get through to him for years. His dear wife had held on in hopes that the Lord would save his soul before he died, but she had seen preachers come and go with little influence upon her hardened husband. It's a story that's told in every church, in every town. But this story is different.

The night before the zealous young gospel preacher was to call upon the old man and his hopeful wife, he had a dream. He saw himself at their home, sitting in the family room visiting with them. He asked, "May I have a glass of water?"

The husband said, "Sure, I'll get it for you."

In the dream the young evangelist saw himself follow the old man into the kitchen. As the two stood chatting, the evangelist said, "You have two of the most beautiful daughters I have ever seen. It's very obvious that you love them and that there isn't anything you wouldn't do for them."

The old man lit up with pride. "Yep, you sure got that right, preacher."

Then in the dream the young man of God saw himself say, "It's really too bad that you can't give them the one thing that they need the most."

"And exactly what would that be?" the man indignantly replied.

The evangelist looked the man right in the eye and answered, "A Christian father!"

To the amazement of the preacher, the man gave his life to Christ right there in the kitchen! Then the dream ended.

The next day the evangelist made the house call. As he sat in the living room visiting with the family, he decided to put his dream to the test. "May I have a glass of water?" he asked, and just as he had dreamed, the husband offered to get it for him. Faith soared in his young heart as he followed the old man into the kitchen. Like an actor performing a script, the young evangelist guided the conversation exactly as he had heard it in the dream. When the old man asked him what it was his children needed the most that he couldn't give them, the young evangelist answered, "A Christian father." The force of these words visibly shook the father. He could not escape from the conviction of the Holy Spirit. There, standing in his kitchen, the old sinner repented and gave his heart to Jesus Christ — just as it had happened in a dream the night before![1]

This story is but one of many dramatic examples, both in Scripture as well as in history, of how God can use dreams or visions to accomplish His purposes in our lives. In the book of Job, held by scholars to be among the oldest books in the Bible, we find the first reference to the use of dreams as a means whereby God communicates to man.

The Whispering Angel

As the narrative unfolds, Job has undergone a hideous and diabolic assault through which he has suffered the loss of everything he held dear. All of his children have been killed in a terrible tragedy. His real estate holdings have been destroyed, all of his livestock have been stolen by bands of thieves, his wealth has been depleted and his credibility throughout the surrounding region has been merci-lessly ruined.[2] In addition, Job's health and well-being are beset with such hellish aggravations so that he despairs even of life itself.[3]

The crowning injury comes from the lips of his beloved wife who, in her own bitterness of soul, says to him, "Are you still trying to be godly when God has done all this to you? Curse him and die."[4]

Finally, as if all this were not enough, Job's three closest friends arrive on the scene with their hearts fully set upon comforting him, but during the initial seven days of mourning they inexplicably turn and condemn him for some hidden sin they feel certain he has com-mitted.[5] Job no doubt expected them to console him in his distress. Can you imagine his shock when they tear into him with their smug accusations and stinging denouncements?

First to speak is Eliphaz. He knew well that his opinion alone could not convince Job, so he frames his remarks in a context that best guarantees their unquestioned authority. He says that God has spoken to him about Job's situation in a dream.

"A word was secretly brought to me, my ears caught a whisper of it. Amid disquieting dreams in the night, when deep sleep falls on men, fear and trembling seized me and made all my bones shake. A spirit glided past my face, and the hair on my body stood on end. It stopped, but I could not tell what it was. A form stood before my eyes, and I heard a hushed voice: 'Can a mortal be more righteous than God? Can a man be more pure than his Maker?'"[6]

Three significant facts are provided in this text. First, the ques-tion asked by the heavenly messenger is not a false or misleading inquiry. It endorses authentic truth and has as its purpose the exclu-sive exaltation of God. So far, so good.

Second, it is clear that no one thought it unusual that a message from God would come "when deep sleep falls upon men." Eliphaz was safe in saying that God spoke to him in a dream, because the practice was common enough to be credible. That claim was never challenged by Job or the others.

Third, in support of the legitimacy of this spiritual visitation, Eliphaz testifies of his fear and trembling in the presence of the heav-enly messenger. This phenomena is consistently supported through-out the Bible. Abraham, Isaac, Gideon, Daniel, the shepherds in the fields keeping watch over their flocks by night, Simon Peter, Paul and John on the Isle of Patmos are among the many who shared a terrifying moment of revelation in which the angel of the Lord had to reassure them with the enduring words, "Fear not."[7]

Once Eliphaz concludes his argument, Job responds with remarkable clarity of thought despite his unbearable suffering. First, he admits that he had spoken rashly because he was in deep grief. "If only my anguish could be weighed and all my misery be placed on the scales! It would surely outweigh the sand of the seas — no wonder my words have been impetuous."[8]

Second, he confronts Eliphaz for his lack of compassion. "One should be kind to a fainting friend, but you have accused me without the slightest fear of God. My brother, you have proved as unreliable as a brook; it floods when there is ice and snow, but in hot weather, disappears."[9]

Finally, Job takes issue with Eliphaz concerning the dream. "When I think my bed will comfort me and my couch will ease my complaint, even then you frighten me with dreams and terrify me with visions."[10]

Notice that Job's rebuttal to Eliphaz did not challenge the dream itself, nor even the message of the dream. Rather, he argues against Eliphaz's insensitive use of the dream to terrify him when he was already suffering great anguish of soul. In essence Job said, "Thanks a lot, pal! The one hope of comfort and relief I have is when I fall asleep. Now you have taken that away by filling me with terrifying thoughts of being tormented by nightmares!"

From this point onward the battle of words raged between Job and his friends. Bildad the Shuhite let Job know exactly how he felt: "How long will you go on like this, Job, blowing words around like wind? Does God twist justice? Your children sinned against God, and He punished them. Admit it!"[11]

Zophar the Naamathite wasted no time in leveling his rebuke against Job: "Shouldn't someone stem this torrent of words? Is a man proved right by all this talk? Should I remain silent while you boast? When you mock God, shouldn't someone make you ashamed? You claim you are pure in the eyes of God! Oh, that God would speak and tell you what He thinks! Oh, that He would make you truly see yourself, for He knows everything you've done. Listen! God is doubtless punishing you far less than you deserve!"[12]

There is no break in the action as the drama unfolds for the next several chapters in the book of Job. The words are bitter, divisive and ultimately futile — typical of all religious debate. The arguments of Job's friends ultimately fail, and a bitter stalemate is reached in the narrative.

The Champion of Truth

Finally, lest we are to think there is no solution, we are introduced to young Elihu — the champion of truth. Though he was a young man, he spoke with great poise in the face of the awkward silence of the aged. He first rebuked Job's friends for condemning Job without giving an answer to him.[13] It was obvious they didn't know what they were talking about, and therefore they had no business being so pushy with their opinions.

Elihu next turned and spoke to Job. The first item on Elihu's list of issues to correct with Job is the matter of dreams and visions.

"But I tell you, in this you are not right, for God is greater than man. Why do you complain to him that he answers none of man's words? For God does speak — now one way, now another — though man may not perceive it. In a dream, in a vision of the night, when deep sleep falls on men as they slumber in their beds, he may speak in their ears and terrify them with warnings, to turn man from wrongdoing and keep him from pride, to preserve his soul from the pit, his life from perishing by the sword."[14]

In this passage of Scripture Elihu touches upon at least seven things that a dream or a vision from God may accomplish in our lives.

1. Dreams provide God's answers to our questions.

In the story of Gideon we find an example of God answering a man in a dream. By the Lord's doing, Gideon had just experienced the alarming reduction of his army from over thirty thousand men to a mere three hundred. On the other hand, the army of the Midianites numbered in excess of fifty-eight thousand well-trained soldiers. To say the least, Gideon was a man with questions.

One night the Lord said to Gideon, "Get up, go down against the camp, because I am going to give it into your hands. If you are afraid to attack, go down to the camp with your servant Purah and listen to what they are saying. Afterward, you will be encouraged to attack the camp."[15]

Gideon *was* afraid, so he and Purah his servant went down to the outposts of the camp. They arrived just as a man was telling a friend his dream. "I had a dream," he was saying. "A round loaf of barley bread came tumbling into the Midianite camp. It struck the tent with such force that the tent overturned and collapsed." His friend responded, "This can be nothing other than the sword of Gideon son of Joash, the Israelite. God has given the Midianites and the whole camp into his hands."

The Bible then says, "When Gideon heard the dream and its interpretation, he worshiped God. He returned to the camp of Israel and called out, 'Get up! The Lord has given the Midianite camp into your hands.'"[16] This is remarkable for several reasons. First, it clearly provided Gideon with the answer he was looking for — the Lord had indeed given the Midianites into his hands.

Second, the fact that God let Gideon overhear the two Midianite soldiers discussing the dream greatly impacted Gideon. Had Gideon dreamed it himself, he could have possibly dismissed it as wishful thinking brought on by the overwhelming stress of the impossible situation. But Gideon didn't dream it; a Midianite soldier did! The dream showed Gideon that he had been afraid of the Midianites for no good reason. The Lord had put the fear of Gideon in their hearts. The dream and its interpretation was God's way of proving that to Gideon.

Finally, God could've just told Gideon all of this, but He chose instead to reveal it through a dream and its interpretation. Why? Because a picture is worth a thousand words — and often much more convincing. Gideon was a man needing a convincing answer, and God gave it to him through an astounding dream.

A century later Saul, the troubled king of Israel, desperate in the final hours of his fallen monarchy, employed a witch to call Samuel from the grave. Astonishingly, Samuel actually appeared (scaring the living daylights out of the witch, by the way), and he challenged Saul, "Why have you disturbed me by bringing me up?" Saul answered him, "I am in great distress. The Philistines are fighting against me, and God has turned away from me. He no longer answers me, either by prophets or by dreams. So I have called on you to tell me what to do."[17]

This text is full of mystery which we shall leave alone. I will, however, make mention of one obvious fact. It was expected in those days that God would answer a man through dreams, and when He did not there was cause for *grave* concern.

The Lost Manuscript

In a less serious and more contemporary example of God answering a man in a dream, let me tell you about a close friend who was quite distraught over the loss of a manuscript he had worked on for several months. He had brought the final transcript home to review it once more before sending it off to the publisher. To his dismay, when he looked in his briefcase that night the papers were missing.

He searched frantically throughout his house, his office, his car and his luggage — all to no avail. The manuscript was gone; he could not find it anywhere. This was but one more thing in a series of diabolical disruptions he had endured while working on the manuscript. It seemed to him that somebody clearly did not want him to finish his book.

That night he dreamed that he was driving along the highway and saw a package by the roadside. When he woke up the next morning, he felt strongly that he should drive along the highway near his home. In doing so he indeed saw a package by the roadside as the dream had indicated.

He stopped to investigate closer and, to his utter amazement, found in the package the very manuscript he had lost! It turned out that it had blown from the top of his car the day before while he had driven from his office to his home. He had forgotten he had placed it there before getting into his car. Remarkably, the papers were undamaged, and he was able to proceed with the publication of his book.[18] God used the dream to lead him to the lost manuscript.

Iti Swhe Reyo Uare — Say, What?

In the summer of 1989 Belinda and I were faced with a major decision. Should we stay with the church in Boulder or accept an invitation to serve at a thriving church in another state? We had been in Boulder for eight years and had seen the Lord bless the work there mightily. They say that the best time to leave is when things are great — that way, you're sure not to be running away from difficulty. Actually, the best time to leave is when the Lord directs — that way, you're not walking in presumption or disobedience.

But I could not tell what the Lord wanted me to do. My heart secretly longed for the position that was open in the distant city, yet

I also had a sense that things weren't quite completed in Boulder. I was divided in my heart, and thus unable to discern God's voice as clearly as when personal opinion isn't in the way.

One night during this time I dreamed I was in a cave searching for the ark of the covenant. (OK, I admit I had recently seen Indiana Jones in *Raiders of the Lost Ark*, but hear me out before you draw any conclusions.) In the dream I came into a large chamber deep in the heart of the cave and I sensed that I was near the ark — I could *feel* its presence.

I looked up and saw a Colorado license plate attached to the roof of the cave. The tag had strange words inscribed where there should have been license numbers. The words were *ITI SWHE REYO UARE*. I tried to sound out the words to see if I could make any sense of them, "Itty sway ray-o oo-er."

What jibberish! Talk about an enigma; I was completely baffled. Still, I kept repeating the strange syllables aloud, "Itty sway ray-o oo-er," hoping to make some sense out of all this. Suddenly, I saw what I had not seen before. The message read, "It is where you are!" The letters of the words were all there; it was the space in between the words that was wrong.

I realized that the license tag was like the proverbial "*X* marks the spot" on treasure maps. The ark was directly over me in the dome, just behind the tag. I excitedly reached up to move the license plate, and as I did a torrent of water rushed over me from above. The dream ended at that moment.

This strange dream provided me with an answer from the Lord that turned out to be of profound significance. Let me explain. First, the ark obviously symbolized the presence of the Lord. The Colorado license tag represented my place of authorization. The cryptic message, "It is where you are," was telling me that I should not leave Colorado to go into another ministry, for the Lord's presence and blessing were with me *here*.

I was deeply impacted by this riddle-like dream; so much so that I indeed did remain in Colorado. How glad I am that I did! Shortly after this dream I became the chaplain for the University of Colorado football team and a close friend to Bill McCartney. The following few years brought tremendous blessings from the Lord which have now resulted in a major move of God across the nation touching the lives of hundreds of thousands of men and their families!

By heeding the dream — "It is where you are" — I was kept from making a colossal mistake. Had I indeed moved away from Boulder at that time, I would be watching from a distance the awesome works of God and regretting that I had ever left. How I praise God for answering me in such an unusual manner — a riddle in the middle of the night.

2. Dreams can give us instruction in the things of God.

One example of God using a dream to give a man divine guidance is known by us all. It happened prior to the birth of Jesus. As we discussed in chapter one, Joseph did not want to expose Mary to public disgrace when he discovered she was pregnant. His intentions were to divorce her quietly so as to prevent a scandal.

While he was considering this, an angel of the Lord appeared to him in a dream and said, "Joseph, son of David, do not be afraid to take to you Mary your wife, for that which is conceived in her is of the Holy Spirit. And she will bring forth a son, and you shall call His name Jesus, for He will save His people from their sins."[19]

It is in dreams that the Lord opens the ears of men and seals their instruction.[20] God removes the hindrances to our hearing and reveals the truth to our spirit — in a dream! Then, according to the word of Elihu, He seals the instruction (i.e., He puts it in and keeps it in). Dreams have a remarkable ability to stay in our memories as though they are events we have actually experienced.

The Trash Can Dream

Once I dreamed I was driving along a narrow road. I came upon a large trash can knocked over in the road, with all its trash strewn about the street. I could not go around it because the road was too narrow, so I had to stop and clean up the mess. As I approached, I saw the face of a man appear upon the surface of the trash can — giving the dream a cartoon-like quality. It made the trash can look like a head lying in the road, with trash coming out the top. I was so startled that I jumped back, and as I did, I heard a voice above me say, "Stop filling your head with trash!" That's when I woke up.

This dream proved itself to be very beneficial in motivating me to correct and moderate my personal walk with the Lord. Following this dream, I identified several examples of how I had been "filling my head with trash."

Believing the lies of Satan, cultivating unhealthy self-talk, receiving accusations against others, holding to the faulty traditions of men, watching distorted and impure things on television and in theaters, harboring hidden things of darkness in my thoughts, turning away from the Lord by little acts of consistent disobedience, being unfaithful in prayer — all of this is trash.

King Hezekiah said to the priests of Israel, "Listen to me, Levites! Consecrate yourselves now and consecrate the temple of the Lord, the God of your fathers. Remove all defilement [i.e., trash] from the sanctuary."[21] This scripture convicted me, and I began to earnestly pursue the Lord. I determined to put into practice in my personal life King Hezekiah's exhortation. Piece by piece I started "taking out the trash."

It was then that the Holy Spirit prompted this joyful thought in my mind: "If you will stop filling your head with trash, I will start filling your heart with treasure." Wow! What a deal! Trash or treasure — indeed, the choice is yours and mine to make.

The Six Barricades to Destruction

A colleague of mine, who was also a close personal friend, had come under suspicion for questionable practices concerning church finances. The situation was further complicated by several reports from individuals who had been significantly wounded by this man's manipulative and domineering style of leadership.

The association of churches to which this man belonged asked me to help with their efforts in bringing him to clear himself of the charges. Their sole motive was to provide vindication to him (believing that he would prove himself to be innocent), and to stop the rumors that were spreading against him.

I met with my friend and urged him to cooperate with the leaders in his denomination, to furnish them with all the information necessary in order to prove that he had indeed conducted himself with integrity and faithfulness. "A good name is to be desired above great riches," I told him.

To my utter dismay, the man completely refused to cooperate. Whether or not he was guilty of the accusations remained to be seen. His behavior, however, lent substantial credibility to the mounting suspicions and escalated the problem to the point where the church officials disfellowshipped him from their association. He has hardened his heart against appeal and remains in resolute defiance to their authority.

Following the disappointing meeting in which these things were finalized with this brother, the Lord showed me a vision. I saw this man speeding on the highway in reckless disregard of all the signs along the way. He veered off the main road and took a side path that was closed. There were six barricades in front of him — each one warning that the bridge up ahead had collapsed.

The man crashed through the first barricade and yelled, "What idiot put that in the road?" He repeated this each time he crashed through another barricade until finally he sped toward the cliff, certain to go over the edge.

As I prayed concerning this vision, the Lord showed me that the barriers He establishes in our lives are there to keep us from recklessly destroying ourselves. It is our disobedience to authority that ultimately jeopardizes our credibility, our effectiveness and quite possibly, even our lives.

I have been able to identify at least six barricades God uses to oppose us when we are engaging in wrong behavior. They are 1) the Bible, 2) the Holy Spirit speaking to our consciences, 3) friends who lovingly protest our mistakes, 4) the church, 5) the law of the land, and 6) the devil himself. Let me explain this briefly.

The Bible is our first line of defense against disobedience. It is objective and unyielding in its righteousness. The Holy Spirit applies truth to our conscience subjectively so as to convict us when we go astray. If we contradict His promptings and stay on course in disobedience, then God uses our close friends to confront us.

Should this fail to turn us around, then the whole church will stand united against our behavior. It is the Lord's intention that this social rejection (i.e., excommunication) will snap us out of our rebellion and turn us back to Him in humble repentance. Sometimes it works; sometimes it does not.

When we persist past the discipline of the church, then the law of the land comes bearing down upon us. Legal questions arise and investigations ensue — each aimed at our error in hope of stopping us from going on in our obstinance. Some, however, have proven clever enough to dance around the law through the loopholes created by legal language. And so the law fails.

Finally, the Lord permits the devil himself to oppose us. Paul enacted this measure of discipline when he "delivered Hymenaeus and Alexander unto Satan, that they may learn not to blaspheme."[22] In another scripture Paul commanded the Corinthian church to "cast out this man from the fellowship of the church and into Satan's hands, to punish him, in the hope that his soul will be saved when our Lord Jesus Christ returns."[23]

The simple vision of the man crashing through the highway barricades provided me with opportunity to seek the Lord for instruction in the things of God. He opened my understanding to see that there are real and consequential barriers set before us for our good. If a man somehow crashes through all these providential obstructions, it is certain that he will indeed plunge into a Christless eternity.

3. God can use dreams to warn us about unseen dangers.

The wise men who sought Jesus by following the star found Him in a house with his mother. They bowed down and worshipped Him, opening their treasures and presenting Him with gifts of gold, incense and myrrh. The Bible tells us that they returned to their country by another route, "having been warned in a dream not to go back to Herod."[24]

As soon as they left, the angel of the Lord appeared to Joseph in a dream and said, "Take the child and his mother and escape to Egypt. Stay there until I tell you, for Herod is going to search for the child to kill him."[25]

After the death of Herod, God told Joseph in another dream to return to the land of Israel — specifically to the parts of Galilee. Joseph obeyed the dream and gave us Jesus of Nazareth, thereby fulfilling the ancient prophecy: "He shall be called a Nazarene."[26] The dreams were warnings from God. By heeding their messages disaster was averted.

Rattlesnakes in the House!

I recall a dream in which I saw a nest of rattlesnakes in my house. I was alarmed at their presence, especially because I had young children in my home. I knew to avoid the snakes, but my children would be unaware of the danger. When I tried to find how the snakes had gotten into my house, I discovered that they had entered through the television. At that point the dream concluded.

Awake, I felt the dream was a warning about leaving my kids to watch television programs without adult supervision. Much of today's programming is like a rattlesnake — coiled and ready to strike the unsuspecting who draw near enough to enter harm's way. Once the poison is in the system, it often proves to be fatal! Adult and child alike are not beyond the danger of being bitten, and there are few antidotes for the poison. Be wise and beware.

A Nest of Rats

One night, in a very unusual manner, a warning came in dreams to both myself and my wife, Belinda. Separately we dreamed the same thing! We didn't realize it, of course, until breakfast the next morning. As we were talking, Belinda told me of the dream she had the night before. I couldn't believe my ears — she was telling me my dream. When I told her this, we both were more than a little awestruck.

We certainly felt that the dream was something we should take seriously. It concerned our church. We dreamed that there was a nest of rats that had been hidden in the building, but which had been discovered and carried out. The dream made us alert over the following days to the possibility of God exposing something of which we had been unaware. Indeed He did, and our church was spared from a potential split through the warning God gave us in the dream.

4. Dreams provide guidance away from wrongdoing.

A father-in-law discovered he had been cheated by his son-in-law. He became furious and vowed revenge. The irony in the situation was that the father-in-law had humored himself by cheating his son-in-law on several occasions. The son-in-law, having had enough, decided to get even. Now that the tables were turned, it wasn't so funny.

The father-in-law gathered several friends and went out into the night looking for the son-in-law, fully set upon exacting his vengeance against the foolish boy. You can read this story in the book of Genesis. It's about Laban and Jacob.[27]

Once Laban was in hot pursuit after Jacob, the Bible says, "Then God came to Laban the Aramean in a dream at night and said to him, 'Be careful not to say anything to Jacob, either good or bad.'"[28] This dream literally saved Laban's life.

It wasn't that Jacob had the power to stop him from whatever he was intending to do, it was that God would not let Laban raise his hand against Jacob without divine consequences. Laban's best and only option was to leave the situation alone. Therefore the Lord warned him in a dream and kept him from doing the wrong thing.

God Confronts a Philistine King

In another story also found in Genesis, Abimelech, king of the Philistines, had ignorantly taken Sarah, Abraham's wife, into his harem. Abraham, of course, was the guilty party for having lied to Abimelech about Sarah in order to save his own life. Sarah was beautiful and desirable; the king's intentions were clear as he retired to the royal bedchamber that night. But the unexpected happened, and the king was kept from doing what was wrong.

"God came to Abimelech in a dream one night and said to him, 'You are as good as dead because of the woman you have taken; she is a married woman.'"[29] Abimelech asserted his innocence in that he had acted ignorantly.

God answered his appeal in the dream, "Yes, I know you did this with a clear conscience, and so I have kept you from sinning against me. That is why I did not let you touch her. Now return the man's wife, for he is a prophet, and he will pray for you and you will live. But if you do not return her, you may be sure that you and all yours will die."[30]

Abimelech probably didn't sleep well the rest of the night. The Bible tells us that he summoned his official "early the next morning" and told them all that had happened — and they were all struck with fear.

King Abimelech confronted Abraham as he returned Sarah to his side. "What have you done to us? How have I wronged you that you have brought such great guilt upon me and my kingdom? You have done things to me that should not be done."[31]

Pontius Pilate's Portentous Predicament

One more example of a warning from a dream comes to mind.

Pontius Pilate, the pompous Roman governor of insignificant Judea, was faced with the responsibility of passing sentence upon Jesus of Nazareth for trumped-up charges of insurrection against Rome.

While Pilate was sitting on the judge's seat, his wife sent him this urgent message: "Don't have anything to do with that innocent man, for I have suffered a great deal today in a dream because of him."[32] Immediately upon hearing this Pilate proposed a release of a prisoner as a show of Roman kindness. He gave the Jews a choice: Jesus or Barabbas. He undoubtedly thought that he had cleverly arranged Jesus' release from judgment. He never imagined that they would actually ask for Barabbas.

When they did, he was forced to follow Roman law and sentence Jesus to death. However, in a desperate attempt to absolve himself of any guilt in the matter, Pilate washed his hands in a basin of water and said for all to hear, "I am innocent of this man's blood. It is your responsibility!"[33]

Pilate, ever the politician, tried to follow the warning of the dream while appeasing the people of the land. His divided heart made him unstable in all his ways. Jesus was crucified, and Pilate, according to history, was called to Rome and executed for his part in the affair.[34]

Julius Caesar and the Ides of March

In the middle of the night on the fourteenth of March, Julius Caesar was awakened by the voice of his wife, Calpurnia, groaning in her sleep. When the day dawned she told him how in her dreams she had held him bleeding and dying in her arms. Her heart was so vexed by the dream that she begged Caesar not to leave the house but to adjourn the meeting which the senate had set for that day, the fifteenth of March.

Caesar, moved by the earnestness of Calpurnia, agreed to her wishes. The conspirators, realizing their plot to assassinate Caesar would be thwarted, quickly sent Brutus, Caesar's close friend, to ask him to reconsider his decision. Brutus succeeded in changing Caesar's mind by showing how foolish it looked for the ruler of Rome to be swayed by the fleeting dream of an emotional woman.

Pride always precedes destruction. It is a fact of life few rulers believe until it is too late. Caesar snapped to his senses, shook the eerie foreboding of the dream out of his mind, adjusted his gait with a suitable strut and walked directly into the cold steel blades of his treacherous assassins! He bled to death in Calpurnia's arms on the senate floor.[35]

This happened less than fifty years before Christ. The story was relatively fresh in the minds of Roman citizens, even more so for their rulers. Certainly Pontius Pilate would have known about it. Could this be one reason why Pilate, upon hearing his wife's troubling dream, sought desperately to free Jesus from condemnation?

5. God can use dreams to keep us from pride.

Nebuchadnezzar, king of Babylon, wrote, "I had a dream that made me afraid. As I was lying in my bed, the images and visions that passed through my mind terrified me."[36] He summoned his officials, advisers and magicians to help him sort out the mystery of the dream. But, in a manner of speaking, all the king's horses and all the king's men couldn't put Humpty together again.

The prophet Daniel was brought before the king and was told the dream. Upon hearing it, Daniel sat there stunned and silent for an hour, aghast at the meaning of the dream. Nebuchadnezzar urged Daniel to speak.

Daniel replied, "Oh, that the events foreshadowed in this dream would happen to your enemies, my lord, and not to you!"[37] The dream revealed how God purposed to humble Nebuchadnezzar, and it came to pass exactly as the dream foretold. Nebuchadnezzar was driven from the palace in madness and lived among the animals of the field, eating grass as though he were an ox. This insanity lasted for seven years.

"At the end of seven years I, Nebuchadnezzar, looked up to heaven, and my sanity returned, and I praised and worshipped the Most High God and honored him who lives forever, whose rule is everlasting, his kingdom evermore."[38]

Here is the humbled king's conclusion: "Now I, Nebuchadnezzar, praise and exalt and glorify the King of heaven, because everything he does is right and all his ways are just. And those who walk in pride he is able to humble."[39]

God humbled the man just as the dream had foretold. Could it be that Nebuchadnezzar would have been spared the fulfillment of the dream by believing it and repenting of his pride? Certainly. God does not take pleasure in our humiliation. But, mark this well, He takes even less pleasure in our pride. God resists the proud but gives grace to the humble.

The Laughing Devil

Years ago I became involved with a church that was embroiled in a bitter disagreement. The congregation was solidly divided and there seemed to be no solution to the conflict. The Bible says, "Only by pride cometh contention."[40] I knew that pride was at the heart of the problem, and that both sides were at fault. I wondered how I would go about convincing them of this and bringing healing to the problem.

That night I dreamed that I was standing by a church that had been burned down. There was nothing left but a pile of smoldering ashes. The people were gathered on either side of the pile screaming at one another. Those on one side cried out to the others, "You did this!" to which those on the other side answered, "No we didn't! You did it!" This bickering went on and on, back and forth like schoolyard children.

Then in the dream I saw Satan standing off by himself, bellowing so hard with laughter that he could hardly speak. Roaring with demonic delight, Satan rose up and mocked the defeated church, saying, "You are both wrong — *I* did it!" He took special pride in saying the word, "I." Satan then laughed so hard he fell to the ground holding his sides. The dream ended.

I shared this with the congregation, and God used it to turn the situation around. The people were able to realize that they were not enemies, but brothers and sisters. They saw that their battle was not against flesh and blood, but against the devil. They rose victorious above the strife and preserved the church from splitting. God used the dream to keep His people from pride and the destruction it brings.

6. Dreams can preserve our soul from the pit.

Captivity, imprisonment, slavery — these are among the most depressing conditions that have ever been inflicted upon man. There is no pit so deep as the pit of bondage. But, as Corrie ten Boom said, "There is no pit so deep that God's love is not deeper still."

The prophet Ezekiel was beside the river Chebar among the captives in Babylon when the heavens were opened and he saw visions of God.[41] These visions flooded his heart with faith and gave him a

51

message of hope that lifted the demoralized remnant of Judah from the bondage of Babylon. Their deliverance became the theme of many songs.

"When the Lord brought back the captives to Zion, we were like men who dreamed. Our mouths were filled with laughter, our tongues with songs of joy. Then it was said among the nations, 'The Lord has done great things for them.'"[42] The Lord has done great things for us, and we are filled with joy — like them that dream.

My wife, Belinda, has cultivated a marvelous intimacy with the Lord in prayer and worship. Over the years Christ has become very close and dramatically real in her life. She is more frequently to be found hastening to the house of the Lord in prayer than any other pursuit. Her countenance glows with the glory she has found in those precious hours spent in God's presence.

One night the Lord dramatically ministered to Belinda through a dream. She saw herself attending a conference with several Christians. During a break from the teaching she walked into the hallway and chanced upon two friends, a pastor and his wife, who live and work near us. Without anything being said in the dream, the three of them walked into a private room and began to pray. Belinda knew that the couple was there to help her work through deep-seated emotional issues she was struggling with at that time in her life. The dream then ended.

When Belinda woke up the next morning, she realized that God had literally used the dream to heal her emotions and remove the turmoil from her heart *while she was sleeping!* The dream brought new understanding to a favorite passage of Scripture: "It is vain for you to rise up early, to retire late, to eat the bread of painful labors; for He gives to His beloved even in his sleep."[43]

7. Dreams can literally save our lives.

Abimelech's life was spared through the dream God gave him concerning Abraham's wife, Sarah, whom he had taken unto himself. The infant Jesus was spared from Herod's horror in Bethlehem by the dream God gave Joseph. Elihu told Job that a dream could keep a man from perishing by the sword. God uses dreams to save our lives. Jack Taylor, a venerable man of God and a trusted mentor in my own life, was literally saved from death by a dream. He had been seriously ill for several weeks, and the doctors were mystified in searching for the cause of the sickness. Consequently, they were unable to prescribe any real cure. Jack's condition deteriorated significantly until one night when he was startled out of sleep by a voice that said, "You are taking a medicine that is killing you." The name of the medicine then came to his mind.

Fully awake in the early morning hours, Jack quickly went to the medicine cabinet to verify if that particular medicine was included in the prescriptions which his doctors had given him. It was. He called the doctors later that morning and asked them what effect the medicine would have on a man in his condition. They immediately confirmed that it would destroy his kidneys and cause him to die. He stopped taking that particular medicine and, thankfully, returned to health and effective ministry. Jack's life was saved by following the voice that came in a dream.

The Car Wreck That Didn't Happen

Evangelist James Robison, known and loved by millions around the world, told me how God saved his life from harm through a dream. James woke one morning from an ominous dream that showed him in a terrible car wreck at a dangerous intersection near his home. He shared this dream with his family and asked them to pray for God's protection over him as he traveled.

A week or so later James stopped at the intersection he had dreamed about. As he prepared to accelerate into the highway traffic, a cargo van approached from James' left. The driver of the van decelerated and signaled that he was making a right turn onto the street that James was exiting. James hesitated to make sure that the van was turning, and when he saw that the van had indeed slowed down he went ahead and accelerated onto the highway.

At that very instant James vividly remembered the dream of the car wreck he had seen at that intersection and he immediately slammed on his brakes. Suddenly, a speeding sports car flashed in front of him and raced on down the highway. James had not seen the car coming; it had been blocked from his view behind the slowing van. Had James not stopped when he did, the wreck that he had seen in his dream would have happened right then. James is convinced that it would have taken his life. The Lord saved him from death through the influence of the dream.

About three weeks later, James was in another state speaking at a conference. He told in detail the story of how God saved his life through a dream.

After the conference, one of the church elders drove James to play in a golf tournament. As they were traveling down the highway, this man was thinking about James's dream and how God had saved his life. He instinctively slowed down as he saw a car pull up to a cross street in the distance, remembering how the car had pulled in front of James in his dream.

As the driver watched the car in the cross road, he realized to his horror that it was pulling out into the highway — directly in his path. He swerved to try to avoid a wreck, but the oncoming car caught the edge of his own car's front bumper, and the two of them collided.

Thankfully, no one was seriously injured. Had the driver of James's car not slowed down, the impact could have been fatal. Why did the driver slow down? After the wreck he said, "If I hadn't been thinking about the dream I would have never seen the other car pulling out in front of us. God only knows how tragic a wreck could have happened."

Now James says that a dream not only saved his life once — it saved it twice.

Conclusion

God speaks in dreams and visions to accomplish many of His purposes in our lives. While there are always those who will doubt it, there are many more who will tell you that He does. Elihu's words of wisdom have stood the test of time — proven over and over again in the lives of countless men and women down through the ages unto the present. "In a dream, in a vision, when deep slumber comes upon men in their beds, God may open their ears."

Does this then mean we should heed every dream as though it is a word from God? Absolutely not! While some dreams do come from God, others stem from far less trustworthy sources. Let's look at some of those now.

Sleep-Fancies and Other Vain Imaginations

Saint Basil the Great, while serving as Archbishop of Caesarea, was being vilified by slander. This is not at all uncommon to men and women of God. But in this particular instance, the evil report against Basil gained its strength through the dreams of certain troublemakers who had set themselves against his ministry and person. Enough momentum had generated from their mystic tales that Basil felt constrained to answer their claims before the notables of Neocaesarea. He eloquently and forthrightly set the record straight.

> I am told the ears of everybody in your town are set a thrilling, while certain tale-mongers, creators of lies, hired for this very work, are giving you a history of me and my doings. I therefore do not think that I ought to overlook your being exposed to the teaching of vile

intention and foul tongue; I think that I am bound to tell you myself in what position I am placed.

I have felt compelled to write to you in these terms, that you may be on your guard against the mischief arising from bad teaching. If we may indeed liken pernicious teachings to poisonous drugs, then, as your dream-tellers have it, their doctrines are hemlock and monkshood, or any other thing deadly to man. It is these that destroy men's souls; not my words, as this shrieking drunken scum, full of the fancies of their condition, make out.

If they had any sense they ought to know that in souls, pure and cleansed from all defilement, the prophetic gift shines clear. In a foul mirror you cannot see what the reflection is, neither can a soul preoccupied with cares of this life, and darkened with the passions of the lust of the flesh, receive the rays of the Holy Ghost. Knowing this, they ought not to have been so lifted up as to ascribe the gift of prophecy to themselves.

Basil concluded his letter with sound advice which stands to this day:

> If then their sleep-fancies do not tally with the commandments of the Lord, let them be content with the Gospels. The Gospels need no dreams to add to their credit. The Lord has sent His peace to us, and left us a new commandment, to love one another, but (the) dreams (of these men) bring strife and division and destruction of love. Let them therefore not give occasion to the devil to attack their souls in sleep; nor make their imaginations of more authority than the instruction of salvation (i.e., the Word of God.)[1]

Back to the Bible

Any serious discussion on the subject of dreams and visions must include a thoughtful examination of what the Scripture teaches with regard to false dreams and pretentious visions. Otherwise it might seem as though the argument for true dreams and visions is superficial, biased and irresponsible. Besides, if our belief that God speaks to us in dreams and visions cannot pass the scrutiny of objective biblical examination, then it is indeed doubtful that God is the author of our thoughts on this matter. So let's take our case before the high court of Scripture.

Four Reasons to Trust the Bible

We turn to the Scripture for several reasons. First, it is the Word of God. As such it is the final authority on all matters of faith and practice. The prophet Isaiah said, "Why are you trying to find out the future by consulting witches and mediums? Don't listen to their whisperings and mutterings. Can the living find out the future from the dead? Why not ask your God?" God was saying, "Check these witches' words against the Word of God! If their messages are different than mine, it is because I have not sent them; for they have no light or truth in them."[2]

Second, we turn to the Bible because it is objective and truthful. It does not change to suit the situation, nor does it pander to the polls, nor does it cower before persons, philosophies or fads. It says what it means and means what it says. Its arguments are irrefutable, its truthfulness is uncompromising, and its findings are faithful and worthy of all acceptance.

Jesus said, "Heaven and earth shall pass away, but my words shall not pass away."[3] He taught us that the man who built his house upon the Word of God would endure the blast of any storm, but the man who rejected the truth of Scripture to follow the opinions of the day would come to sure and sudden ruin.[4] So we must build our case upon the Word of God, or it cannot stand at all.

Third, we turn to the Scripture because there is a power in the Bible not found in any other document known to man. It is a living word with eternal authority and profound spiritual energy. Jesus said, "The Spirit gives life; the flesh counts for nothing. The words I have spoken to you are spirit and they are life."[5]

Finally, we turn to the Bible because it alone has the unique ability to divide between soul and spirit and to discern the thoughts and intents of the heart. The writer of Hebrews said, "Whatever God says to us is full of living power: it is sharper than the sharpest dagger, cutting swift and deep into our innermost thoughts and desires with all their parts, exposing us for what we really are."[6]

This is more than helpful, considering that "the heart is deceitful above all things and beyond cure."[7] The prophet Jeremiah pondered the complexity and perversity of man's sinful heart and asked, "Who can understand it?" The Holy Spirit provided the perplexed prophet with the only answer that can suffice: "I the Lord search the heart and examine the mind, to reward a man according to his conduct, according to what his deeds deserve."[8]

Think about it. When one has something so subjective and intensely private as a dream, cradled within the bosom of something so deceptive and incurable as a sinful heart — the need for God's holy Word becomes profoundly evident! If dreams and visions are the product of our own hearts, then we would be fools indeed to rely on something so uncertain. But, thank God, we are not left to our own thoughts and desires. We have the Word of God, a more sure word of prophecy, that discerns our hearts.

What Does the Bible Say?

This brings us to the teaching of Scripture concerning false prophets, deceptive dreams and pretentious visions. Make no mistake about it — there are false prophets in the church and in the world. Peter wrote, "But there were also false prophets among the people, just as there will be false teachers among you. They will secretly introduce destructive heresies, even denying the sovereign Lord who bought them — bringing swift destruction on themselves. Many will follow their shameful ways and will bring the way of truth into disrepute. In their greed these teachers will exploit you with stories they have made up."[9]

False prophets are greedy. They want power, fame, wealth, attention, loyalty and service. They make up dreams and visions and deliver their messages couched in the language of secrecy and special revelation. They use these things to manipulate those who trust them into doing their personal bidding. They are deceitful, destructive and damnable.

The Bible does not pull punches on this matter. It delivers stern denunciations against false dreams, and it demands severe penalties against those who deceitfully engage in the practice of promoting them. "If a prophet, or one who foretells by dreams, appears among you and announces to you a miraculous sign or wonder, and if the sign or wonder of which he has spoken takes place, and he says, 'Let us follow other gods' (gods you have not known) 'and let us worship them,' you must not listen to the words of that prophet or dreamer."[10]

Is everybody clear in their minds about this? The bottom line is, *don't follow those who lead you away from God* — even if they have credentials which make them seem godly. And what exactly are those credentials? Dreams that come to pass! You see, the credentials are honorable — the issue here is one of character and motive.

Good Cop, Bad Cop

Look at it this way. When a police officer goes bad, he gives all cops a bad name and brings dishonor to the badge of authority they wear. In the same manner, when a false prophet uses dreams as the basis of his authority, it gives all dreamers a bad name and brings distrust to legitimate dreams and visions.

In both scenarios (policeman and prophet), there is nothing wrong with the badge. The issue is the character and conduct of the one who wears it. A crooked cop should be discharged from his duty and punished for his crimes. Likewise, false prophets who make themselves appear truthful by the misuse of dreams and visions should be firmly rejected.

Indeed, under the Law the people were commanded to take drastic measures to eradicate such deceit from their society: "That prophet or dreamer must be put to death, because he preached rebellion against the Lord your God, who brought you out of Egypt and redeemed you from the land of slavery; he has tried to turn you from the way the Lord your God commanded you to follow. You must purge the evil from among you."[11] Obviously we are not to go around murdering false prophets (although I've met a few who, passing through my church, have tempted me!).

How then does this scripture apply to us today? Practically speaking, our obedience to the spirit of the Law is fulfilled when we reckon false prophets as though they are dead to us. What can a dead man say? Nothing. What can a dead man do? Nothing. So be it of all who peddle falsehood in the church through the misuse of dreams and visions.

Visions From Their Own Minds

The Bible makes it quite clear what God thinks about false dreams and those who promote them. "This is what the Lord Almighty says: 'Do not listen to what the prophets are prophesying to you; they fill you with false hopes. They speak visions from their own minds, not from the mouth of the Lord.'"[12]

A few verses later the Lord says it again. "I have heard what the prophets say who prophesy lies in my name. They say, 'I had a dream! I had a dream!' How long will this continue in the hearts of these lying prophets, who prophesy the delusions of their own minds? They think the dreams they tell one another will make my people forget my name, just as their fathers forgot my name through Baal worship."[13]

Moreover, the Lord confronts a third time the deceit of false prophets: "The Lord Almighty, the God of Israel, says: 'Don't let the false prophets and mediums who are there among you fool you. Don't listen to the dreams they invent, for they prophesy lies in my name. I have not sent them.'"[14] It is quite evident that the Lord has no intention of letting such rascals get away without rebuke and exposure.

Come to the Light

Truth holds up to scrutiny; falsehood does not. It is only the counterfeit that fears close examination. In the teachings of Jesus we read, "Everyone who does evil hates the light, and will not come into the light for fear that his deeds will be exposed. But whoever lives by the truth comes into the light, so that it may be seen plainly that what he has done has been done through God."[15]

The apostle John, one of Jesus' closest friends, said, "This is the message we have heard from Him and declare to you, that God is light and in Him is no darkness at all. If we say that we have fellowship with Him, and walk in darkness, we lie and do not practice the truth. But if we walk in the light, as He is in the light, we have fellowship with one another, and the blood of Jesus Christ His Son cleanses us from all sin."[16]

Whether it be dreams and visions, or sermons, plans, thoughts and deeds — let's bring them all to the light to see if they are done through God. The Psalmist said, "In thy light shall we see light."[17] Commenting on this text Spurgeon said, "We need no candle to see the sun, we see it by its own radiance, and then see everything else by the same luster. The knowledge of God sheds light on all other subjects."[18] Rightly, therefore did the Psalmist sing, "Thy word is a lamp unto my feet, and a light unto my path."[19]

A few years ago I was rummaging through the books in an antique store and came upon a small volume entitled *The Hyacinth: or Affection's Gift,* by Henry F. Anners. The book, published in 1845, is a collection of poems and short stories aimed at youth to provide moral inspiration and practical instruction. I was intrigued by the little book, so I bought it and took it home. Perusing through its pages, I came upon this wonderful poem.

The Boy and the Fire-flies

An inexperienced boy, one night
through lonely paths returning,
Had taken to guide his steps aright,
a lantern brightly burning.

And safe he traveled by its ray,
until, before him glancing,
He saw, along the doubtful way,
the sparkling fire-flies dancing.

Then he discarded with disdain
his lantern calmly beaming,
To follow this resplendent train,
in fitful radiance gleaming.

But, ere a second step he took,
he found his folly humbled:
The flying lights his path forsook,
and in a ditch he tumbled.

Then bitter anger he expressed
against these guides beguiling;
Who thus the simple boy addressed:
"Nay, cease this vain reviling!

> "The blame remains with you alone;
> and half the ills men reckon,
> Proceed from leaving lights well known,
> to follow some false beacon."

We Must Make a Distinction

In a rationalistic society such as ours, spiritual things like dreams and visions are generally regarded with condescending skepticism. That's understandable, for not all men have faith. But this attitude is pervasive within the church as well. The result is to first dismiss dreams entirely since they occur outside of logic and self-control. Secondly, we are taught to view dreams and visions as deceptive and heretical, for they dare to imply that revelation from God can occur *outside* of Scripture. Please take note that I said "outside of" Scripture, rather than "in contradiction to" Scripture. There is an obvious and important difference.

Certainly God speaks through the Scripture, for it is the Word of God. However, God also speaks through dreams and visions, as well as by many other means, but *never* to the contradiction of Scripture nor to add to the Scripture — but only to *illustrate* it! For this reason it behooves us to use the Scripture to make a clear distinction between that which is true and that which is false in all matters of enlightenment — especially in the matter of dreams and visions.

"But," someone may ask, "since the Bible is so direct in denouncing those who foretell by dreams, shouldn't we reject dreams altogether, just to be safe and sure?" No, we should reject *false* dreams altogether. It is important that we distinguish between true and false dreams in this discussion. Otherwise we might inadvertently lump them together and reject all dreams. This would be a mistake, because some dreams are indeed from God.

No serious student of Scripture would deny this fact. The Bible expressly demonstrates that God is pleased to reveal Himself to us in the mystery of a dream and through the wonder of a vision. This in itself could explain why false prophets rely so heavily upon dreams and visions in their repertoire of alleged revelations. It may be, in the final analysis, the only way they have to lend any sense of credibility to their fraudulent messages.

The people in the Bible clearly understood and expected that God would speak to them through dreams and visions. He had done it so many times. How deceitful, therefore, it was for a false prophet to use this legitimate means of revelation to peddle his illegitimate wares upon a trusting flock. No wonder the Lord was so adamant about this practice and so severe in His judgments against it. We each should follow the Lord's leading and do all we can to distinguish the true from the false, and hold fast to that which is good.

How to Discern When a Dream Is False

Jesus said, "Watch out for false prophets. They come to you in sheep's clothing, but inwardly they are ferocious wolves. By their fruit you will recognize them."[20] Good trees produce good fruit; bad trees produce bad fruit. The same is true of dreams and visions. We discern them by the fruit they produce.

False dreams and visions have two things in common: deception and discord. Let's take a closer look at these evil twins.

Deception

Jesus said, "I am the way, the truth, and the life: no man cometh unto the Father, but by me."[21] Jesus did not say that He was the only way into the spiritual realm, rather that He is the only way a person may pass *through* that realm and safely reach the true God.

There are all kinds of doors into the spiritual dimension; dreams and visions are but two of them. Walking through the door is not the issue. Where one goes *is*. Therefore, the first test of any dream or vision is: does it lead us exclusively to Jesus Christ in love and obedience?

The second test is, does the dream or vision adhere faithfully to the Bible, and does it stay within the teachings of Scripture? Here is where Joseph Smith, founder of the Church of Jesus Christ of Latter Day Saints (commonly known as the Mormon Church), went astray. Smith professed having a vision in which an angel from heaven appeared to him and showed him secret tablets which supposedly "updated" the gospel of Jesus Christ.

In the Bible the apostle Paul wrote, "I am astonished that you are so quickly deserting the one who called you by the grace of Christ and are turning to a different gospel — which is really no gospel at all. Evidently some people are throwing you into confusion and are trying to pervert the gospel of Christ. But even if we or an angel from heaven should preach a gospel other than the one we preached to you, let him be eternally condemned!"

Lest his readers should misunderstand exactly what he meant, Paul repeated himself emphatically, "As we have already said, so now I say again: If anybody is preaching to you a gospel other than what you accepted, let him be eternally condemned!"[22]

This singular verse of scripture exposes both the absurdity and the audacity of Joseph Smith's claims. To contradict such a clear directive of holy Scripture borders on insanity. John the Beloved on the isle of Patmos received *the* revelation of Jesus Christ. After he had faithfully penned all that God had shown him, John summarized in the epilogue a warning which holds true for the entire canon of Scripture.

"I warn everyone who hears the words of the prophecy of this book: If anyone adds anything to them, God will add to him the plagues described in this book. And if anyone takes words away from this book of prophecy, God will take away from him his share in the tree of life and in the holy city, which are described in this book."[23]

Had Joseph Smith weighed carefully the warning of John the Beloved and heeded the admonition of the apostle Paul, he would have saved himself and all his followers from the inevitable consequence of their folly. As Paul would say of the Jews in his day, so we may say of the Mormons today:

"Brethren, my heart's desire and my prayer to God for them is for their salvation. For I bear them witness that they have a zeal for God, but not in accordance with knowledge. For not knowing about God's righteousness, and seeking to establish their own, they did not subject themselves to the righteousness of God."[24]

With all due respect to the dear people who honestly believe that Mormonism is true, the fact remains that its inception stands in direct violation of the Word of God and is therefore false. Certainly it has some truth within it; otherwise no self-respecting person would have anything to do with it at all.

But how can so many good people be so wrong? The answer in a word — *deception*. This is the firstfruit of falsehood. And the second is much the same.

Discord

Discord is the fruit of anything false — be it a sermon, a prophecy, a teaching, a dream or a vision of an angel from heaven. If it causes discord in the body of Christ, it is false.

There is a manifest disharmony in deception. What fellowship does light have with darkness? What communion does Christ have with Satan? There is no compromise, no negotiation, no diplomatic treaty, no peace between good and evil, no ceasefire between truth and falsehood. Whenever and wherever they chance to meet, there is *war*. The fallout is felt in our spirits, our minds and sometimes even our bodies.

When deception is present, discord is close at hand. The peace is broken, the joy is lost and the vitality fades away when error enters into anything. Like cancer to the body, so is falsehood to the soul. Discord is disruptive, debilitating and detestable.

Solomon said, "There are six things the Lord hates, seven that are detestable to him: haughty eyes, a lying tongue, hands that shed innocent blood, a heart that devises wicked schemes, feet that are quick to rush into evil, a false witness who pours out lies and a man who stirs up dissension among brothers."[25]

There are seven deadly sins lurking in the darkness of sleep fancies and other vain imaginations. They are pride, deceit, hatred, treachery, rebellion, betrayal and strife. Such things as these are not the fruit of God's kind of wisdom but are earthly, unspiritual and inspired by the devil. And wherever these things arise, there will be disorder and every other kind of evil.

Spotting the Counterfeit

The surest way to spot the counterfeit is by being thoroughly acquainted with the genuine article. For this reason we must seek the wisdom that truly comes from heaven. We shall know when we have found it, for it is first of all pure and gentle. Then it is peace-loving and courteous.

Furthermore, those who hold to the wisdom that comes from God are characterized by an ability to openly discuss matters in honest disagreement, while displaying a gracious willingness to yield to others who speak the truth. They are genuinely full of mercy and good deeds. They are wholehearted, straightforward and sincere.

These, unlike those who are false and argumentative, patiently plant the seeds of peace whereby they ultimately reap a harvest of goodness.[26]

Six Ways to Recognize False Dreams and Visions

There are at least six distinctive characteristics commonly found in false dreams and visions. Awareness of these traits will aid us in discerning when a dream is not from God.

1. They are seductive.

In the beginning when the serpent first whispered to Eve, "Yea, hath God said...?" there was a strange seduction taking place. He aroused her curiosity and stimulated her doubts. He dazzled her with lies and led her into deception.

After all these years, the devil still employs the same tactics. He uses dreams and visions to fill people with vanity and deceit. He gives a false sense of confidence and well-being, the promise of power and riches, fame and glory. He isolates people from those in authority and whispers alternatives to God's expressed will.

On the other hand, Satan also uses dreams and visions to create unfounded fears and debilitating anxieties. Have you ever had a nightmare that scared the living daylights out of you? It was the devil's work. It disturbed your sleep for nights to come and dogged your steps throughout the day. While it had your attention you were effectively rendered inactive for the Lord — precisely what the devil wanted all along.

Dreams of vain glory or visions of terror — in either case a satanic seduction is taking place. The effect of these kinds of dreams and visions is that they lead people astray from the truth and into ruin. "This is what the Lord Almighty says: 'Do not listen to what the prophets are prophesying to you; they fill you with false hopes. They speak visions from their own minds, not from the mouth of the Lord.'"[27]

2. They are corrupt.

There is a moral pollution that happens through false dreams and visions. The Bible says, "Regard not them that have familiar spirits, neither seek after wizards, to be defiled by them: I am the Lord your

God."[28] A defilement occurs whenever Satan is at work. Whether it is in the mind, or in relationships with others, in the church or beyond — Satan walks with filthy feet and leaves corruption everywhere he steps.

Many people responded to a survey in which I asked several questions concerning their experiences in dreams and visions. One of the frequent comments was of waking out of a disturbing dream feeling defiled and sinful. Interestingly enough, this happened most often after they had a special time with the Lord in church or some other form of ministry. It was Satan's way of trying to steal, or at least spoil, the blessing they had experienced.

3. They are contradictory.

Satan is defiant against the truth and deliberate in his attempt to pervert the minds of unsuspecting people. He will first use flattery, and when it fails, he resorts to mockery. Sarcastic charm has served the devil well through the ages, for most people are sufficiently self-doubting that they are rendered virtually incapable of answering his lies.

The devil contradicts truth, even when he partially employs it to spread his lies. "They keep saying to those who despise me, 'The Lord says: You will have peace.' And to all who follow the stubbornness of their hearts they say, 'No harm will come to you'"[29] Though the Lord does speak peace to His people and promise them freedom from harm, this was not what the Lord was saying to the people who were in rebellion to His will. The false prophets, motivated by Satan, deliberately contradicted the truth with brazen self-confidence and deceitfully framed it in words the Lord had spoken before. Nonetheless, the contradiction was evident to those who had discernment. It is the same even to this day.

4. They are discouraging.

"The idols speak deceit, diviners see visions that lie; they tell dreams that are false, they give comfort in vain. Therefore the people wander like sheep oppressed for lack of a shepherd."[30] A dream or vision that does not come from God will be false, reckless and detrimental.

It provides no solace to the suffering that people endure. It negates true leadership and cultivates depression. It promotes a lie and crushes the spirits of those who believed it was true. When something you have hoped for fails to happen over and over again, you ultimately give up and become caustic and cynical. This is exactly what the devil wants, and thus he perverts dreams and visions in order to achieve it.

5. *They are unproductive.*

The Lord said, "If they had stood in my council, they would have proclaimed my words to my people and would have turned them from their evil ways and from their evil deeds."[31] When a dream or a vision is truly from the Lord, it will proclaim God's Word to His people and turn them away from sin unto the Lord. That is the purpose of God's Word. It goes forth and does not return to Him without first accomplishing the purpose for which He sent it.

Dreams and visions that are not from God cannot accomplish the purposes of God. That's why the Lord said, "Let the prophet who has a dream tell his dream, but let the one who has my word speak it faithfully. For what has straw to do with grain?"[32]

It is true that straw will fill you up, but who wants to eat straw? Especially when you are offered *grain* from the Lord! Straw and grain may look alike, and perhaps may even taste the same, but once they are in the belly there is no mistake about which was the better choice for dinner! As straw would be unproductive to the body, so false dreams and visions are unproductive to the soul.

6. *They are destructive.*

"'Indeed, I am against those who prophesy false dreams,' declares the Lord. 'They tell them and lead my people astray with their reckless lies, yet I did not send or appoint them. They do not benefit these people in the least,' declares the Lord."[33]

The apostle Peter warned us against false prophets who would "secretly introduce destructive heresies...bringing swift destruction on themselves."[34] False dreams and visions cultivate recklessness and irresponsibility. They are unprofitable and destructive.

Six Questions That Must Be Answered

Here is a simple test you should apply to every dream or vision you have or hear about. You can also extend this to sermons, teachings, books, songs, movies, paintings or anything else that invites itself into your imagination through the doorway of sight and sound.

1. Does this lead me to Jesus Christ and fill me with love for His church?

2. Does this promote righteousness and purity in my life?

3. Does this align itself with the clear and emphatic teachings of the Bible?

4. Does this strengthen my faith and fill me with the sense of a noble destiny and an honorable purpose in life?

5. Does this turn me from sin and selfishness to seek the Lord and serve Him in faithfulness and love?

6. Does this build up the body of Christ and equip believers to do the work of the ministry?

If the answer is yes to the above questions, then the dream or vision is from God.

Conclusion

Since there are false dreams, then there must be *true* dreams as well. One cannot exist without the other, or else the Scripture would speak simply of dreams as either altogether false or altogether true. That it distinguishes them from one another is yet more proof that true dreams do come from God.

We have a proverbial saying, "Don't throw out the baby with the bathwater." Actually, no one would ever really do such a thing — so why the proverb? It corrects the tendency we have to be less than selective in our dismissal of things for which we think we have no use. Just because the water is dirty and should be discarded, one must not be extreme and toss away with it that which is precious and irreplaceable!

This is true of dreams and visions as well. The Lord spoke to Jeremiah, "If you return, then I will restore you — before Me you will stand; and if you extract the precious from the worthless, you will become My spokesman."[35] We must realize that there are both precious and worthless dreams — the grain and straw, as Jeremiah put it, or to use a New Testament figure of speech — the wheat and the tares. Both grow together, but only one is of any merit.

Let's now look at some of the dreams and visions that God has used to bless and benefit His beloved people.

PILLOWS OF STONE

The cool night was a welcomed reprieve from the exhausting heat of the long day's journey. The strange band of wanderers ventured onward into the unknown countryside — looking for a land that would belong to them. As night began to fall, the nomadic chieftain gathered his weary clan near a cluster of great oak trees. It would provide them with some form of shelter from the threatening storm off in the distance. Each peal of thunder seemed to be getting closer as the wind picked up and blew dust and weeds across the barren expanse. The tents were pitched, and a perimeter security was posted to insure the tribe against beasts and bandits. The plains of Mamre were notorious for both.

The crackling fire became the gathering place for the tribe when night fell. Children's faces would glow with wonder as they listened to the elders tell stories of heroes and villains, and they would quickly drift off to sleep when talk turned to more mundane matters. Eventually, they would retire to their own places of rest, safe under the vigilant eyes of those that kept watch. Oddly enough, their heads rested well on the pillows of stone as they slept through the night.

The venerable patriarch himself, once assured that all under his care were provided for, would then close his eyes in sleep. Often the night would pass as any other — uneventful, and far too quickly. But on this particular evening history was about to be made. A voice was soon to speak to the slumbering elder, filling his heart with childlike wonder. It sounded like the wind. Perhaps that's all it was to the others who slept nearby, but to the man who led this pilgrim clan it was unmistakable — *Somebody* called his name: "Abram."

The Dreams of the Patriarchs

The word *patriarch* comes from the Latin *pater*, "father," and the Greek verb *archo*, "to rule." A patriarch is thus a ruling ancestor who may have been the founding father of a family, a clan or a nation. In the Bible, Abraham, Isaac and Jacob (and the twelve sons of Jacob) were the patriarchs of Israel. The Bible says, "Long ago God spoke in many different ways to our fathers through the prophets [in visions, dreams, and even face to face], telling them little by little about his plans."[1]

By studying the dreams and visions of those who heard the word of the Lord in days gone by, our primary purpose is to gain insight into the dreams and visions we may have today. Perhaps it could be that God is speaking to us as He did unto them. Our focus will be primarily upon Abraham, Jacob and Joseph. We omit Isaac and the others not because they are unimportant, but because we have no biblical record of God speaking to them specifically through dreams and visions.

Abraham

"The Lord had said to Abram, 'Leave your country, your people and your father's household and go to the land I will show you. I will make you into a great nation and I will bless you; I will make your name great, and you will be a blessing. I will bless those who bless you, and whoever curses you I will curse; and all peoples on earth will be blessed through you.'"[2]

No explanation is given as to how the word of the Lord had come to him. There was no Bible in those days, so how did God's word come? Was it a dream, or a vision or a trance? Was it merely a thought in Abraham's mind? Or was it an audible voice from heaven, or an angelic visitation of some sort?

The answer is found in Stephen's sermon, preached centuries later to the joint session of the Jewish high council. "Brothers and fathers, listen to me! The God of glory appeared to our father Abraham while he was still in Mesopotamia, before he lived in Haran. 'Leave your country and your people,' God said, 'and go to the land I will show you.'"[3]

Stephen uses the Greek word *optanomai* to describe Abraham's encounter with God. It means "letting oneself be seen." The word is used elsewhere in the New Testament of the angel Gabriel appearing to Zechariah beside the altar of incense (Luke 1:11), of Moses and Elijah appearing with Jesus at the Transfiguration (Matt. 17:3), and of Jesus Himself appearing to Saul of Tarsus on the Damascus road (Acts 9:3-5).

In each instance the recipients *saw* that which was before them. The word of the Lord came to Abraham in a similar manner. Stephen spoke of Abraham's first encounter with God as being in a vision. None present in the council argued with him on this point, because they all knew it was true.

Abraham saw the Lord — not once, but several times! In fact, upon his obedience to the call of God, Abraham was again visited by the Lord specifically in a vision. "The Lord appeared to Abram and said, 'To your offspring I will give this land.' So he built an altar there to the Lord, who had appeared to him." The word *appeared* literally means "to see," either actually or in a spiritual vision. The Bible says that from this time onward Abraham "called on the name of the Lord."[4]

The Promised Land

The word of the Lord came again to Abraham and reaffirmed God's promise to bless him. "Lift up your eyes from where you are and look north and south, east and west. All the land that you see I will give to you and your offspring forever. I will make your offspring like the dust of the earth, so that if anyone could count the dust, then your offspring could be counted. Go, walk through the length and breadth of the land, for I am giving it to you."[5]

Once again we are not told specifically how the word of the Lord came to Abraham — only that it did. We can safely conclude that it was in a vision, based not only upon the previous encounter but also upon the fact that God told Abraham to "lift up his eyes and look." As we will see, this is a classic example of what happens in a vision. But whether it was a vision or not, one thing is certain — the Lord spoke, Abraham believed Him, and the blessings of God continued to increase in his life.

The Covenant of Faith

"After this, the word of the Lord came to Abraham in a vision: 'Do not be afraid, Abram. I am your shield, your very great reward.' But Abram said, 'O Sovereign Lord, what can you give me since I remain childless and the one who will inherit my estate is Eliezer of Damascus?'"[6] It's evident that Abraham was holding firm to God's earlier promise, "I will make you a great nation." Without showing any disrespect to the Lord, Abraham now wanted to know what God was going to do (practically speaking) to make the promise come true.

I find it noteworthy that Abraham responded to God's grand promises with down-to-earth practicality. It is a pattern we each should follow, set for us by the father of faith. Too often someone has a dream or a vision and they lose touch with day-to-day priorities. Often it seems that people of faith take liberty by being irresponsible in matters of fact. This was not the case with Abraham.

Custom dictated that Eliezer of Damascus would be the rightful heir, so Abraham asked God if this was the way God would do it. Since there is no immediate answer from the Lord, Abraham concluded, "You have given me no children; so a servant in my household will be my heir."[7] Abraham's reasoning was honorable and his conclusions logical. But he was wrong.

"Then the word of the Lord came to him: 'This man will not be your heir, but a son coming from your own body will be your heir.'"[8] Keep in mind that the vision is still taking place as Abraham speaks his mind about who would be his heir. God answered Abraham's thoughts and thereby corrected his wrong conclusions *while he was having a vision.*

The word *vision* means to gaze at, to perceive mentally, or to contemplate with pleasure. Specifically, it means; "to behold, to look up and see."[9] This vision was not a figment of Abraham's imagination. He was fully awake and conversant with the Lord. His senses were not dulled by wine nor in any other way fatigued. He was cognitive and reposed. Abraham *saw* with his eyes, *heard* with his ears, *reasoned* with his mind and even *spoke* to God in his vision. All of these factors show that his will, emotions and understanding were fully involved in the process.

The Bible says that God then took him outside and said, "Look up at the heavens and count the stars — if indeed you can count them." Pausing long enough to let the full scope of the promise settle upon Abraham's heart, the Lord then said to him, "So shall your offspring be."[10] Abraham believed the Lord, and God credited it to him as righteousness.

The Blood Covenant

The Lord spoke to Abraham again and said: "'I am the Lord, who brought you out of Ur of the Chaldeans to give you this land to take possession of it.' But Abram said, 'O Sovereign Lord, how can I know that I will gain possession of it?'"[11] Having faith does not mean one does not have questions. It means that one trusts God even if no answers are given to the questions one does have. Abraham had many questions, and on this occasion the Lord answered Abraham in a most peculiar manner.

God instructed Abraham to cut the sacrificial animals down the middle and lay the pieces opposite one another. Abraham then stood in the midst of the carcasses, driving away the vultures while he waited for God to speak to him again.

That evening as the sun was going down, a deep sleep fell upon Abraham, and a vision of terrible foreboding, of darkness and horror, came to Abraham as he slept. God said to Abraham in the dream: "Know for certain that your descendants will be strangers in a country not their own, and they will be enslaved and mistreated four hundred years. But I will punish the nation they serve as slaves, and afterward they will come out with great possessions."[12]

Five Distinguishing Facts About Abraham's Dream

This encounter of Abraham with God provides us with several insights into how God may speak to us through a dream. First, it happened after a deep sleep came upon him. The Hebrew word translated "deep sleep" means a lethargy or trance. It comes from the root word which means to stun, to stupefy, or to be cast into a deep sleep.[13] Unlike other visions in which Abraham was sharp-witted and watchful, here he is unconscious and overcome with holy dread.

Second, this dream is distinctly prophetic. In a wondrous moment of revelation God let Abraham see the future history of his children's children when as yet he was without a child! A casual reading of the book of Exodus will provide the remarkable account of this prophecy's precise fulfillment.

Third, this dream gave Abraham personal assurance of God's commitment to bless him with a long and fruitful life. "You, however, will go to your fathers in peace and be buried at a good old age."[14] This undoubtedly calmed his troubled spirit. He may have wondered, "If this great bondage is coming upon my descendants, then what will happen to me?" The dream gave him an answer.

Fourth, the dream provided Abraham with an explanation for why his descendants would be kept out of their Promised Land for so long before they could inherit it. "In the fourth generation your descendants will come back here, for the sin of the Amorites has not yet reached its full measure."[15]

Finally, this remarkable dream instituted three profound truths that become thematic throughout the remainder of Scripture. They are: 1) God is the initiator of covenant, not man; 2) the one requirement of covenant is blood sacrifice; and 3) God is sovereign and faithful in administrating the outcome of His promises.

The Sign of the Covenant

"When Abram was ninety-nine years old, the Lord appeared to him and said, 'I am God Almighty; walk before me and be blameless. I will confirm my covenant between me and you and will greatly increase your numbers.'"[16]

As before, God let Himself be seen by Abraham. The Bible says that Abraham fell face down before the Lord and heard these words: "As for me, this is my covenant with you: You will be the father of many nations. No longer will you be called Abram; your name will be Abraham, for I have made you a father of many nations."[17]

While Abraham was on his face, the Lord revealed to him the sign of the covenant — circumcision (cutting the foreskin from the male sexual organ). This is God's wisdom, for no man would have *ever* thought to do this to himself. It was revealed by God in a vision to Abraham. In this single act of submission the identity and the virility of manhood are rightfully surrendered to God.

How amazing that today millions of men and boys from nations all around the world bear the sign of circumcision in their bodies. And how fascinating that the practice was revealed in a vision to Abraham so very long ago! Doctors say it's for the purpose of hygiene (as indeed it is), but the Bible says it is a sign of God's covenant to make Abraham the father of many nations — which He has indeed done.

The Birth of Isaac

"The Lord appeared to Abraham near the great trees of Mamre while he was sitting at the entrance to his tent in the heat of the day. Abraham looked up and saw three men standing nearby. When he saw them, he hurried from the entrance of his tent to meet them and bowed low to the ground."[18]

As it unfolds, we discover the purpose of this remarkable visitation was to announce that Sarah, though barren and aged, was to conceive and bring forth a son. Though it was impossible for man, God kept His promise. Sarah became pregnant and bore a son to Abraham in his old age, at the very time God had promised it would happen. Abraham named him Isaac and circumcised him on the eighth day as God commanded him.[19] Both God and Abraham were promise keepers.

The record of Scripture is indisputable. We have at least seven documented cases where God spoke to Abraham through dreams and visions. By this means God lifted a man out of paganism and directed him towards greatness. Such is the power of vision. Abraham believed God and obeyed Him. His life was forever changed as a result of the dreams and visions God gave him. So, for that matter, was the history of the world.

Jacob

"We are climbing Jacob's Ladder." What child attending Sunday school hasn't heard the little chorus? It's a cute song, but what does it mean? What exactly are we singing about? In one word: Jesus! In the New Testament, when Nathaniel met Jesus, he was astounded by the Lord's insight into his life and exclaimed, "Rabbi, you are the Son of God! You are the King of Israel!" Jesus downplayed Nathaniel's astonishment and said, "I tell you the truth, you shall see heaven open, and the angels of God ascending and descending on the Son of Man."[20]

This is an unmistakable reference to Jacob's dream centuries earlier, in which he saw a stairway resting on the earth, with its top reaching to heaven, and the angels of God ascending and descending upon it. At the top of the stairs stood the Lord in His majesty, and in the dream He spoke to Jacob, just as He had spoken to Abraham.[21]

The ladder in Jacob's dream at Bethel was a symbolic revelation of Jesus Christ — the way, the truth and the life! The angels are the messengers who bring God's word from heaven and return to God with our prayers — through Jesus Christ alone. "Salvation is found in no one else, for there is no other name under heaven given to men by which we must be saved "[22]

Jacob woke up from his dream and was filled with holy fear. So moved was he that he took the stone he had used as his pillow and poured oil on top of it, thereby making this vow to God: "If God will be with me and will watch over me on this journey I am taking and will give me food to eat and clothes to wear so that I return safely to my father's house, then the Lord will be my God and this stone that I have set up as a pillar will be God's house, and of all that you give me I will give you a tenth."[23]

God brought Jacob into the covenant by speaking to him through a dream. He can — and does — do the same today!

The Speckled Rams

After spending several years with Laban, his father-in-law, and prospering through the blessing of the Lord, the time came for Jacob to move on. He made a deal with Laban that he would only take from the flocks those animals that were spotted, streaked or in any way discolored. Laban agreed and then hid all the spotted livestock from Jacob so that there were none for him to take.

The Bible tells us that Jacob put spotted sticks in the drinking water and in the food troughs of the remaining herds, and the animals gave birth to spotted offspring![24] What? Why on earth would he think that spotted sticks would make animals give birth to spotted offspring? And, seeing that it worked, how is this possible!?

Indeed, like us, Jacob's wives also wanted to know how he had pulled this off and thereby taken the greater part of their father's herds. Jacob told them the answer.

"In breeding season I once had a dream in which I looked up and saw that the male goats mating with the flock were streaked, speckled or spotted. The angel of God said to me in the dream, 'Jacob.' I answered, 'Here I am.' And he said, 'Look up and see that all the male goats mating with the flock are streaked, speckled or spotted, for I have seen all that Laban has been doing to you. I am the God of Bethel, where you anointed a pillar and where you made a vow to me. Now leave this land at once and go back to your native land.'"[25]

We now understand that the spotted sticks held no magical power, nor were they responsible for the amazing alteration of nature in the breeding animals. Why Jacob even used spotted sticks is unclear. Perhaps they were simply a point of reference by which he acted out his faith in God's Word. The point is that *God* turned the offspring speckled in response to Jacob's faith, which he came by in a dream.

The Angels of God

Once Jacob successfully separated from Laban there remained one more relationship he had to face — Esau, the brother he had cheated out of his birthright. To prepare Jacob for the moment of reconciliation with Esau, the "angels of God met him"[26] as he traveled from Padan Aram. The word *met* is used to describe an unexpected encounter which is inevitable and cannot be avoided.

This meeting with the angels triggered something in Jacob's heart toward Esau, for the next thing he did was to send a message to Esau asking for favor in his sight. When Jacob heard that Esau was approaching him with an army of four hundred men, fear struck his heart. He quickly devised a plan whereby he would appease his brother with gifts, or at least be able to escape with half his camp intact.

This brings us to perhaps the most renowned of all Jacob's encounters with God. Having sent his great family ahead in two companies, Jacob was left alone. Little did he know that yet another inevitable meeting was about to take place.

Your Name Is Israel

Alone in the darkness of what he feared would be his last night on earth, Jacob was suddenly face to face with a terrifying stranger. No sooner had they met than the man began to wrestle with Jacob. The word *wrestle* means to pulverize. We can deduce that God was grinding Jacob to powder!

Jacob put up a good fight, as so many do, and the Lord concluded that the match was over. He would leave Jacob as he was, crippled in his calling. A fear greater than anything Jacob had ever known seized his heart, and he grabbed hold of the Lord, crying out, "I will not let You go until You have blessed me!" The Lord responded with the final blow that completely brought Jacob to the end of himself.

"What is your name?" the Lord asked him. For the first time in his life Jacob knew that he would have to admit who he was — *what* he was — a deceitful, contriving, manipulating coward who lived only for himself. He answered the Lord, "My name is Jacob." The name was built on the Hebrew noun for "heel" meaning, "he grasps the heel" or "he cheats, supplants."[27] From the moment he was born holding onto his brother's heel, throughout his life, Jacob was a deceiver.

By confessing his name to the Lord, Jacob was finally broken from the independence that kept him away from the higher call of God upon his life. It was at that moment the Lord said, "Your name will no longer be Jacob, but Israel because you have struggled with God and with men and have overcome."[28] You see, by losing the wrestling match, Jacob won.

Jesus taught, "If any man will come after me, let him deny himself, and take up his cross, and follow me. For whosoever will save his life shall lose it: and whosoever will lose his life for my sake shall find it."[29] Jacob leaned upon his staff the remainder of his days; it was the only way he could walk upright after the Lord had touched his thigh. Today you and I must lean upon the cross as the only means whereby we may walk worthy of our high calling. Yes, we are climbing Jacob's ladder and every step goes higher, higher — soldiers of the cross!

After the bout had finished, Jacob named the place where it happened Peniel, saying, "It is because I saw God face to face, and yet my life was spared."[30] It is at the cross we meet God, and there our lives are spared through Jesus. Now, like Nathaniel, we see the angels of God ascending and descending upon the Son of Man, our Savior and our King, our great Redeemer and our Friend. Jesus is our Peniel!

Jacob and Esau were reconciled, by the way, and both went their separate ways in peace. Esau became the patriarch of the Edomites, and Jacob became father to the children of Israel. The nation Israel today owes its existence and its very name to the outcome of Jacob's ancient wrestling match with God.

Jacob's Final Vision

Jacob's final vision came when he and his family were invited to live in the land of Egypt by his son Joseph. "God spoke to Israel in a vision at night and said, 'Jacob! Jacob!' 'Here I am,' he replied. 'I am God, the God of your father,' he said. 'Do not be afraid to go down to Egypt, for I will make you into a great nation there. I will go down to Egypt with you, and I will surely bring you back again. And Joseph's own hand will close your eyes.'"[31]

As he had always done, Jacob obeyed the Lord and went to Egypt. This set the stage for the fulfillment of the prophecy God had given to Abraham in the disturbing dream so long ago.

Joseph

Joseph, eleventh son of Jacob, was destined by God to be one of the greatest of Israel's patriarchs. His ascendancy to greatness, however, was not exactly a stroll through the park. He was indignantly bullied by his brothers, mercilessly sold as a slave, falsely accused as a rapist, unjustly imprisoned as a criminal and completely forgotten like a bad memory. But at no time was he ever forsaken by God. Nor did he at any time during the unbearable process turn away from trusting the Lord. What was his secret? Where did he come by such staying power? It happened in a dream!

"Now Joseph had a dream."[32] The primary root meaning of the word translated *had* is "to bind firmly."[33] Thus it could be said that Joseph became firmly bound up in the dream that God had given him. Having *had* dreams myself I can attest to the accuracy of this definition. Dreams that come from God transcend simple thought and mere human aspirations. They are spiritual experiences. They become rooted in your heart as though they actually happened to you. Though your body is at rest with your eyes firmly closed, your spirit meets with God, and the eyes of your heart record all that is set before you. When you wake up, you never forget the dream. The years may pass like days in a week, but you still recall with vivid clarity the smallest details of a dream from God.

When Baptist Preachers Dream

The Rev. A. J. Gordon, the renowned Baptist preacher and author from Boston, and one of the founders of the highly respected Gordon Conwell Seminary, told of a dream he had that dramatically changed the course of his ministry, even though he had never paid any attention to his dreams before.

> It was Saturday night, when wearied from the work of preparing Sunday's sermon, that I fell asleep and the dream came. I was in the pulpit before a full congregation, just ready to begin my sermon, when a stranger entered and passed slowly up the left aisle of the church looking first to the one side and then to the other as though silently asking with his eyes that someone would give him a seat. He had proceeded nearly halfway up the aisle when a gentleman stepped out and offered him a place in his pew, which was quietly accepted.
>
> Excepting the face and features of the stranger, everything in the scene is distinctly remembered — the number of the pew, the Christian man who offered his hospitality,

the exact seat which was occupied. Only the countenance of the visitor could never be recalled. That his face wore a peculiarly serious look, as of one who had known some great sorrow, is clearly impressed on my mind. His bearing too was exceeding humble, his dress poor and plain, and from the beginning to the end of the service he gave the most respectful attention to the preacher. Immediately as I began my sermon my attention became riveted on this hearer. If I would avert my eyes from him for a moment they would instinctively return to him, so that he held my attention rather than I held his till the discourse ended.

To myself I said constantly, "Who can that stranger be?" And then I mentally resolved to find out by going to him and making his acquaintance as soon as the service should be over. But after the benediction had been given, the departing congregation filed into the aisles and before I could reach him the visitor had left the house.

The gentleman with whom he had sat remained behind, however, and approaching him with great eagerness I asked: "Can you tell me who that stranger was who sat in your pew this morning?" In the most matter-of-course way he replied: "Why, do you not know that man? It was Jesus of Nazareth."

With a sense of keenest disappointment I said: "My dear sir, why did you let Him go without introducing me to Him? I was so desirous to speak with Him." With the same nonchalant air the gentleman replied: "Oh, do not be troubled. He has been here today, and no doubt He will come again."

And now came an indescribable rush of emotion. As when a strong current is suddenly checked, the stream rolls back upon itself and is choked in its own foam, so the intense curiosity which had been going out toward the mysterious hearer now returned upon the preacher — and the Lord Himself. "Whose I am and Whom I serve" had been listening to me today. What was I saying? Was I preaching on some popular theme in order to catch the ear of the public? Was it "Christ crucified preached in a crucified style," or did the preacher magnify himself while exalting Christ?

So anxious and painful did these questionings become that I was about to ask the brother with whom He had sat if the Lord had said anything concerning the sermon, but a sense of propriety and self-respect at once checked the suggestion. Then immediately other questions began with equal vehemence to crowd into the mind. We speak of a "momentous occasion." This, though in sleep, was recognized as such by the dreamer — a lifetime, almost an eternity of interest crowded into a single solemn moment.[34]

A.J. Gordon was never the same after his dream. Neither was Joseph after his.

Joseph had a dream. Perhaps we could more accurately say that the dream *had* Joseph! That's where he got his staying power which carried him through all that happened to him over the years. Indeed, the story of Joseph is one of the most inspiring examples of the power of a dream.

Joseph's Dream of Greatness

Joseph said to his brothers, "Hear, I pray you, this dream which I have dreamed." Why, Joseph seems so polite and proper in this request, as if nothing is wrong with what he is about to do. Indeed, the refinery of the King James English makes it virtually impossible for anyone to sound like a jerk. But that is exactly what Joseph was being, and his brothers knew it. And Joseph *wanted* them to know it. Listen to how the Living Bible puts it:

"One night Joseph had a dream and promptly reported the details to his brothers, causing even deeper hatred. 'Listen to this,' he proudly announced. 'We were out in the field binding sheaves, and my sheaf stood up, and your sheaves all gathered around it and bowed low before it!' 'So you want to be our king, do you?' his brothers derided. And they hated him both for the dream and for his cocky attitude."[35]

The boy just didn't know how to leave things alone. He no sooner finishes one dream than he returns with yet another. We can almost hear him saying *nah-na-nah-na-naah-na* (to the tune of "Ring Around the Rosies").

"'Listen to my *latest* dream,' he boasted. 'The sun, moon, and eleven stars bowed low before me!' This time he told his father as well as his brothers; but his father rebuked him. 'What is this?' he asked. 'Shall I indeed, and your mother and brothers come and bow before you?' His brothers were fit to be tied concerning this affair, but his father gave it quite a bit of thought and wondered what it all meant."[36]

Jacob, though displeased with Joseph's immature behavior, recognized the familiar quality of a dream from God. He rebuked the boy, but carefully considered the revelation God had given his son in a dream. Perhaps it brought to mind affectionate memories of Bethel and Peniel where he had himself met the Lord in dreams.

While there was not much need for interpretation, seeing that everybody clearly understood what Joseph was saying, Jacob pondered long over the application of the dream. How would this dream come to pass? Indeed, how could this dream come to pass? The remainder of the book of Genesis is devoted to answering that very question.

Kill the Dreamer!

Jacob sent his sons, excluding Joseph, to herd their flocks in Shechem, a city about one hundred miles north of Hebron, where Jacob lived. Obviously a journey of that distance would take some time to accomplish. Evidently it took longer than Jacob thought necessary, so he sent Joseph to check on his brothers. This was not a smart thing to do.

The brothers spotted Joseph in the distance long before he reached them. His brightly colored coat gave him away. "Here comes that dreamer!" they said to each other. "Come now, let's kill him and throw him into one of these water cisterns and say that a ferocious animal devoured him. Then we'll see what comes of his dreams."[37]

The devil is forever trying to put an end to the dreams that come from God. Joseph's brothers become co-conspirators in a diabolic plot to thwart the purposes of God in Joseph's life. Little did they (or the devil, for that matter) know that they were playing right into the very hand of the Lord. The decisions made in that moment by these brothers set in motion a chain of events which ultimately brought these very men to bow in the presence of Joseph — just as he had dreamed!

The last sight the treacherous brothers had of Joseph was of him begging them not to sell him into slavery. The memory of his terror and anguish would haunt them for years to come. In fact, standing condemned before the ruler of Egypt years later they confessed, "Surely we are being punished because of our brother. We saw how distressed he was when he pleaded with us for his life, but we would not listen; that's why this distress has come upon us."[38] They were never able to rid their consciences of what they had done to Joseph, and to their father who loved him so much.

Joseph in Egypt

Joseph was led away into Egypt where he was sold to Potiphar, an officer of Pharaoh.[39] Potiphar found him so trustworthy that he put Joseph in charge of his household, and he entrusted to his care everything he owned. Things were going along fine until Potiphar's wife, a desperate woman, took offense at Joseph's refusal of her sexual advances. In a moment of bitter rejection she accused Joseph of trying to rape her. Her accusations were sufficient to send him to prison without trial. "From the pit to the purchase block to the prison. This just isn't my decade," Joseph may have thought. But God was with Joseph and prospered him in the prison. He was put in charge over all the other prisoners.

The Cupbearer and the Baker

Joseph noticed that the two of the inmates were acting quite dejected one morning, so he inquired as to the cause of their sadness. "We both had dreams," they answered, "but there is no one to interpret them." Then Joseph said to them, "Do not interpretations belong to God? Tell me your dreams."[40]

The story of Joseph not only validates that God speaks to us through dreams and visions, it also introduces something new to the discussion: the interpretation of dreams. This is significant because it shows that our dreams often need to be interpreted. That is to say, they don't always come in clear and easy-to-understand pictures.

Well, why not? some might ask. Why doesn't God just tell us plainly what He has on His mind? Why fool around with wheat bundles bowing down, and ladders going into heaven, and speckled goats jumping around during mating season? Why show us sheets filled with pigs and catfish let down from heaven, or Macedonians calling us across the sea, or hippos in our gardens? Why does He give us weird dreams in the first place?

The answer is a single word: economy. A picture is worth a thousand words. Words may soon be forgotten, but a vision or a dream will stick deep within the soul of the one to whom it came.

Well, then why do we have to interpret the dreams? Why doesn't God make the meanings obvious? The Bible says, "It is the glory of God to conceal a matter; to search out a matter is the glory of kings."[41] God uses the mystery of a dream not only to capture our hearts, but also to call us into the noble pursuit of wisdom.

Yet Joseph assures us that we cannot find the answer on our own. "Do not interpretations belong to God?" Indeed they do. But God is pleased to share them with us if we would turn our hearts toward Him with inquiry. If we seek, we will find.

"So the chief cupbearer told Joseph his dream. He said to him, 'In my dream I saw a vine in front of me, and on the vine were three branches. As soon as it budded, it blossomed, and its clusters ripened into grapes. Pharaoh's cup was in my hand, and I took the grapes, squeezed them into Pharaoh's cup and put the cup in his hand.'"[42] *Hmmmm.* What do you think *that* means?

"This is what it means," Joseph said to him. "The three branches are three days. Within three days Pharaoh will lift up your head and restore you to your position, and you will put Pharaoh's cup in his hand, just as you used to do when you were his cupbearer."[43]

Joseph quickly added a personal appeal for the cupbearer to remember him when he stood again before Pharaoh, "When all goes well with you, remember me and show me kindness; mention me to Pharaoh and get me out of this prison."[44]

The baker listened intently to every word Joseph said to the cupbearer. His dream had so many similarities that he surely thought the interpretation would be as hopeful for him as it had been for the cupbearer. He said to Joseph, "I too had a dream: On my head were three baskets of bread. In the top basket were all kinds of baked goods for Pharaoh, but the birds were eating them out of the basket on my head."[45] *Hmmmm.* What do think *that* means?

"This is what it means," Joseph said. "The three baskets are three days. Within three days Pharaoh will lift off your head and hang you on a tree. And the birds will eat away your flesh."[46] Yikes!

The dreams came to pass within three days. It happened exactly as Joseph had said. With the cupbearer restored to the palace, and Pharaoh celebrating a birthday, Joseph's hopes were high for justice, knowing that the cupbearer would tell Pharaoh about his unjust situation. But the days turned to weeks, the weeks to months, and the months to years. No word from the palace. No reprieve. No appeal. No release from prison. Joseph had been forgotten. How awful. This had to be the darkest period of Joseph's life.

Shake Well Before Using

A Hebrew in an Egyptian prison did not fare well. It is true that the jailer showed some kindness to Joseph, but whatever measure of mercy he was allotted could not have softened the blow of his unjust imprisonment. The Psalmist gives us some insight into Joseph's treatment while in the prison. "They bruised his feet with shackles, his neck was put in irons, till what he foretold came to pass, till the word of the Lord proved him true."[47]

Did you catch that? The word of the Lord proved *him* true. It had been many years since Joseph had boasted in his boyish manner of the dreams of greatness that God had given him. Though his childish behavior clouded the issue, Joseph's dreams were from God. But Joseph's attitude was not. The years were not for the sake of proving the dreams were true, but for the sake of proving Joseph to be true. The refining process of the Lord does the same in our lives today.

There are many in the church today who themselves are much like Joseph. They truly receive dreams and visions from God, but conduct themselves with such immaturity that it stirs their brethren to reject them. Perhaps, like Joseph, they too must go through some agonizing years of proving before their words can be believed. There is a pit, a purchase block and a prison before there is a palace!

Pharaoh's Double Feature

The dreams of Pharaoh are the turning point of God's intervention on Joseph's behalf. Pharaoh dreamed he was standing by the Nile, when out of the river there came up seven cows, sleek and fat, and they grazed among the reeds. After them, seven other cows, ugly and gaunt, came up out of the Nile and stood beside those on the riverbank. And the cows that were ugly and gaunt ate up the seven sleek, fat cows. Then Pharaoh woke up. He fell asleep again and had a second dream: Seven heads of grain, healthy and good, were growing on a single stalk. After them, seven other heads of grain sprouted — thin and scorched by the east wind. The thin heads of grain swallowed up the seven healthy, full heads.[48]

Most people would wake up from a dream like this, scratch their head a couple of times, review what they had for dinner the night before, shrug their shoulders and go on about the day. Why didn't Pharaoh? Why give these weird dreams a second thought? The Bible says he was "troubled." The word means to be agitated. It would be like listening to a faucet drip all night long. The more you try not to hear it, the louder it sounds. The more Pharaoh tried not to think about the dreams, the more they dominated his thoughts and troubled his soul.

His agitation was further compounded by the fact that no one could explain what the dreams meant — if, indeed, they meant anything at all. Everything in the palace came to a halt, a sense of irritation permeated the air, and the officials, ignorant of the dream's meaning, were wise to keep their distance.

Finally, what Joseph had asked for two years earlier was about to happen. The cupbearer remembered him before Pharaoh. "Now a young Hebrew was there with us, a servant of the captain of the guard. We told him our dreams, and he interpreted them for us, giving each man the interpretation of his dream. And things turned out exactly as he interpreted them to us."[49] That's all the king needed to hear. He immediately sent for Joseph, and they quickly brought him to the palace.

Pharaoh said, "I had a dream, and no one can interpret it. But I have heard it said of you that when you hear a dream you can interpret it."[50] Joseph's answer reveals how deeply God had worked in his heart. "I cannot do it," Joseph replied.[51] How different this was from the young smart-aleck who knew the interpretation to his own dreams as a boy. Maybe the years of reflection had brought Joseph to such humility. How many times had he thought through his own dreams and wondered what they could possibly mean, seeing he obviously misinterpreted them the first time around.

"I cannot do it." This is the answer of humility and truth. Joseph quickly added, "But God will give Pharaoh the answer he desires."[52] Pharaoh then told his dreams to Joseph, and God opened his understanding. "And for that the dream was doubled unto Pharaoh twice; it is because the thing is established by God, and God will shortly bring it to pass."[53] Make note of that, for it provides us with a key to how God speaks. The repetition of a revelation becomes its confirmation.

Joseph told Pharaoh that Egypt would have seven years of prosperity, followed by seven years of famine. Pharaoh was first perplexed by the dreams; now he was stunned by their meaning. "What should I do?" he asked. Joseph set forth a savings plan that would take the abundance of the first seven years and provide for the nation during the successive years of the operation.

Pharaoh turned to his officials and asked, "Can we find anyone like this man, one in whom is the spirit of God?"[54] It was unanimous, and Pharaoh said to Joseph, "Since God has made all this known to you, there is no one so discerning and wise as you. You shall be in charge of my palace, and all my people are to submit to your orders. Only with respect to the throne will I be greater than you. I hereby put you in charge of the whole land of Egypt."[55]

"Then Pharaoh took his signet ring from his finger and put it on Joseph's finger. He dressed him in robes of fine linen and put a gold chain around his neck. Pharaoh gave Joseph the name Zaphenath-Paneah," which means *"God Speaks and He Lives!"*[56] May God hasten the day when once again the kings of earth take note of the servants of the Lord and mark them with such a name as Pharaoh gave to Joseph!

The seven years of plenty came and were followed by a severe famine that reached far beyond Egypt's border. Once word spread that there was food in Egypt, many people came to Joseph to buy grain and supplies. Imagine the moment when Joseph looked from his throne to behold his very own brothers bowing before him asking for grain![57]

Lessons for Dreamers From the Life of Joseph

Joseph held to the vision God gave him for his life. It kept him through everything he experienced. He was restrained from sin, redeemed from sorrow and restored to honor by holding on to the dreams from God. There are five helpful guidelines that we learn from Joseph.

1. Stay the course (Gen. 37:5-10).

God puts His word in our hearts through the inspiration of vision. We hear a sermon that calls us into the service of the Lord, or meet a missionary who opens our eyes to worlds we know not, or in some other way, even in a dream, the thought enters into our hearts of how we may serve the Lord and be used mightily by God for His glory. Stay the course like Joseph, no matter what may befall you. Remember, between the promise and the promised land there is a desert filled with fiery serpents and grumbling unbelievers. Let your eye be fixed upon the faithfulness of the Lord. He will accomplish what He has spoken.

2. Serve the Lord (Gen. 39:4, 21).

Joseph made the most out of every bad situation. His focus was always toward the Lord. Whether in Potiphar's house or in the federal prison, Joseph served the Lord and was lifted above the circumstances. Do whatsoever your hand finds to do as though it were for the Lord. It will cause the standard of your life to be above the common, and may in fact be the very means the Lord employs to turn the hearts of others favorably towards you.

3. Shun wickedness (Gen. 39:9).

When faced with the provocative and powerful temptation pressed upon him by Potiphar's lusty wife, Joseph stood firm as a man of integrity and purity. You must do the same. The dreams and visions of God in our lives can be sabotaged by the undermining work of sin. Do not think that there is no longer any reason for you to stay faithful just because the Lord delays in his work. The vision is for the appointed time; though it tarries, wait for it. It will surely come. But you must have pure hands with which to hold it when it arrives.

4. Share the truth (Gen. 41:14-57).

One great lesson we learn from Joseph's life is that the truth always prevails. We should not only know the truth, but share it every chance we have. And most certainly we are to speak the truth whenever we are faced with opportunities to speak for God, whether it be to cellmates or to kings on their thrones.

5. Succeed with God (Gen. 45:7–50:20).

The testimony of Joseph girds our feet with glad resolve to run with vision, faith and courage whatever course lies before us. Come what may, we fully believe we shall stand triumphant in the fulness of God's faithfulness, there proclaiming loudly for all to hear that whatsoever others had meant unto us for evil, God had meant for good and thereby accomplished glorious things in our hearts and lives. Praise be to God!

Conclusion

Abraham, Jacob and Joseph are the fathers of our faith. As such, they set for us the spiritual genetic code for our walk with God. We see that dreams and visions factored significantly in their lives, and thus we should expect that it would be the same in our lives today. We have good cause to believe as much, because that which God started with the patriarchs He continued with Moses, Samuel and the prophets. Let's turn our attention there and see what awaits us.

THE ALL-SEEING EYE

One day Miriam and Aaron "began to talk against Moses because of his Cushite wife, for he had married a Cushite. 'Has the Lord spoken only through Moses?' they asked. 'Hasn't he also spoken through us?' And the Lord heard this. (Now Moses was a very humble man, more humble than anyone else on the face of the earth.)

"At once the Lord said to Moses, Aaron and Miriam, 'Come out to the Tent of Meeting, all three of you.' So the three of them came out. Then the Lord came down in a pillar of cloud; he stood at the entrance to the Tent and summoned Aaron and Miriam. When both of them stepped forward, he said, 'Listen to my words: When a prophet of the Lord is among you, I reveal myself to him in visions, I speak to him in dreams. But this is not true of my servant Moses; he is faithful in all my house. With him I speak face to face, clearly and not in riddles; he sees the form of the Lord. Why then were you not afraid to speak against my servant Moses?' The anger of the Lord burned against them, and he left them."[1]

This story reveals at least three important facts for us to consider. First, it shows the preeminent privilege granted to Moses to speak to the Lord face to face. Truly, the Lord resists the proud but gives grace to the humble. The second fact that must be noted is that God takes great offense when people speak against those to whom He has chosen to reveal Himself. The third significant detail given in this story is that God does speak to prophets through dreams and visions. The Lord Himself clearly said so, and for that matter He has certainly done so throughout history.

"I have also spoken by the prophets, and I have multiplied visions, and used similitudes, by the ministry of the prophets."[2]

Even though they are from God, prophets and visionaries are seldom greeted with wide acceptance. Rather, they are often angrily rejected, or worse yet, murdered! Why is this? Why do people venerate prophets *after* they have been martyred?

In Hosea's day the Lord gave this answer: "Because your sins are so many and your hostility so great, the prophet is considered a fool, the inspired man a maniac."[3] Is it possible that godly men, anointed by the Holy Spirit and speaking for the Lord, could be considered as nothing more than foolish maniacs? So much for the latest opinion poll.

God, by His own admission, makes Himself known in visions, and He speaks in dreams. The word *known* means "to know; to ascertain by seeing." Thus, while we are dreaming or having a vision it is possible that we can find out something the Lord wants us to know about Himself. The word *speak* means "to arrange words for the purpose of answering, appointing, commanding, communing, declaring, promising or teaching."[4] This definition opens the door on at least seven possible benefits that God may give through dreams or visions should He decide to speak to us in this manner.

When someone says that God spoke to them in a dream, they could mean that He has: 1) answered a question they have had, 2) appointed them to a task or mission, 3) commanded them concerning something in their lives, 4) communed with them the secrets of His heart, 5) declared to them some aspect of His will, 6) promised them something that is to come, or 7) taught them about a matter of truth. These are the kinds of things that God says to us in our dreams. In no instance will any of these things violate Scripture if they are from God. They will not detract from nor add unto the holy Bible. They serve primarily to expound and illustrate the truth which God has spoken. This is a good test to determine if the dreams we have are from God or not.

Moses, the Man of God

Moses was uniquely set apart by the Lord and spoken to by God. Modern translations have it "face to face," but this is misleading. The Lord told Moses, "No man shall see me and live."[5] Therefore, when the Bible says God spoke to Moses "face to face," it does not mean that Moses and God looked each other in the eye and talked. Rather, it means that God revealed Himself to Moses "apparently, and not in dark speeches."[6]

In other words, the Lord did not mince words with Moses: He talked to him straight up, without riddles, proverbs or word puzzles like those that occur in dreams and visions. Moses did, in fact, have visionary experiences, but they were not veiled in symbolism. He actually beheld the appearance of the Lord — first in the burning bush, next upon the mountain of fire, and finally, while hidden in the cleft of the rock as the glory of the Lord passed by him.

These things make us cast a wishful glance back and sigh, "Oh, I wish God would talk to me like that." But, doesn't the writer of Hebrews say that "God had some better thing for us?" Don't mislead me now. Do you think that we are to have a relationship with God that *exceeds* that which Moses had? Evidently so. Then why are so many today *not* experiencing a walk with the Lord that is better than that of Moses? Let's go back to the bush and see what happened there. Maybe we can find an answer.

The Burning Bush

"And the angel of the Lord appeared unto him in a flame of fire out of the midst of a bush. And he looked, and, behold, the bush burned with fire, and the bush was not consumed. And Moses said, 'I will now turn aside, and see this strange and marvelous sight, why the bush is not burnt.' And when the Lord saw that he turned aside to see, God called unto him out of the midst of the bush, and said, 'Moses, Moses.' And he said, 'Here am I.'"[7]

The curiosity of a burning bush intrigued Moses. It proved to be a sufficient enough mystery to catch his attention and turn him aside. Notice that the Lord didn't call to him *until* Moses "turned aside to see." Could it be the same for us today? I believe so.

In any vision or dream that comes from the Lord there is an invitation for us to turn aside and see what He will say. If we will take the time to turn aside, the Lord will speak to us. Don't despise your dreams; don't dismiss them; don't wake up and slough them off because they are weird or disturbing. Take the invitation in hand and turn to the Lord. If there is any meaning to be found, He will "speak" to you. He will arrange the dream for the purpose of answering, appointing, commanding, communing, declaring, promising or teaching you something about Himself.

I wonder how many "burning bushes" we may have walked past in our busy schedules? How many times have we missed out on a life-changing conversation with God because we didn't turn aside to see the strange sight? Moses teaches us by his example the importance of humble curiosity before the Lord. If we, like Moses, would just start *there,* we would be amazed at how much better our relationship with the Lord would be.

More Than a Fable

Mere folklore does not transcend cultural boundaries. The traditions and practices of one people do not become the standard for all people of the world. Human ideology is not that powerful. What came from Moses came from God. As such, the ideas generated in his encounters with the living God have not only transcended culture, they have endured for all time, defining civilization as we know it.

The Ten Commandments, profoundly simple and uncompromisingly direct, frame the civil laws of virtually every nation in the free world today. The Passover stands out as one of the pre-eminent religious holidays of all time. Tabernacles and temples alike owe their foundations to the word of God given to Moses. Principles of business management stem from the counsel of Jethro and the establishing of seventy elders. Even medicine bears witness to Moses, with the serpent coiled about the doctor's caduceus as the symbol of healing. Moses is clearly a man who cannot be dismissed by anyone other than a complete fool.

Samuel and the Prophets

From the lofty heights of the patriarchal beginnings and the glory of Moses, the man of God, we come down through the deep valleys of the Judges unto Samuel, the great prophetic reformer of Israel. Many colorful personalities have passed upon the pages of biblical history during this time: Joshua, Moses' successor, who led the people into the promised land; Balaam, the false prophet, whom God rebuked through the mouth of a donkey; Deborah, the great prophetess, who led Israel to victory against the treacherous Canaanites; Samson, the mighty man, who overthrew the Philistines and destroyed the Temple of Dagon; and Ruth, the Moabitess, who pledged herself to the God of Israel and became the grandmother of King David and a forebear of Jesus Christ.

Yet, despite the tireless efforts of faithful men and women over the years, Israel had degenerated morally and politically. They had left their first love and fallen far from the glory and wonder of earlier days. Samuel signaled a new chapter in God's dealings with His people — a new beginning, a fresh start. Many other prophets would follow in Samuel's footsteps, but few would have such a significant place of leadership with God's people.

Samuel the Seer

"Formerly in Israel, if a man went to inquire of God, he would say, 'Come, let us go to the seer,' because the prophet of today used to be called a seer."[8] How interesting that men would call them *seers.* This undoubtedly came as a result of what they did — *see* (i.e., dreams and visions). The Bible identifies by name nine different seers. They are Samuel, Zadok the priest, Gad, Heman, Iddo, Hanani, Asaph, Jeduthun and Amos.[9] The list expands considerably when you add to it all the prophets.

No Open Vision in Those Days

The Bible warns us against doing what seems right in our own eyes, teaching that the end of such behavior can often result in death.[10]This was graphically illustrated during the time of the Judges. Because there was no king in Israel, every man did that which was right in his own eyes, and the summary result of that period in Israel's history was famine throughout the land.[11] It was a natural sign of what was happening in the spiritual world.[12]

"'The days are coming,' declares the Sovereign Lord, 'when I will send a famine through the land — not a famine of food or a thirst for water, but a famine of hearing the words of the Lord. Men will stagger from sea to sea and wander from north to east, searching for the word of the Lord, but they will not find it.'"[13]

Such were the days when Samuel was a boy. "In those days the word of the Lord was rare; there were not many visions."[14] Eli, the high priest, was virtually blind, and his sons were perverted beyond recovery. It was one of the darkest moments in Israel's history. But God intervened and saved the undeserving nation by speaking to Samuel through dreams and visions.

"One night Eli, whose eyes were becoming so weak that he could barely see, was lying down in his usual place. The lamp of God had not yet gone out, and Samuel was lying down in the temple of the Lord, where the ark of God was. Then the Lord called Samuel. Samuel answered, 'Here I am.'"[15]

The lamp of God had not yet gone out. What a picture this paints! The flickering candle burning down to its final moments illustrated the condition of the nation before God. But God, ever rich in mercy, called out in the night to a small child who was himself but a flickering light in the things of God. "Now Samuel did not yet know the Lord, neither was the word of the Lord yet revealed unto him."[16] His childlike response, "Speak, Lord, for your servant is listening," inaugurated one of the most remarkable prophetic ministries of all time. "

The Lord was with Samuel as he grew up, and he let none of his words fall to the ground. And all Israel from Dan to Beersheba recognized that Samuel was attested as a prophet of the Lord. The Lord continued to appear at Shiloh, and there he revealed himself to Samuel through his word."[17]

A careful study of this scripture will show that God fathered Samuel in the things of the Spirit, that He continued giving him visions at the tabernacle of Shiloh, and that He revealed Himself to Samuel through the word of the Lord. These three dynamic realities are still available for us who love the Lord today! *Speak, Lord, for Your servants are listening!*

The Prophet Isaiah

Rick and Susan knew it was time for a change in their lives. They both had wandered far from the Lord, and their marriage was on the rocks. Oh, sure, they were successful in their professional careers and enjoyed popularity with their friends, but something was missing. They agreed to go to church one Sunday and see if it would help them get their lives back on track.

The parking lot was full as they arrived, and the swarm of glowing strangers made them feel out of place. They paused momentarily and considered turning around to go back home. "Let's go through with it," Susan said. "We've come this far, and we really need help." Rick nodded in agreement and parked the car. They quietly entered the church, taking the back pew near the door to ensure a quick exit — just in case they changed their minds.

The people were friendly enough, and the minister seemed genuine and disarming. The bulletin was tastefully done, and the many activities available through the church were impressive. Rick even chuckled as he read the joke on the back of the bulletin. "Maybe these people aren't as weird as I thought," he mused to himself. The choir made an orderly entrance, and the service officially began. Suddenly, the sanctuary filled with the glorious sounds of the choir singing, "Holy! Holy! Holy! Lord God Almighty!" Rick and Susan were totally unprepared for what happened next.

The presence of the Holy Spirit swept over them and they both began to sob uncontrollably before the Lord. They embraced one another and forgave each other for all that had happened to drive them apart. And they repented for having turned away from the Lord. God forgave them and restored them, filling them with joy and hope.

All this, and the pastor had not yet even preached his sermon! Such wonder filled their hearts as the choir concluded the song — a revival had stirred within their souls! What was in that song that it could do so much in such a short amount of time? Little did they know that they were singing a song that was written by angels and revealed in a dream!

I Saw the Lord!

"In the year that King Uzziah died, I saw the Lord seated on a throne, high and exalted, and the train of his robe filled the temple. Above him were seraphs, each with six wings: With two wings they covered their faces, with two they covered their feet, and with two they were flying. And they were calling to one another: 'Holy, holy, holy is the Lord Almighty; the whole earth is full of his glory.'"[18]

This was Isaiah's defining moment. It provided the momentum for his lifelong devotion to God as a prophet of the Lord. "Then I heard the voice of the Lord saying, 'Whom shall I send? And who will go for us?' And I said, 'Here am I. Send me!'"[19] Yes, Isaiah *saw* the Lord. Isaiah's many prophecies, some legendary, must all be viewed in light of this single vision. It not only set the standard of his faith, it also maintained the intensity of his faithfulness over sixty years of tireless and thankless service. Tradition has it that Isaiah was martyred during the reign of Manasseh, son of King Hezekiah. His legacy has lasted through the ages.

Seven Outstanding Visions

"The vision of Isaiah, son of Amoz."[20] Vision, as it is used in this verse, is a Hebrew word meaning a divine revelation of truth. Isaiah's prophecies, contained in 66 chapters, were revealed to him by God. Here, for your personal study, are seven of the more renowned of Isaiah's visions:

- A virgin shall conceive (7:14)
- His name shall be called Wonderful (9:6)
- The ministry of Jesus (61:1-3)
- The crucifixion (52:13—53:12)
- The Gentiles are redeemed by the Lord (60:1-3)
- The Redeemer's glorious return (63:1-5, 64:1-5)
- The new heaven and earth (66:22)

"No Old Testament book, with the possible exception of Psalms, speaks more powerfully and appropriately to the modern-day church than the book of Isaiah. He has been called the 'messianic prophet' and the 'evangelical prophet.' He prophesied for all future ages, predicting both the first and second coming advents of Christ."[21] Not bad for a "maniac!"

Jeremiah Was Not a Bullfrog

Jeremiah, like Samuel, was but a boy when the Lord called him to be a prophet. He recounts for us the manner of his call: "The Lord said to me, 'I knew you before you were formed within your mother's womb; before you were born I sanctified you and appointed you as my spokesman to the world.' 'O Lord God,' I said, 'I can't do that! I'm far too young! I'm only a youth!' 'Don't say that,' he replied, 'for you will go wherever I send you and speak whatever I tell you to. And don't be afraid of the people, for I, the Lord, will be with you and see you through.' Then he touched my mouth and said, 'See, I have put my words in your mouth! Today your work begins, to warn the nations and the kingdoms of the world. In accord with my words spoken through your mouth I will tear down some and destroy them, and plant others, nurture them, and make them strong and great.'"[22]

Teenagers are typically given to visions of grandeur, but this was a tall order that only God could fill! And Jeremiah knew it. (If Jeremiah was a bullfrog, he would have croaked right there!) The Lord gave him every assurance he needed to receive the call of God upon his young life. And then, having settled the young prophet's misgivings, the Lord put him to work immediately by showing him a vision of an almond branch and asking, "What do you *see,* Jeremiah?" Once again we have a clear reference to vision. It is an established method God uses to make His word known.

I Am Watching My Word

A delightful play on words takes place between the Lord and Jeremiah, and a lifelong promise is thereby lodged deep within the heart of the young man of God. "I *see* the branch of an almond tree,"[23] Jeremiah says to the Lord. And the Lord enthusiastically responds, "You have seen correctly, for I am *watching* to see that my word is fulfilled!"[24] (Read that again.)

I can picture the look on your face, dear reader, for I have seen it countless times in seminars as I have shared this verse with others. It is a look of total bewilderment. No matter how many times we read the above scripture, it just does not make sense to us. What does the branch of an almond tree have to do with the Lord watching over His word to perform it? Why would God give Jeremiah such a mystifying vision?

I assure you, Jeremiah was not at all mystified. If anything, he was delightfully amused at the Lord's sense of humor. You see, the Hebrew word for almond is *shaqed* (pronounced 'shaw-kade'), which describes the almond tree when it is in early bloom. When the Lord told Jeremiah, "I am *watching* My word," He used the Hebrew word *shaqad* (pronounced 'shaw-kad'), which means to be alert and sleepless, always on the lookout. *Shaqed; shaqad.* It was a pun — an unforgettable gift from the Lord to a young, budding prophet, assuring him of God's faithfulness to perform everything He says.

In the cold of winter, when all else lay dormant beneath the chilled earth, the early blossom of the almond tree would always remind Jeremiah of his call into the ministry. It would keep him assured of God's faithfulness to fulfill His word even when it looked as though the word could never come to pass. This undoubtedly brought much comfort to Jeremiah throughout the forty years of his ministry to God's people. Some of Jeremiah's visions included:

* The Boiling Pot (1:13-14)

* The Broken Wells (2:13)

* The Rotten Girdle (13:3-7)

* The Potter's Wheel (18:1-5)

* The Two Baskets of Figs (24:1-3)

* The Yoke Upon His Neck (27:2)

* The Destruction of Babylon (51:37-40)

An Enduring Promise to All People

"Call unto Me, and I will answer you, and show you great and mighty things, which you do not know."[25] Why on earth would anybody bother with psychic hotlines, when they can put a direct call into the Lord! (By the way, the reason they are called *hotlines* is because they originate from hell!) Don't turn to the devil for answers; call upon the Lord! Someone might say, "I've tried calling, but I can't get through to Him." We must call upon Him in *truth* if we want to make a connection. "The Lord is nigh unto all them that call upon him, to all that call upon him in truth."[26]

Maybe someone else would say, "He doesn't want to talk to me, for I have sinned against Him." When King David had sinned against the Lord, he, too, thought it was all over — until he made that call. That's when he discovered the Lord's love and mercy. "For thou, Lord, art good, and ready to forgive; and plenteous in mercy unto all them that call upon thee."[27]

Perhaps someone else may suppose that they are in too much trouble to bother the Lord, that He wouldn't want to be disturbed with their problems. The Lord says, "Call upon me in the day of trouble: I will deliver thee, and thou shalt glorify me."[28] There is simply no reason for you not to make that call! Do it now; operators are standing by!

"But, what will I say? I'm not very spiritual, and I really don't know the Bible very well at all." The Lord said, "I will answer you, and show you great and mighty things, which you do not know." If we will call upon the Lord, He will show us things that we do not know. The word *show* means "to put in front; to cause to stand out boldly." A good paraphrase would read, "I will put it right in your face." The word *great* means strange and marvelous; it's the same word used by Moses to describe the burning bush.[29] The word *mighty* could be rendered "isolated" or "inaccessible". The idea is that God would reveal things to Jeremiah that would otherwise be isolated or inaccessible. Does this promise stand true for us today? Jesus said, "Ask, and it shall be given you; seek, and ye shall find; knock, and it shall be opened unto you."[30] So, what are you waiting for, friend? Make that call today; you'll be glad you did!

Ezekiel the Charismatic

Ezekiel stands out among the prophets as being the most *charismatic*. Even Daniel, though he had phenomenal insights into the last days, does not seem to be as mystical and ecstatic as Ezekiel. We look back and admire Ezekiel as a man of God, a true prophet of the Lord, but were he ministering among us today we would all be having a fit. How do you pastor someone who is picked up by their hair and carried by the Holy Spirit to the riverside? Good grief!

There is a saying that goes, "You never get a second chance to make a first impression." The opening verse in Ezekiel states the case up front, without apology — in our face. "In the thirtieth year, in the fourth month on the fifth day, while I was among the exiles by the Kebar River, the heavens were opened and I saw visions of God."[31] Ezekiel never was one to beat around the bush. He was a man on a mission with a message. Small talk would have to wait.

Ezekiel saw visions of God. His book is the record of what he saw. Yet, even with the inspiration of the Holy Spirit upon him as he wrote, Ezekiel still labored to put into words the indescribable sights that opened before him. He concludes his introductory chapter saying, "This was the appearance of the likeness of the glory of the Lord."[32] Oh, Ezekiel didn't actually see the Lord, what he saw was the *glory* of the Lord. No, wait a minute; actually, he saw the *likeness* of the glory of the...no, that's not it either. What Ezekiel saw was the *appearance* of the likeness of the glory of the Lord. There, that's it. Rather indescribable wouldn't you say? (Show a little patience when someone is trying to tell you something that the Lord has shown them — it's not always so easy.)

Ezekiel said the heavens were opened. This means that God removed the barrier that separates the natural from the spiritual realm and let Ezekiel see into the other side. The word *opened* is first used to describe the flood of Noah: The heavens opened, and the rain came down (Gen. 7:11). Ezekiel's visions and Noah's flood were both a mighty outpouring from heaven. Later, Noah opened the window on the ark and the light shone inside after forty days (Gen. 8:6). Likewise, after a period of stormy darkness, God broke the seal and opened the hearts of His people to receive fresh insight from His Word through the visions of Ezekiel. In another place Joseph opened the storehouse in Egypt and gave grain to the people (Gen. 41:56). In the same manner, God was providing abundance of spiritual grain through the visions of Ezekiel. But, as it turned out, the people were not that hungry for the things of God.

Some of Ezekiel's visions included:

- The Hand and the Scroll (2:9-3:4)

- The Abomination in the Temple (8:1-6)

- The Mark Upon the Forehead (9:1-4)

- The Glory Departs from the Temple (10:18)

- The Eagles and the Vine (17:1-10)

- The Two Harlot Sisters (23:1-4)

- The Cooking Pot (24:1-5)

- The Valley of Dry Bones (37:1-14)

- The New Temple of God (chs. 40–43)

- The River of Life (47:1-12)

They Shall Know That I Am the Lord

For twenty years Ezekiel prophesied to the people. His many sermons, illustrated by visions and signs, can be summarized in three words — *know the Lord*. "We do not have to look deeply to find the key idea and the focal message of Ezekiel. It confronts us on almost every page. With slight variations, the expression, 'They shall know that I am the Lord,' occurs no less than seventy times in his book. To see this is to see the heart of Ezekiel's prophetic ministry." (J. Sidlow Baxter).[33] Furthermore, Ezekiel shows us that knowing the Lord will be evidenced in our lives by three things: 1) Personal responsibility in cultivating moral faithfulness, 2) Humility in submitting to the discipline of the Lord, and 3) Faith in trusting God to ultimately exalt and establish righteousness over evil — in our lives and in the world.

Daniel, in a League All His Own

Josephus calls Daniel one of the greatest of the prophets. Daniel's ministry occurred in the courts of some of history's great monarchs — Nebuchadnezzar, Cyrus and Darius. Leaders, take note of this: God has *never* left Himself without a witness in the halls of power. Those who govern are, therefore, without excuse if they forge their empires without holding converse with God. (We will examine this in detail in the following chapter.)

Daniel lived as a prime minister but was not ashamed to humbly identify with his God in public. Nor was he hardened to the unusual manifestations of the Spirit that can attend some prophetic visitations. Daniel would tremble, lose all strength and faint under the power of the Holy Spirit. He, being a highly dignified man, did not deem it undignified to be thus embraced by God. In this, Daniel stands in glaring contrast to high-minded men today who regard themselves above such behavior. "God doesn't do *those* kinds of things anymore," they assert, "and He certainly will never do them to me!" I once heard a trusted pastor say, "Never say never." It's good advice.

We are told of Daniel that God gave him knowledge and skill in all learning and wisdom, and, specifically, that Daniel had understanding in all visions and dreams.[34] His character and gifting were renowned throughout the kingdom. "In every matter of wisdom and understanding about which the king questioned them, he found them ten times better than all the magicians and enchanters in his whole kingdom."[35] A sampling of dreams and visions in Daniel includes:

- The Seven-year Itch (4:1-37)

- The Handwriting on the Wall (5:1-30)

- The Four Beasts (7:1-8)

- The Ancient of Days and the Son of Man (7:9-22)

- The Ram and the Goat (8:1-14)

- The Visit From Gabriel (9:20-27)

- The Vision of the Glorious Man (10:1-9)

Many authors have written great volumes expounding upon the prophecies of Daniel. Some are worthy of wide acceptance while others belong with books like *Eighty-eight Reasons Why Jesus Will Return in 1988.* (When Jesus didn't return, one opportunistic writer came out the following year with *Eighty-nine Reasons Why He Didn't.*).

I shall leave the ten toes of the great statue for others to manicure, along with the four beasts that rose out of the stormy sea, the seventy prophetic weeks of Israel, and the heavenly war of Michael with the prince of Persia. My purpose is to simply show the substantial role of dreams and visions as a means whereby God speaks to us. Daniel illustrates this with class.

Amos, the Non-prophet Prophet

Perhaps you may be thinking, "I could never be like Daniel."

Maybe. Maybe not. But perhaps you could be like Amos. "I am not really one of the prophets," Amos wrote. "I do not come from a family of prophets. I am just a herdsman and a fruit picker. But the Lord took me from caring for the flocks and told me, 'Go and prophesy to my people.'"[36] (It would help you get the impact of Amos' words if you would read them as though you were listening to Forrest Gump!)

I've always liked Amos. He was a very down-to-earth, pragmatic prophet. Though he downplayed his qualifications and did not possess academic or theological training, Amos displayed great common sense and was very creative in his use of words.

"The style of Amos may not be marked by sublimity, but there is a clearness and regularity, an elegance and color and freshness about him, which give him a literary charm all his own. His vocabulary, his figures of speech, his illustrations, are all redolent of the country life from which he came. There was an unconventional bluntness about him which must have been disconcerting to the college-trained professional prophets of Baal."[37] Imagine the shock of the upper class when Amos called the women a bunch of fat cows![38]

The five visions of Amos included:

- The Grasshoppers Turned Back by Prayer (7:1-3)

- The Fire Quenched by Intercession (7:4)

- The Plumb Line of God's Standard (7:7-17)

- The Basket of Summer Fruit (8:1-14)

- The Lord Beside the Altar (9:1-10)

We have a final word from Amos that stirs our hearts with dreams of great things. He prophesied of a time to come when the Lord would build up the tabernacle of David (9:11). For the Christian, this clearly refers to the church of the Lord Jesus, David's greater Son. As proof of this, James quoted this promise in the book of Acts to settle a dispute that arose when the Gentiles began to be included in the spread of Christianity (Acts 15:16).

Five Great Promises for the Church

The prophecy of Amos concerning the tabernacle of David

provides five promises concerning the church in the last days. According to his vision the church will be:

1. Strengthened: "In that day I will restore David's fallen tent. I will repair its broken places, restore its ruins, and build it as it used to be" (9:11, NIV).

2. Enlarged: "That they may possess the remnant of Edom and all the nations that bear my name," declares the Lord, who will do these things" (9:12, NIV).

3. Enriched: "'The days are coming,' declares the Lord, 'when the reaper will be overtaken by the plowman and the planter by the one treading grapes. New wine will drip from the mountains and flow from all the hills'" (9:13, NIV).

4. Populated: "I will bring back my exiled people Israel; they will rebuild the ruined cities and live in them. They will plant vineyards and drink their wine; they will make gardens and eat their fruit" (9:14, NIV).

5. Planted: "'I will plant Israel in their own land, never again to be uprooted from the land I have given them,' says the Lord your God" (9:15, NIV).

I offer this brief outline to inspire leaders and lay people alike with a vision of what the Lord can do (and *wants* to do) in the church. What a great blessing awaits those who will turn to the Lord and trust Him to bring this vision to pass.

The Power of Vision

Few things can challenge and inspire us to complete the task that God has given us like a dream or a vision. "Where there is no vision, the people perish."[39] The word *perish* means "to cast off restraints; to live without direction or discipline." God supplies us with vision so as to secure us with discipline. Vision inspires us to hold the course until we reach the goal. It enables us to say no to lesser things. Take away vision and you will destroy vigor. Visionaries lead the way to greatness, for they dare to dream of achieving things beyond what is conventional and routine. They live with extraordinary restraint in the singleness of their goal. Such is the power of vision.

Soon after the completion of Disney World in Orlando, one of the dignitaries present at its opening commented, "Isn't it sad that Walt didn't live to see this?" Mike Vance, creative director of Disney Studios, replied, "Walt did see it — that's why it's here."[40] If a vision could inspire Walt Disney to provide for the building of something so curious as Disney World, how much more should we seek vision for the extraordinary task of building the glorious church of Jesus Christ!

Zechariah, the Dreaming Prophet

In the truest sense of the word, Zechariah was a seer. The book of Zechariah opens with no less than eight distinct visions shown to him by the angel of the Lord. Each vision is given with some explanation of its meaning and application.

The first vision of the man and the horses, standing among the myrtle trees, served as a reminder to the people that God was always watching over them with loving concern even though He was often hidden from their sight, and it seemed that He had forsaken them. The vision gave them reassurance that the Lord would again be merciful to Jerusalem and rebuild the Holy City.[41]

The second vision of the four horns and four craftsmen served as reminders of God's righteous judgments. The four horns represented the nations that the Lord had used to bring judgment upon Judah. In turn, the craftsmen represented the judgment which the Lord was bringing upon the nations that had scattered Judah during their time of trial.[42]

In the third vision of the man with the measuring line there is an unmistakable promise that Jerusalem, though presently in ruins, would be rebuilt and settled. The Lord Himself would be a wall of fire about the city.[43] The imagery here is rich in prophetic significance. It not only applies to Jerusalem in the time of Zechariah, but also reaches far into the future when the beautiful city of God, the new Jerusalem, as a bride adorned for her groom, will come down out of heaven and be established upon the new earth.[44]

In the fourth vision we see Joshua the high priest dressed in filthy garments and accused by Satan. This captivates our hearts because we see ourselves in Joshua. What happens next in the vision fills us with inspiration because there we see the Lord. The vision portrays the mercy and power of God in providing for our cleansing from sin and our freedom from accusation.[45] Like Joshua in the vision, we all have soiled garments and are constantly accused by Satan before God. But God, who is rich in mercy, turns and rebukes Satan. As for us who have been defiled — the vision reveals that God will cleanse us, clothe us, crown us and commission us to serve Him anew in faithfulness and power. Praise be to God!

The fifth vision of the lampstand among the olive trees was given to show that God's purposes will only be accomplished by His Spirit moving in power among His people.[46] Most people are familiar with this portion of Scripture, for it is where we find the famous quote, "It's not by might nor by power, but by My Spirit, says the Lord."[47]

The sixth vision of the flying scroll announces God's judgment against deceitful behavior of all kinds.[48] The Lord has sent an ominous and all-inclusive curse throughout the whole earth against the thief and the liar (i.e., the devil). There is no escape from the heavenly scroll. It is the word of the Lord which brings judgment against evil — a judgment which will consume and destroy the strongholds of darkness.

The seventh vision of the woman in the basket signifies the holiness of God and the removal of wickedness.[49] The woman, symbolizing wickedness, is placed in a basket and covered with a lid made of lead. This symbolizes being sealed shut. The purpose of the lid is to keep mankind from looking upon wickedness, which is attractive and seductive. How interesting it is that man is forever trying to pry the lid off so he can see what is inside. How tragic it is when he succeeds.

And, finally, the eighth vision of the four chariots displays God's sovereign control over all the earth — north, south, east and west.[50] There is no place exempt from the presence of the Holy Spirit, nor are any excluded from the judgments of the Lord. He is God. He is Holy. He is just. And He is coming!

Interactive Tell-a-Vision

It is of particular interest to read how Zechariah would interact with the messengers in his visions. He was not simply a passive observer, like someone watching a movie in a darkened theater. He would ask questions of the angels while the vision was taking place, and he would get answers.

"Then I looked and saw four animal horns! 'What are these?' I asked the angel. He replied, 'They represent the four world powers that have scattered Judah, Israel, and Jerusalem.' Then the Lord showed me four blacksmiths. 'What have these men come to do?' I asked. The angel replied, 'They have come to take hold of the four horns that scattered Judah so terribly, and to pound them on the anvil and throw them away!'"[51]

In the vision of Joshua being cleansed from his filth and clothed with new garments, Zechariah is so excited by what he sees that he blurts out his own advice about what should happen next. "Then I said, 'Put a clean turban on his head.' So they put a clean turban on his head and clothed him, while the angel of the Lord stood by."[52] This is interactive "tell-a-vision" at its finest!

The Tip of the Iceberg

We have touched upon no less than fifty-five dreams and visions in this chapter alone. Overall, the book thus far has provided reference to at least ninety-seven dreams and visions. This does not include the visions that were written by the prophets under the heading, the "burden of the word of the Lord."[53] Though this seems like much, it is, in fact, but the tip of the iceberg. The greater body of documentation remains as yet untouched — though readily available for all who would seek to know more. My point is simple. Here is provided such preponderance of evidence that it demands a verdict, and the only verdict that can be given is that God clearly speaks through dreams and visions.

Though we have looked at the patriarchs and the prophets, God does not exclude Himself to them alone. He is rich in mercy to *all* who call upon Him. The standing orders of the universe, unrescinded and unopposed, echo throughout the ages — "Let there be light!" There is no class of person exempt from the probing love of the God who longs to reveal Himself to man, whether we be awake or asleep. Young and old, male and female, bond and free, rich and poor alike may all meet with the Lord in the wondrous world of dreams and visions. There you will find the ground is level between pauper and prince, commoner and king.

THE CONFESSION
OF KINGS

The astonished king fell to his knees and lay prostrate upon his face in the presence of the man of God. All of his royal advisors were shocked, but none of them dared interrupt this moment of humility and confession. The king opened his mouth and said, "Surely your God is the God of gods and the Lord of kings, and a revealer of mysteries."[1] The king was Nebuchadnezzar of Babylon. The man of God before whom he yielded was Daniel the prophet. Here are the circumstances of that amazing moment in history.

A Dream to Remember

A bewildering anxiety seized Nebuchadnezzar's heart when he could not remember a haunting dream he had. All the magicians, astrologers and the sorcerers were summoned before the king and given a very disturbing order — they were to tell the king his forgotten dream or else be put to death! They were, of course, unable to comply, and so the executioner's blade began falling upon their heads. It was a desperate moment in Babylon.

Daniel turned to the Lord and sought God's mercy concerning this situation, and God answered him by giving Daniel the king's dream and its interpretation! "During the night the mystery was revealed to Daniel in a vision. Then Daniel praised the God of heaven."[2] Daniel went before the king and said: "The secret which the king has demanded, the wise men, the astrologers, the magicians, and the soothsayers cannot declare to the king. But there is a God in heaven that reveals secrets, and He has made known to King Nebuchadnezzar what will be in the latter days. Your dream, and the visions of your head upon your bed, were these."[3]

A hush fell upon the throne room as the anxious king leaned forward to hear what Daniel seemed so confident to tell. As it turned out, Daniel's confidence was justified. He unfolded the significance of the king's dream after all others had failed to provide any clue into its makeup or meaning. When Daniel had finished, he gave all the credit to God. The king of Babylon was awestruck.

The prophet Daniel has left a standard that all servants of the Lord should strive after. His integrity, humility, courage and faithfulness turned the heads of heathens and captured their hearts for God. According to Scripture, Daniel was a man of "an excellent spirit, and knowledge, and understanding, interpreting of dreams, and showing of hard sentences, and dissolving of doubts."[4] For this reason the kings of the world called upon him in their times of need.[5]

A Preview of Coming Attractions

In Nebuchadnezzar's dream he saw a great statue with a head of gold, shoulders and arms of silver, a torso made of brass, legs of iron and feet made of iron and clay mixed together.[6] There, in a single picture, is the comprehensive summary of the rise and fall of four successive world empires spanning several thousand years! Libraries today are filled with the details of what God revealed in a single image through a dream. Truly, a picture is worth a thousand words! Tens of thousands.

History unfolded exactly as Daniel foretold. The Babylonian empire (the head of gold) was followed by the Persian empire (chest and arms of silver), which was followed in turn by the Grecian empire under Alexander the Great (the torso of brass). The Roman empire (legs of iron) rose after the death of Alexander. We are now at the feet of the great statue, feet made of iron and clay mixed together — an unstable alliance of things which cannot be united, and an apt description of today's global community. It only remains for the great Stone to come from heaven, as Daniel said, and strike the feet, bringing the entire statue tumbling down. Afterward, the mountain of the Lord will fill the earth. This is none other than the coming kingdom of Jesus Christ. As surely as the four earthly powers have come and gone, so also will the kingdom of Christ come and remain forever!

Baxter said, "Never did a more epochal dream come to a man. Moreover, it was just as necessary that Nebuchadnezzar should forget it as that he should dream it. Had the king himself been able to relate the dream, there might have been competing interpretations; but that it should become a sheer blank and then be recalled by the inspired Daniel was proof beyond question that both the dream and its interpretation were from the Most High."[7]

After Daniel delivered unto the king both the dream and its meaning, Nebuchadnezzar fell prostrate and made what has been, in so many words, the confession of kings and rulers through the ages — "Surely God is the God of gods and the Lord of kings, and He is a revealer of mysteries!"

Joshua, Son of Nun

Obviously Joshua never held the title of king, but he unquestionably functioned in a leadership role that was an empirical prototype for future monarchs. As such he merits due regard for how he began his rule over Israel. After the death of Moses, the Lord said to Joshua, "Moses my servant is dead. Now then, you and all these people, get ready to cross the Jordan River into the land I am about to give to them."[8] Only a fool would seek to govern without a word from God. Joshua was no fool. He waited until the Lord spoke before he took the reins of leadership into his capable hands.

The Lord then said to Joshua, "Today I will begin to exalt you in the eyes of all Israel, so they may know that I am with you as I was with Moses."[9] Joshua led the children of Israel across the Jordan River, reminiscent of Moses at the Red Sea. While this was wondrous, in itself it was not enough to solidify Joshua's leadership apart from Moses. Something more was needed. The defining moment came at the walled city of Jericho. This miracle, a theme of song to this very day, would validate Joshua's authenticity as the Lord's appointed leader and launch Israel into a new era of conquest and national identity.

The Captain of the Hosts

While positioned outside the city of Jericho, surveying the situation so as to devise a strategy for conquest, Joshua was visited by an unusual being. "Joshua looked up and saw a man standing in front of him with a drawn sword in his hand. Joshua went up to him and asked, 'Are you for us or for our enemies?' 'Neither,' He replied, 'but as commander of the army of the Lord I have now come.' Then Joshua fell facedown to the ground in reverence, and asked him, 'What message does my Lord have for his servant?' The commander of the Lord's army replied, 'Take off your sandals, for the place where you are standing is holy.' And Joshua did so."[10]

That this was a vision is undeniable.[11] That this was the Lord *Himself* standing before Joshua is equally beyond question, for He says to him the very words that were spoken to Moses at the burning bush. This vision became Joshua's personal induction into leadership, his own baptism by fire.

The vision came to Joshua at the beginning of his rule so as to strengthen him for the duration and the challenges that lay ahead. To do the impossible, we must see the invisible. Joshua saw the Lord and was thereby set upon the highway of kings. His obedient, seven-day march around the fortified city of Jericho not only brought the walls down, it also pioneered a path for all those who would follow him in leadership of God's people through the ages. To lead, we must follow. To follow, we must see.

King David's Royal Shepherd

David was a runt. There's just no other way to describe him in the humble days of his boyhood. His seven older brothers were of superior stature and ability, making his chances for any recognition remote at best. Even Samuel was certain that one of them was God's chosen successor to Saul when he first arrived at Jesse's home to anoint the new king. There was no question in anybody's mind that the choice would *not* include David, so they didn't even bother bringing him to the meeting.

But when the Lord stopped Samuel from proceeding, he turned to Jesse and asked, "Are these all your sons?" "Oh, no," Jesse answered, "I have one more — but he's just a boy, and really doesn't have much to offer. He couldn't possibly be the one you are looking for; trust me." Samuel sat down and said, "Bring him to me; I will not leave until I see him." They fetched David from the fields, and as he drew near Samuel rose and said, "Behold the king of Israel!" He anointed David in the midst of his brothers and spoke into his heart the secret of the Lord.[12]

Years later David recounted before the Lord the promise which He had revealed through Samuel. "In a *vision* you spoke to your prophet and said, 'I have chosen a splendid young man from the common people to be the king — he is my servant David! I have anointed him with my holy oil. I will steady him and make him strong. His enemies shall not outwit him, nor shall the wicked over-power him. I will beat down his adversaries before him and destroy those who hate him. I will protect and bless him constantly and sur-round him with my love; he will be great because of me.'"[13]

You can be sure that David referred to this vision many times dur-ing the years of his reign. It cultivated within him a quiet trust in the word of the Lord. That's the purpose of a dream or a vision — to direct us to the word of the Lord so that our faith may be strength-ened by holding onto God's faithfulness to what He has promised.

David, the Visionary Leader

King David, like most leaders, was a visionary man. How right therefore that God would speak to him in visions. David showed his own tendency towards the emblematic language of visions when he wrote, "The Lord is my shepherd." David, himself a shepherd, found an easy comparison to the Lord in the rich imagery of the shepherd's life.

David believed in dreams and visions, as he was no stranger to their godly influence. Psalm 139 stands out like a torch among candles, giving strong reason to believe that David was describing a dream he may have had. Note his confession, "How precious to me are your thoughts, O God! How vast is the sum of them! Were I to count them, they would outnumber the grains of sand. *When I awake,* I am still with you."[14] The Reverend George Gilfillan, a contemporary of Spurgeon, wrote a beautiful summary of David's sublime Psalm, capturing the dream-like quality of its imagery.

> Here the poet inverts his gaze, from the blaze of suns, to the strange atoms composing his own frame. He stands shuddering over the precipice of himself. Above is the all-encompassing Spirit, from whom the morning wings cannot save; and below, at a deep distance, appears amid the branching forest of his animal frame, so fearfully and wonderfully made, the abyss of his spiritual existence, lying like a dark lake in the midst.
>
> How, between mystery and mystery, his mind, his wonder, his very reason, seem to rock like a little boat between the sea and the sky. But speedily does he regain his serenity; when he throws himself, with childlike haste and confidence, into the arms of that Fatherly Spirit, and murmurs in His bosom, "How precious also are Thy thoughts unto me, O God."[15]

Charles Spurgeon himself turned this Psalm into a personal prayer and wrote,

> Thy thoughts of love are so many that my mind never gets away from them, they surround me at all hours. I go to my bed, and God is my last thought; and when I awake I find my mind still hovering about His palace gates. God is ever with me, and I am ever with Him. This is life indeed. If during my sleep my mind wanders away into dreams, yet it only wanders upon holy ground, and the moment I wake my heart is back with the Lord.

Then Spurgeon added this commentary:

The Psalmist does not say, "When I awake I *return* to Thee," but, "I am *still with* Thee," as if his meditations were continuous, and his communion unbroken.[16]

Only a dream could accomplish them.

Whether the Psalm was born of a dream or not, there is absolutely no doubt that David was inspired with insight about God and himself, which he could not have known apart from some form of direct revelation. This is something David would be quite conversant with, seeing that his reign as king was complimented by the visionary ministry of no less than three prophets: Nathan, Gad and Zadok.[17] In addition to the influence of his prophetic friends, we also have David's own writings that reveal the high esteem he had for spiritual revelation:

- I will bless the Lord who counsels me; he gives me wisdom *in the night.* He *tells* me what to do.[18]

- You have tested me and seen that I am good. You have come *even in the night* and found nothing amiss and know that I have told the truth.[19]

- *On my bed* I remember you; I think of you through the watches of the night.[20]

- My eyes anticipate *the night watches,* that I may meditate on thy word.[21]

- But as for me, my contentment is not in wealth but in *seeing you* and knowing all is well between us. And *when I awake* in heaven, I will be fully satisfied, for I will see you face to face.[22]

The Sword of the Lord

We have as a final consideration the actual record of Scripture confirming to us that David himself did indeed have at least one unforgettable open vision. The story given in the Bible is quite astonishing.[23]

A devastating plague broke out among the Israelites, and several thousand died. King David admitted it was his sin that brought the plague, and he turned to God in repentance. Gad, the king's seer, brought God's perplexing answer to David's prayer. He was given three choices of punishment: 1) three years of famine, 2) three months of defeat at the hands of his enemies, or 3) three days under the sword of the Lord. David cast himself upon the Lord's mercy and chose the three days.

God sent an angel against Jerusalem to destroy it, and seventy thousand men of Israel fell. The Lord said to the angel, "It is enough. Restrain your hand." The angel stopped and stood by the threshing floor of Ornan. At that moment David "looked up and saw the angel of the Lord standing between heaven and earth, with a drawn sword in his hand extended over Jerusalem. Then David and the elders, clothed in sackcloth, fell facedown."[24] David interceded for the nation and asked that judgment fall upon him alone.

The angel instructed David to build an altar to the Lord, which David did. As soon as he sacrificed upon the altar, God answered him by fire from heaven. Then the angel put his sword to its sheath. The incident was over.

David was so moved by this that he immediately set in motion the preliminary provisions for building the temple of the Lord. "Then David said, 'The house of the Lord God is to be here, and also the altar of burnt offering for Israel.'"[25] This would be the greatest temple ever built in the history of man for the glory of God — how profoundly significant that it was God who chose the site and revealed it to David through the angel's instructions!

Blueprints From Heaven

The temple would actually be built by Solomon in the years to come, but the blueprints were given to David in a vision. "Then David gave Solomon the blueprint of the Temple and its surroundings — the treasuries, the upstairs rooms, the inside rooms, and the sanctuary for the place of mercy. He also gave Solomon his plans for the outer court, the outside rooms, the Temple storage areas, and the treasuries for the gifts dedicated by famous persons. *For the Holy Spirit had given David all these plans.*"[26]

David rose to greatness under the blessing of God. He held sway from the Euphrates River to the Mediterranean Sea. The Lord anointed his head with oil and caused his cup to overflow. King David was rightfully feared by all nations around him, for the Lord, his royal Shepherd, prepared a table before him in the presence of his enemies. Goodness and mercy followed him all the days of his life. He finished out the years of his reign with dignity and diplomacy, and closed his eyes in peaceful death. A ruddy shepherd boy, the runt of Jesse, now dwells in the house of the Lord forever.

King Solomon's Gold Mine

The air was filled with a lingering doubt in the aftermath of King David's death. He was, after all, the greatest king Israel had ever crowned. Oh, sure, the days of Saul were heady and somewhat illustrious, but once David ascended the throne there was no comparison between the two. Did not the people sing, "Saul has slain thousands, but David his ten thousands"?

Greatness is a hard act to follow. This is why headline entertainers never open for "wanna-be's." Having seen the main attraction, who cares about a nobody? You never follow a steak dinner with a baloney sandwich. Surely Solomon, in all his proverbial wisdom, would agree.

Solomon, son of David. Well, actually, son of David and Bathsheba — and *everybody* in the kingdom knew all about that sordid story. Ah, if only Absalom had lived, he would now be the king. He was clearly the popular choice, and the most qualified to follow his famous father. But his pride and ambition twisted his mind and defiled his soul. He died on the run after a failed military coup.

The next most likely candidate was Adonijah. But he, too was premature in his quest for the royal throne. Even before David died, Adonijah had gathered the government leaders and military commanders at the palace to celebrate his self-installment as the new king. The only problem with this is that he wasn't the king! David had promised Bathsheba that Solomon would be the king.

"Solomon? You gotta be kiddin' me! The guy is a mamma's boy! You expect *him* to lead Israel's army against her enemies? To stand before kings and command their respect? To solve our domestic problems with the shrewdness and wit necessary for men of high office? *Puh-leeeeze,* give me a break!" Such were the likely sentiments of the populace at the time of Solomon's ascendancy. As I said earlier, the air was filled with a lingering doubt in the aftermath of King David's death. And nobody knew it better than Solomon.

Hail to the Chief

The pomp and circumstance of ceremonial celebrations have a way of glossing over even the deepest of our darkest fears. The sound of trumpets and drums, the electrifying magic of royal pageantry, the astounding beauty of kingly glamour and affluence, the hopeful rhetoric of political speeches and the overall feeling of success portrayed by such national pride — it's enough to quell even the most vocal of critics. But, as they say, the honeymoon will soon be over. Reality will come and, when it gets here, it bites!

At Gibeon, the place where kings traditionally sacrificed to the God of Israel, Solomon drew a deep breath in the privacy of his royal bedchamber. It was the first time he had to himself in the fanfare of all the festivities. Tomorrow would bring the final step of his installment; his "swearing into office upon the Bible," as it were. For the people of Israel to see their king sacrifice unto the Lord would complete the formalities of Solomon's inauguration. Yet it would be no mere ceremony for Solomon. He eagerly anticipated the moment of sacrifice, hoping for some sign from God of His divine favor. *That's* what made David so great, and Solomon knew that he would not succeed without the same.

He drew yet another deep breath and slowly let it out in a sigh. His entire body seemed to melt in the comfort of his bed. But suddenly, unexpectedly, and in a most commanding manner — there, standing before Solomon the king of Israel, was the Lord Himself, the King of heaven and earth! Solomon was understandably speechless, and so the Lord spoke first. "Ask Me," He said, "for whatever you will. What do you want Me to give to you?"[27]

"Solomon replied, 'You were wonderfully kind to my father David because he was honest and true and faithful to you, and obeyed your commands. And you have continued your kindness to him by giving him a son to succeed him.

'O Lord my God, now you have made me the king instead of my father David, but I am as a little child who doesn't know his way around. And here I am among your own chosen people, a nation so great that there are almost too many people to count! Give me an understanding mind so that I can govern your people well and know the difference between what is right and what is wrong. For who by himself is able to carry such a heavy responsibility?'"[28]

The Lord was pleased that Solomon had asked for this, and said, "Since you have asked for this and not for long life or wealth for yourself, nor have asked for the death of your enemies but for discernment in administering justice, I will do what you have asked. I will give you a wise and discerning heart, so that there will never have been anyone like you, nor will there ever be. Moreover, I will give you also what you have not asked for — both riches and honor — so that in your lifetime you will have no equal among kings."[29]

And now for the moment of truth. The Bible says, "Then Solomon awoke — and he realized it had been a dream."[30] I had never noticed this before. I've heard the story of Solomon many times throughout my life. I've even studied it and have actually preached sermons about him — but I never noticed that this historical meeting with the Lord happened in a dream.

I must admit that my first thought was one of disappointment. "Ah, shucks," I said, "All this time I thought the Lord actually appeared to Solomon. I didn't realize that it was only a dream." But then it hit me. The Lord *did* appear to Solomon! Just because it happened in a dream did not make it any less *real*.

After all, was Solomon the wisest of all kings?

Yes.

Wasn't he also the wealthiest?

Yes.

Didn't he, in fact, have fame and honor beyond all who came before or after him?

Yes.

Well, how real is *that?*

My disappointment turned to wonder as I saw that the Lord's word is so spiritually powerful that it can enter our hearts whether we are awake or asleep. (This has brought me great comfort during those times my sermons have been delivered to snoozing parishioners!) Think about this. The Lord appeared to Solomon in a dream, spoke to him concerning his life and Solomon awoke and walked into history. The dream came true. Every proverb in the Bible is a testimony to the God who speaks in dreams! *That* was King Solomon's gold mine, and you and I may stake our claim there today.

The Rubble of Zerubbabel

The glorious temple of Solomon lay in ruins. The people of Judah had been held captive for seventy years in Babylon, during which time the city of Jerusalem had been overrun with thieves and beasts. When the captivity ended by the sovereign intervention of God, the happy Jews, under their new governor Zerubbabel, returned to their homeland with high hopes of rebuilding the destroyed temple and restoring worship in Jerusalem. But their enthusiasm was short-lived.

No sooner had they arrived in Jerusalem than they were faced with the impossibility of their task. The temple had suffered extensive destruction and was virtually unrecognizable as it lay in a massive heap of burnt stones, dusty from the desert winds. Zerubabbel didn't know where to start; the mountain of devastation was insurmountable, the ruins too great. But, before despair set in, God sent the prophet Zechariah with a pocket full of visions.

In one of the visions a conversation unfolded between Zechariah and the angel of the Lord. It is as though the purpose of the vision was two-fold: first, to show Zechariah the vision; and second, to teach him how to interpret what he saw. "Then the angel who had been talking with me woke me, as though I had been asleep. 'What do you see now?' he asked. I answered, 'I see a gold lampstand holding seven lamps, and at the top there is a reservoir for the olive oil that feeds the lamps, flowing into them through seven tubes. And I see two olive trees carved upon the lampstand, one on each side of the reservoir. What is it, sir?' I asked. 'What does this mean?'

"'Don't you really know?' the angel asked. 'No, sir,' I said, 'I don't.' Then he said, 'This is God's message to Zerubbabel: Not by might, nor by power, but by my Spirit, says the Lord Almighty — you will succeed because of my Spirit, though you are few and weak. Therefore no mountain, however high, can stand before Zerubbabel! For it will flatten out before him! And Zerubbabel will finish building this Temple with mighty shouts of thanksgiving for God's mercy, declaring that all was done by grace alone.'"[31]

Zechariah delivered the mail. The rubble of Zerubabbel didn't stand a chance before the God of Israel! The exasperated leader was filled with renewed faith in God's word and rose to the occasion. Like the flame of a candle, supplied with abundance of oil and shining bright in the darkness, Zerubbabel set himself to accomplish everything that God had called him to do. He was empowered through the vision to believe in the provision of the Holy Spirit. The temple was built, and God filled it with His glory, making it even greater than it had been in the days of Solomon.

Highlights From History

We now move cautiously from the pages of Scripture to the pages of history, to give supplemental testimony from the archives of antiquity of how some of the world's prominent kings and leaders were aided or deceived in crucial battles through the influence of dreams and visions.[32] Hannibal invaded Rome, Xerxes invaded Greece, Alexander the Great conquered Tyre and Napoleon was shaken at Waterloo. Even the despicable Adolf Hitler believed himself to be on a divine mission after an alleged dream supposedly saved his life (proving that a madman empowered with thoughts of divinity is a terror indeed). Others, however, had dreams that truly did come from God.

Two Dreams That Saved Jerusalem

Flavius Josephus, the renowned Jewish historian, wrote in the Antiquities a fable-like account of a remarkable deliverance for the Jews in Jerusalem. It happened during the time of Alexander the Great. Here is Josephus' account, as translated by A.R. Shilleto.

> Alexander the Great, when he had taken Gaza, made haste to go up to Jerusalem. And Jaddus the high priest, when he heard that, was in an agony and dread, not knowing how he should meet the Macedonians, since the king was displeased at his previous defiance. He therefore ordered the people to make supplications, and to join him in offering sacrifice to God, whom he besought to protect and deliver the nation from further perils that were coming on them.
>
> Thereupon God warned him in a dream, as he was asleep after he had offered sacrifice, to take courage, and to adorn the city, and open the gates; that the rest were to appear in white garments, but that he and the priests were

to meet the king in the garments proper to their order, without dread of any evil consequences, which the providence of God would prevent.

Upon this, when he rose from his sleep, he greatly rejoiced; and declared to all the warning he had received from God, and acted entirely according to his dream, and waited for the coming of the king. And when he heard that the king was not far from the city, he went out in procession with the priests and mass of the citizens.

The procession was imposing, and the manner of it different from that of other nations. It reached a place called Supha, which word, translated into Greek, signifies a prospect, for you have thence a prospect both of Jerusalem and of the temple. Now when the Phoenicians and Chaldeans that followed the king thought they should have liberty to plunder the city, and torture the high priest to death, which the king's displeasure made probable, the very reverse of this happened.

For Alexander, when he saw the multitude at a distance in white garments, while the priests stood clothed in their fine linen, and the high priest in purple and gold robes, with his mitre on his head, and the golden plate in it whereon the name of God was engraved, he approached by himself, and adored that Name, and first saluted the high priest.

The Jews also with one voice saluted Alexander, and surrounded him, whereupon the Kings of Syria and the rest were astonished at what Alexander had done, and supposed him disordered in mind. However, Parmenio alone went up to him, and asked him, 'How it comes to pass, that when all others adored him, he should adore the high priest of the Jews?' To whom he replied, 'I did not adore him, but that God who has honored him with the high priesthood.'

For I saw this very person in a dream in these very robes, when I was at Dium in Macedonia, who, when I was considering with myself how I might obtain the dominion of Asia, exhorted me to make no delay, but boldly to cross over, for he would conduct my army, and would give me the dominion over the Persians.

And so having seen no other in such robes, and now seeing this person in them, and remembering that vision, and the exhortation which I had in my dream, I believe that I bring this army under the divine conduct, and shall conquer Darius, and destroy the power of the Persians, and that all things will succeed according to what is in my mind.[33]

The Flaming Cross of Constantine

One of the more famous accounts of kings and their visions is told of the Roman emperor Constantine the Great. As history has it, Constantine, the son of Helena, herself a devout Christian woman, was proclaimed king after the untimely death of his father, Constantius I. A vicious rivalry for the vacated throne ensued, forcing the young ruler into a desperate battle at the Milvian Bridge near Rome in A.D. 312.

Constantine, who was already sympathetic toward Christianity through the godly influence of his mother, is said to have seen in a vision a flaming cross in the sky. Later that night he dreamed that Christ appeared to him, holding the same emblem he had seen in the vision, saying, "Under this banner conquer."[34]

As a result of the vision and dream, Constantine adopted the sign of the cross and was indeed victorious. The battle is regarded as a turning point for Christianity. Although events within the lofty chambers of imperial power had already begun softening the hearts of the emperors to the cause of Christ,[35] this astounding victory of Constantine signaled the dawn of a new day for the church.

The Edict of Milan, which Constantine issued within a year of his victory, brought a new era in the church's life. The persecuted saints of the Lord soon became the celebrated citizens of Constantine's vast empire. Kelsey writes,

> There was a burst of activity within the church that brought a flow of new literary work. Great Christian leaders arose to solve a host of religious problems. Athanasius laid the foundation for all subsequent Christian thinking, while Augustine in his voluminous

writings set the general direction of the Western church for the next thousand years.

Under Chrysostom and the great Capadocians the mold was also formed for all Eastern Christianity down to the present day. Not one of these great leaders ignored the subject of dreams. Rather, we find each of them taking the trouble to show, often many times, that the dream is one significant way in which God reveals Himself to man. Indeed, this new era of Western civilization was opened by the dream-vision that came to Constantine before his battle for Rome.[36]

What About the Crusades?

Contrary to popular thought, Constantine was not responsible for the so-called Holy Crusades. Those atrocities didn't occur until five hundred years after Constantine died. By that time the church had become corrupted with adherents who knew nothing of the saving grace of Jesus Christ, nor had any regard for the works of the Lord. In the year A.D. 450, a priest named Salvian wrote,

> Rich and poor, pagan and Christian alike in this Empire are sunk in a slew of immorality rarely known in history. Adultery and drunkenness are fashionable vices; virtue and temperance are the butt of all jokes. The name of Christ has become a profane expletive among those who call Him God.[37]

The lure of power and the deceitfulness of riches drew men of ambitious evil into the ranks of religion. Claiming to honor the cause of Christ, they in fact did so much harm that the world has yet to recover from the wounds of their religious apostasy.

Emperor or Church — Who's in Charge Here?

A successor to Constantine, Emperor Theodosius was regarded as a devout man. However, when news reached him that a mob had savagely murdered the Roman governor of Thessalonica, Theodosius became so enraged that he sent soldiers to revenge his death. Over seven thousand citizens were killed in one day!

News of the massacre spread quickly, and when Ambrose, the Bishop of Milan, heard it he was sickened. The Lord spoke to Ambrose in a dream, revealing that he was to call the emperor to repent publicly and confess his sin against God and the nation.

In his letter to the emperor, Ambrose gave several examples of kings who had repented and received God's blessings.

> I have written this, not to confound you, but that by the example of these kings may stir you to put away this sin from your kingdom. For you will do it away by humbling your soul before God.
>
> You are a man, and it has come upon you — conquer it. I urge, I beg, I exhort, I warn — for it is a grief to me that you, who were an example of unusual piety, who were conspicuous for clemency, should not now mourn that so many have perished. Conquer the devil whilst you still possess that wherewith you may conquer.

To enforce the order, Ambrose was forbidden by the Lord to conduct any religious service in the presence of the king — especially the serving of Communion. As the apostle wrote, "Whoever eats the bread or drinks the cup of the Lord in an unworthy manner will be guilty of sinning against the body and blood of the Lord"[38] Ambrose could have no part in mocking the table of the Lord by offering the blood of One who was innocent to one who himself had murdered thousands of innocent citizens.

Ambrose tells the emperor why he will oppose him.

> Lastly, I am writing with my own hand that which you alone may read. As I hope that the Lord will deliver me from all troubles, I have been warned, not by man, but plainly by Himself that it is forbidden me. For when I was anxious, in the very night in which I was preparing to set out, you appeared to me in a dream to have come into the Church, and I was not permitted to offer the sacrifice.

The letter concludes frankly,

> I dare not offer the sacrifice if you intend to be present.

Our God gives warnings in many ways, by heavenly signs, by the precepts of the prophets; and by the visions even of sinners. He wills that we should understand, that we should entreat Him to take away all disturbances, to preserve peace for you emperors, so that the faith and the peace of the church, whose advantage it is that emperors be devout Christians, may continue.[39]

Ambrose followed the warning from God in his dream, as did all the other bishops throughout the Roman empire. After some months the rejected monarch went before Ambrose and repented, confessing his sin.

This was a most telling moment in history, for it set the pendulum in motion to swing back and forth between church and state for the next several centuries. It raised a question that draws fire and blood to this very day — "Does the emperor empower the church, or does the church empower the emperor?" We ask it in a slightly different way now, "Does the government obey the church, or does the church obey the government?" The answer is neither! They both are to obey God by serving and blessing His people!

Nicholas, Bishop of Myra

One of the happy recipients of Constantine's charity was a man by the name of Nicholas, who was Bishop of Myra in Asia Minor. The young bishop was imprisoned in the year 303, during the reign of Emperor Diocletian, when many Christians were persecuted. He was freed when Constantine proclaimed the imperial toleration of all religions.

Nicholas was the only child of wealthy Christian parents, born about A.D. 280 in Patara, in the province of Lycia in Asia Minor. When his parents both died in a plague the boy was left with a good deal of wealth. Young Nicholas dedicated his life to God's service and moved to Myra, chief city of his province. There, after the death of their bishop, members of the council balloted unsuccessfully, for some time, trying to choose a successor.

Finally, in a dream, the oldest official was told to stand the next day at the cathedral door and select as the new bishop the first man named Nicholas who entered. When the young Christian went to the church as usual for morning prayers, he was asked his name, and soon afterward he was selected by the council and consecrated to the high office. Nicholas, because of his youth, tried to refuse the position, but he was overruled.

Early in his new career, during a visit to the Holy Land, he was so impressed by the places connected with Christ's life that he decided to resign from his bishopric at Myra and remain at Palestine. But God commanded him in a dream to return to Asia Minor. He obeyed the Lord and labored faithfully among the people of Myra.

Nicholas was very popular as a Bishop, and several stories of his ability to perform miracles have come down to us through church tradition. On his return from the Holy Land, it is said that a mighty storm arose, and the ship was almost wrecked. Nicholas calmly prayed to God, and the sailors were astonished when the wind suddenly abated, and their lives and ship were saved.

There is a legend that he restored to life a sailor who had died as a result of falling from a high mast. Also, on this same voyage, it was revealed to Nicholas in a dream that the ship's master was planning not to return him to Patara, but to sell him as a slave. Again Nicholas was successful through his prayer, for a heavy wind forced the vessel back to Asia Minor.

Another miracle attributed to him happened in A.D. 325, when the sons of a rich Asiatic, on their way to study at Athens, were killed and robbed by a wicked innkeeper who had previously been guilty of similar offenses. This man hid the boys' bodies in casks of brine.

Nicholas, on his way to the council of Nicaea, stopped at this inn, and that night in a dream the crime was revealed to him. He forced the wicked man to confess, then Nicholas made the sign of the cross over the casks, prayed earnestly to God, and, as the story has been told, immediately the three boys were restored to life.

One of Nicholas' chief characteristics was his unsurpassed generosity. In his youth he had learned by going around among the people how many were oppressed by poverty. Realizing God had blessed him with riches that he might be a blessing to others, Nicholas often went about in disguise and distributed presents, especially to children. Such things endeared him to the discerning adults who saw through the disguise, but for the sake of the children, he kept his identity secret.

There have been many stories generated through the centuries about this fascinating character — some unquestionably legendary and fictitious. But the fact remains that the man lived and impacted his world with his gentle, Christlike spirit. After his death, and upon validation of testimonies concerning his ministry, Nicholas was named as the patron saint of children. We know him today as jolly old Saint Nick — more commonly called Santa Claus![40]

I found this story rather fascinating and, after some thought, decided to include it in this book for your consideration. At the very least it serves as an example of the mythical nature of dreams and visions throughout history. There is one other dream that stands out in history, and seems almost too legendary to believe. Yet, the documentation is too substantial to dismiss. It happened to the president of the United States in the year 1865.

Abraham Lincoln

Ward Hill Lamon, the president's confidant and lifelong friend, tells in his journals of the night Mr. Lincoln had "his personal Patmos." Lamon wrote,

> The most startling incident in the life of Mr. Lincoln was a dream he had only a few days before his assassination. To him it was a thing of deadly import, and certainly no vision was ever fashioned more exactly to the actual tragedy which occurred soon after. Mr. Lincoln seemed unable to keep the dream a secret. I give it as nearly in his own words as I can, from notes which I made immediately after its recital.[41]

The president spoke in slow and measured tones as he braced Lamon for what he was about to say. "It seems strange how much there is in the Bible about dreams," Lincoln stated.

> There are, I think, some sixteen chapters in the Old Testament and four or five in the New in which dreams are mentioned; and there are many other passages scattered throughout the book which refer to visions. If we believe the Bible, we must accept the fact that in the old days God and His angels came to men in their sleep and

made themselves known in dreams. Nowadays dreams
are regarded as very foolish, and are seldom told, except
by old women and by young men and maidens in love.

Mrs. Lincoln here remarked, "Why, you look dreadfully solemn.
Do you believe in dreams?"

I can't say that I do," returned Mr. Lincoln, "but I had
one the other night which has haunted me ever since.
After it occurred, the first time I opened the Bible,
strange as it may appear, it was at the twenty-eighth
chapter of Genesis, which relates the wonderful dream
Jacob had. I turned to other passages, and seemed to
encounter a dream or vision wherever I looked. I kept on
turning the leaves of the old book, and everywhere my
eyes fell upon passages recording matters strongly in
keeping with my own thoughts, supernatural visitations,
dreams, visions and the like."

The president now looked so serious and disturbed that Mrs.
Lincoln exclaimed: "You frighten me! What is the matter?"
"I am afraid, " said Mr. Lincoln, observing the effect his words
had upon his wife, "that I have done wrong to mention the subject
at all."
This only inflamed Mrs. Lincoln's curiosity the more, and while
bravely disclaiming any belief in dreams, she strongly urged him to
tell the dream which seemed to have such a hold upon him, being
seconded in this by another listener. Mr. Lincoln hesitated, but at
length commenced very deliberately, his brow overcast with a shade
of melancholy.

Lincoln Dreams of His Assassination

Ward Hill Lamon recorded for all posterity the words that
Lincoln spoke:

About ten days ago, I retired very late. I had been up
waiting for important dispatches from the front. I could
not have been long in bed when I fell into a slumber, for
I was weary. I soon began to dream. There seemed to be

a deathlike stillness about me. Then I heard subdued sobs, as if a number of people were weeping. I thought I left my bed and wandered downstairs. There the silence was broken by the same pitiful sobbing, but the mourners were invisible.

I went from room to room; no living person was in sight, but the same mournful sounds of distress met me as I passed along. It was light in all the rooms; every object was familiar to me, but where were all the people who were grieving as if their hearts would break? I was puzzled and alarmed. What could be the meaning of all this? Determined to find the cause of a state of things so mysterious and so shocking, I kept on until I arrived at the East Room, which I entered. There I met with a sickening surprise.

Before me was a corpse wrapped in funeral vestments. Around it were stationed soldiers who were acting as guards, and there was a throng of people, some gazing mournfully upon the corpse, whose face was covered, others weeping pitifully. "Who is dead in the White House?" I demanded of one of the soldiers. "The president," was his answer; "he was killed by an assassin!" Then came a loud burst of grief from the crowd, which awoke me from my dreams. I slept no more that night, and although it was only a dream, I have been strongly annoyed by it ever since.[42]

"That is horrid!" said Mrs. Lincoln. "I wish you had not told it. I am glad I don't believe in dreams, or I should be in terror from this time forth." "Well," responded Mr. Lincoln thoughtfully, "it was only a dream, Mary. Let us say no more about it, and try to forget it. I think the Lord in His own good time and way will work this out all right. God knows what is best."

Indeed.

Long Time No See

The great crowd of priests dutifully gathered in front of the temple in preparation for the casting of lots. Only one among them could be chosen to go into the holy place to burn incense before the Lord, and once they had been chosen they could never do it again. It seemed fitting that old Zechariah, who had been waiting for over sixty years, would finally be selected. He had thought it would never happen, but on this day when the lot fell, he was the chosen one.

Sixty years is a long time to wait for anything, but it seems relatively brief compared to the four hundred years that span the time between Malachi's closing promise of the Old Testament and the dawn of the new day ushered in by the coming of Christ in the New Testament.

During that period there were no words from heaven, no prophecies, no dreams or visions, no stirrings of God among the people. Nothing. Four centuries of prophetic silence. Long time no see. The people had no choice but to go forward in faith, holding firmly to the memories and promises of the past. They knew not when God would speak again; they only knew that He would.

The old man's heart raced with youthful excitement as he prepared to enter where so few had ever gone. He felt privileged knowing he would soon stand before the great purple veil that guarded the ark of the covenant from carnal curiosity. Standing at the golden altar of incense, he would be just one curtain away from the manifest presence of God. Zechariah drew a deep breath as he entered into the solitude of that sanctuary. His ritual service would last only a few moments, but he intended to savor every precious second. He knew he would never pass this way again.

The people waited expectantly outside, and when Zechariah lingered well beyond the allotted time, they wondered what was wrong. There were nervous glances exchanged among the attending priests, each waiting for the other to take the initiative to go inside the temple to see what was the matter. Had Zechariah violated the sacred barrier between the holy place and the holy of holies? Did he in some way offend the Lord Almighty? Was he to be found dead before the ark of the covenant? Why did he tarry so long inside the temple? The questions raced in the minds of all who waited outside.

No one thought for a moment that the aged man was receiving a word from the Lord. The years of silence had taken a toll upon the expectancy of the people's hearts. But on this day the silence was being broken! Gabriel, the angel of the Lord, appeared to Zechariah standing on the right side of the altar of incense and told him that his wife would bear him a son named John, who would be the forerunner of the Lord and "turn the hearts of the fathers unto the children."[1] The angel, to whom four hundred years were but a blink in eternity, quoted the closing promise of the Old Testament and thus turned the first page of the New.

Zechariah was dumbstruck by the experience and, being unable to speak when he exited the temple, he gestured to the people in such a way that they concluded he had seen an angel. I wonder, did he flap his arms like wings and point to heaven? The people marveled at the unusual activity of that day's temple proceedings. Was this a sign that God was about to visit Israel once again?

Over the next few months an outpouring of revelatory visitations would occur as God continued speaking to His people. Mary received the announcement of the birth of Christ by a vision of Gabriel in her home. Joseph received guidance in four separate dreams concerning Jesus. The Magi visiting from afar were warned by God in a dream not to trust Herod, for he was seeking an occasion to murder Jesus.

Thus the New Testament opens with a cluster of visionary experiences, all centered around Jesus Christ. Throughout its development, dreams and visions factor highly at significant junctures in the history of the New Testament. Saul of Tarsus is converted to Christianity, Simon Peter is sent to the Gentiles, the apostles are led across the Aegean Sea into Europe and the church is strengthened by the surge of prophetic insights given in dreams and visions. Finally, the wondrous era closes out with perhaps the most famous of all dream/vision experiences — the Revelation of Jesus Christ given to His servant John, who was imprisoned on Patmos Island.

These facts are incontrovertible. Dreams and visions are a significant feature of the New Testament, just as they were in the Old. In vain do men dispute the record of Scripture. Thomas Paine expressed the sentiments which came with the Age of Reason when he wrote that biblical dreams and visions were in fact not divinely inspired, but mere human contrivances for the sake of coded communication during times of war or peril. Thus did Paine opine:

> The writings of Ezekiel, Daniel and John on Patmos arose from the situation the writers were in as prisoners of war, or prisoners of state, in a foreign country, which obliged them to convey even the most trifling information to each other, and all their political projects or opinions, in obscure and metaphorical terms. They *pretended* to have dreamed dreams and seen visions, because it was unsafe for them to speak facts or plain language. We ought, however, to suppose that the persons to whom they wrote understood what they meant, and that it was not intended anybody else should.[2]

This presumptuous observation concerning biblical dreams is characteristic of the rationalist philosophy that dominates modern thinking in some churches today. A few of our less illustrious seminary professors have molded the minds of zealous young ministers with their own biased traditions of hermenutical, exegetical and systematic dissection of Scripture — so that dreams and visions, along with other miraculous phenomena, are no longer regarded with any measure of credence. Though disguised in the garments of reason and objectivity, this approach to the Scripture is one of the most blatant examples of prejudice and subjectivity to be found anywhere.

Any honest person will tell you that we are never to interpret the Bible with our minds already made up concerning what it has to say. Rather, we are to let the Bible change our minds where we are wrong and shape our character where we go astray. If the Bible teaches about something that is not normative to our lives, we are to turn to the Lord and seek His grace in changing our lives to the norm of Scripture. We cannot make the Bible say what we have already made our minds believe. Certainly not! We ourselves must be changed by the unchangeable truth of God's holy Word.

When, therefore, the Bible speaks of dreams and visions, it is not for us to say that they no longer occur simply because we ourselves do not experience them. We ought instead to pray that God might choose to speak to us in a dream or in a vision. We may be delighted by His response! Also, it is not our place to reject dreams and visions simply because deceivers, witches and occultic charlatans exploit people through the pretentious use of such things.

One does not discard every twenty-dollar bill given to him simply because a counterfeiter has introduced his forgeries into the market. That would be absurd. It is equally foolish to reject genuine dreams and visions in an overreaction to those who use dreams and visions to practice divination and sorcery. The Bible instructs us to not treat prophecies with contempt. We are to "test everything, and hold on to the good." Evidently, some prophecies are from God, while others are not. The same is true of dreams and visions. By rejecting the bad, and holding to the good, we will not "put out the Spirit's fire."[3]

Opponents may argue, "We have the Bible and do not need for God to speak to us in dreams and visions." One could follow that line of thinking and easily answer that we therefore do not need preachers either. After all, now that the Bible is so readily available, why must I sit and listen to someone else tell me what it says? Obviously, preachers are used by God to explain the Scriptures in such relevance that we readily see their redemptive connection to our lives. Dreams and visions do the same thing! They are God's messengers of the night, His nocturnal preachers. They illustrate the truth of God's holy Word in truly unforgettable ways. Sometimes they even exceed the capabilities of a preacher, because a picture is worth a thousand words!

Besides this, the Bible itself says that in the last days God *will* speak to us in dreams and visions. Those who believe the Bible but do not believe that God speaks in dreams and visions are faced with an enigma. This reminds me of the perplexity of Lactantius, a third century church father who dreamed that he was not supposed to believe in dreams.[4] What's a fellow to do?

A favorite text of those who debate the point is a passage from the epistle to the Hebrews. "In the past God spoke to our forefathers through the prophets at many times and in various ways, but in these last days he has spoken to us by his Son, whom he appointed heir of all things, and through whom he made the universe."[5] The assumption of some interpreters is that this means God no longer speaks now that Christ has come and we have the Bible. They reason that since Jesus is the final word from God, there is nothing else to be said.

Let me offer but three brief thoughts on this. First, the phrase "in these last days" encompasses ourselves as well as those who walked with Christ in the first century. If not, then could someone please tell us exactly *when* did the last days end? Are we now living in "the after-the-last-days days"? The fact is, the last days have not ended just yet. When they do, everybody will know it! Thus, God speaks today just as He spoke then, for it is the same dispensation.

Second, when the Bible says that God spoke in various ways in the past, but now has spoken to us in His Son, it means that all the ways by which God speaks are now to be found in His Son alone. This includes the preaching of sermons, prophecies, dreams and visions, parables, commandments, oracles, revelations, statutes, testimonies and any other means of communication available to God for the exaltation of Jesus Christ and the edifying of His church.

138

Third, let's ask a simple question here. If God decided to stop speaking in dreams and visions once Christ came, then why did dreams and visions continue *after* Jesus ascended into heaven? Consider the following examples from the text of New Testament Scripture.

Standing Too Close to the Flame

The young attendant held the coats and watched as the elders stoned the blasphemer. He had heard of stonings but had never before been witness to one at ringside. It was gruesome. The frenzy of Middle Eastern fanaticism was at its hottest pitch as the angry zealots pounded the skull of Stephen with stones. Young Saul seemed enchanted at the sight of blood and bone. He vowed in his heart to carry this campaign of retribution throughout the whole of Israel, to rid the Holy Land of those deceivers called by the name of the false prophet Jesus.

There was one thing, however, that Saul could not get out of his mind. It was the look on Stephen's face as he died. He seemed almost angelic despite the hellish fire of hatred that burned hot about him. And his words seemed truer to the heart of Moses' teachings than anything Saul had ever heard from his rabbinical masters.

Stephen had exclaimed, "Look! I see the heavens opened and the Son of Man standing at the right hand of God!" That proved to be the damning moment in his trial. The elders rushed upon him and began their dread act of execution. But Stephen knelt down and cried out in a loud voice, "Lord, do not charge them with this sin."[6] These were not the words of a man dying in cowardly fear, nor even in torturous pain. These were the words of faith and vision.

Somehow young Saul was able to shake from his own conscience the haunting image of Stephen's death and to fuel his anger against the Christians by seeking the approval of his elders. They were only too happy to underwrite his brief reign of terror. Armed with papers authorizing his random acts of cruelty, Saul headed for Damascus where a large community of believers lived. It was his intent to see that it would also be where they died.

As he journeyed toward Damascus, suddenly a brilliant light shone around him from heaven, and Saul fell to the ground. A voice spoke, and everybody froze in their tracks. Saul asked, "Who are You, Lord?" The answer would rock him to the depths of his heart — "I am Jesus, whom you are persecuting." Trembling and astonished, Saul replied, "What do You want me to do?" The Lord said to him, "Arise and go to the city, and you will be told what to do."[7]

Is That You, Lord?

Have you ever sensed the Lord telling you to do something that seemed so unlikely that you had to double check to make sure it was really the Lord who put the thought in your heart? Imagine how Ananias must have felt when the Lord spoke to him in a vision, "Ananias, arise and go to the street called Straight, and inquire at the house of one called Judas for one called Saul of Tarsus, for behold, he is praying." I can just imagine the thought that might have entered Ananias' mind: "Yeah, right." Then the Lord added, "He has seen in a vision a man named Ananias coming in and putting his hand on him, so that he might receive his sight." This is interesting because both Saul and Ananias, though separated in the city, were having essentially the same vision.

Ananias tried his best to convince the Lord that this was not a smart thing to do. "Lord," he appealed, "I have heard from many about this man, how he has done much harm to Your saints in Jerusalem. And he is here with authority from the chief priests to bind all who call upon Your Name." The Lord was unmoved by the argument. "Go," He said, "for he is a chosen vessel of Mine to bear My name before Gentiles, kings and the children of Israel. For I will show him how many things he must suffer for My name's sake."[8]

Ananias obeyed the Lord and went to Saul. That took a lot of courage and faith. If Ananias was wrong — if the vision he had seen was false — he would be the first Christian arrested in Damascus by the infamous persecutor. He entered the house and said, "Brother Saul, the Lord Jesus sent me to you."[9] In effect he was asking, "Are you my brother? and, Is Jesus your Lord?" These two questions ought to be asked today by opponents in the church who seem more ready to stone one another than to love one another. May God give us all the same courage and faith displayed by Ananias.

When Ananias laid hands on Saul the scabs that were upon his eyes fell to the floor and he received his sight. This was a prophetic type of how the Lord was opening Saul's spiritual eyes to know the mysteries of the kingdom. Little wonder that years later he would write to those whom he had converted to Christ, "I pray also that the eyes of your heart may be enlightened in order that you may know the hope to which he has called you, the riches of his glorious inheritance in the saints, and his incomparably great power for us who believe."[10]

The Eyes of Your Heart

The conversion of Saul was accomplished by four visions. The first one was given to Stephen as he was being stoned, which undoubtedly had its effect upon Saul. The second one took place on the road to Damascus, the third one in the house of Judas as Saul was praying, and the fourth one was given to Ananias leading him to go and pray for Saul that he might see. In the following years, each time Saul would tell his testimony he was careful to point out that the Lord had spoken to him in a vision. Furthermore, he made it a case for his defense against those who thought him to be a heretic — "I was not disobedient unto the heavenly vision."[11]

As it turns out, Paul (the name which Saul preferred) was a Christian influenced greatly by visions. Including those already touched upon here, the New Testament documents no less than fourteen specific encounters Paul had with visions.[12] He was a man who saw with the eyes of his heart. Shortly after his conversion Paul returned to Jerusalem filled with an evangelistic zeal that could have converted the entire nation. But sometimes people aren't as eager to be saved as we are to save them. One day while he was praying in the temple, Paul fell into a trance and heard the Lord say to him, "Make haste, and get out of Jerusalem quickly, because they will not accept your testimony about Me."[13]

He left Jerusalem and spent the following three years in the Arabian desert, receiving revelations from the Lord Himself. Here, in his own words, is a brief testimony of those mysterious days. "I want you to know, brothers, that the gospel I preached is not something that man made up. I did not receive it from any man, nor was I taught it; rather, I received it by revelation from Jesus Christ."[14]

To confirm this Paul wrote the Ephesian church and said, "Surely you have heard about the administration of God's grace that was given to me for you, that is, the mystery made known to me by revelation, as I have already written briefly. In reading this, then, you will be able to understand my insight into the mystery of Christ, which was not made known to men in other generations as it has now been revealed by the Spirit to God's holy apostles and prophets."[15]

On Your Mark. Get Set. Wait!

Paul lived in Antioch for the next fourteen years, experiencing the trying of his faith. Often the Lord follows dreams and visions with tent-making. He would not have us be so heavenly minded that we are no earthly good. A man named Barnabas, who would become Paul's dearest friend, met him in Antioch and encouraged him in his time of obscurity.

One day as they were worshipping the Lord together with the prophets and teachers in the church at Antioch, the Holy Spirit said, "Dedicate Barnabas and Paul for a special job I have for them."[16] Being directed by the Holy Spirit, they went to Seleucia and then sailed for Cyprus. The time of his vision had come!

After a prosperous missionary journey, Paul and Barnabas returned to Antioch only to become embroiled in a religious controversy stirred up by the Jews. It was then that yet another vision came by which it was determined that Paul and Barnabas should travel to Jerusalem and present their views before the leaders of the church. Concerning this trip Paul wrote, "I went in response to a *revelation* and set before them the gospel that I preach among the Gentiles."[17]

The Greek word Paul used was *apokalupsis,* meaning "disclosure, appearing, to lighten, make manifest, to be revealed, a revelation."[18] It was first used in the New Testament by old Simeon when he took the baby Jesus and lifted Him up in the temple, saying that He would be "a Light of *revelation* to the Gentiles."[19] Paul also used the word in the epistle to the Corinthians, listing it as one of the four ways a preacher may profit the church — revelation, knowledge, prophesying, doctrine.[20]

It is interesting to observe how the traditional evangelical church has held tenaciously to knowledge and doctrine, while standing respectably aloof from revelation and prophecy. Perhaps we feel that the first two are objective and rational, while the latter two are more subjective and mystical. The fact remains, however, that they come together in a cluster of four — and we need all four to fully benefit the church with the preaching of God's holy Word.

To my charismatic brothers who speak of nothing but revelation and prophecy, I urge you to set your hearts also upon knowledge and doctrine. That way, you truly will be preaching the full gospel.

How Lovely on the Mountains

Everywhere in the world hungry hearts are longing for the living bread of heaven. Paul challenged his readers, "How shall they ask the Lord to save them unless they believe in him? And how can they believe in him if they have never heard about him? And how can they hear about him unless someone tells them? And how will anyone go and tell them unless someone sends him? That is what the Scriptures are talking about when they say, 'How beautiful are the feet of those who preach the Gospel of peace with God and bring glad tidings of good things.' In other words, how welcome are those who come preaching God's Good News!"[21]

This was more than a theory to Paul. He actually did it himself. The most notable instance was when he and his fellow missionaries were at their wits' end trying to preach the gospel in Asia and Bithynia. For some strange reason they were "forbidden by the Holy Spirit to preach the Word" in these places.[22] Jesus had said, "Go," but now the Holy Spirit was saying, "No!" This was not a contradiction, but a clarification. They were to go into all the world, but right now they were not to go specifically into Asia. The timing of preaching is as crucial as the gospel itself.

Backed up against the Aegean Sea with nowhere to turn, the missionaries received light in their time of darkness. During the night Paul had a vision of a man of Macedonia standing and begging him, "Come over to Macedonia and help us." Luke, the inspired historian, added, "After Paul had seen the vision, we got ready at once to leave for Macedonia, concluding that God had called us to preach the gospel to them."[23]

Once they had arrived in Macedonia and saw the effectiveness of their preaching, the mission team set out for other cities in the region. Paul went to Corinth and was initially met with a fire-storm of resistance. He was on the verge of leaving the city when God once again changed Paul's travel plans. "One night the Lord spoke to Paul in a vision: 'Do not be afraid; keep on speaking, do not be silent. For I am with you, and no one is going to attack and harm you, because I have many people in this city.' So Paul stayed for a year and a half, teaching them the word of God."[24] Thus, the great church of Corinth was founded and became a major force for Christianity in the first century.

Not every city would be so open as Corinth. At one place, a town named Iconium, a band of religious opponents stirred up a mob against Paul, and they stoned him and dragged him out of the city, supposing him to be dead.[25] It is widely held that this was the time Paul referred to later when he wrote, "This boasting is all so foolish, but let me go on. Let me tell about the visions I've had, and revelations from the Lord. Fourteen years ago I was taken up to heaven for a visit. Don't ask me whether my body was there or just my spirit, for I don't know; only God can answer that. But anyway, there I was in paradise, and heard things so astounding that they are beyond a man's power to describe or put in words."[26]

There was another time when Paul stood before a Jewish mob, and as he was not too keen on being stoned, he tried to calm them with reason. He was doing fine until he tapped into their bigotry by saying that the Lord had told him to go unto the Gentiles. The crowd would have torn him to pieces had not the Roman soldiers intervened by arresting him. The following night, while he lay in the county jail, the Lord stood by him and said, "Take courage! As you have testified about me in Jerusalem, so you must also testify in Rome."[27]

All Other Ground Is Sinking Sand

The storm lashed against the ship with a fury born in hell. The apostle on board was headed for the heart of the Roman Empire, and Satan would do whatever he could to stop this mission. His preaching had stumped Felix and Festus and almost persuaded Agrippa. Caesar must not be bothered by the convicting truth of the Nazarene.

The sky grew darker, and the wind howled like an army of demons at war. Seasoned sailors turned pale with fear; they knew they were in over their heads. Panic broke out, and all on board were in great distress of soul, knowing that death in a watery grave was imminent.

Suddenly, Paul stepped into the midst of the chaos and said, "Cheer up! Not one of us will lose our lives, even though the ship will go down. For last night an angel of the God to whom I belong and whom I serve stood beside me and said, 'Don't be afraid, Paul — for you will surely stand trial before Caesar! What's more, God has granted your request and will save the lives of all those sailing with you.' So take courage! For I believe God! It will be just as he said!"[28]

As it turned out, he was right. The vision was not a hallucination of a dying man; it was a revelation of the living God. It filled Paul with faith and courage and seized the sailors with awe.

A few men tried to jump ship, and Paul warned them that they would perish if they set out on their own. They took his advice and stayed on board. This is a message many need to hear today as they forsake the church and go off to do their own thing. The songwriter phrased it well, "On Christ the solid rock I stand, all other ground is sinking sand." Keep the faith, hold the course, finish the race. We shall be saved! It will turn out just as God has said!

Counsel for the Defense

Rome spared no expense in surrounding their Caesar with the luxurious trappings of power. They thought him to be a god and therefore lavished upon him the splendor befitting divinity. Paul was little impressed standing in the palace courts, for it didn't come anywhere near the glory of the temple of the Lord.

The air was thick with political power. Soldiers' footsteps echoed throughout the massive hallways as they marched prisoners to and from their dungeon cells. Senators and scribes walked with deliberate and guarded steps as they entered into the presence of the Roman tribunal. One false move, one misguided word, one slight act of indecorum, and they would feel the full wrath of the monster Rome.

There, in the middle of the court, standing completely alone was the prisoner Paul. Charged with insurrection against the emperor by preaching another King, there were no attorneys willing to stand at his side. The risk of associating with rebellion against Rome was too great. That's when it happened. Paul felt a presence he had come to know so well. Lifting up his eyes, Paul saw the Lord standing beside him!

After he was returned to his cell, Paul excitedly wrote to his young disciple, Timothy, and said, "The first time I was brought before the judge, no one was here to help me. Everyone had run away." Yet Paul was not bitter. He added, "I hope that they will not be blamed for it." Then he gets to the point. "The Lord stood with me and gave me the opportunity to boldly preach a whole sermon for all the world to hear. And he saved me from being thrown to the lions."

Paul had witnessed a judicial miracle. The magistrate of the Roman court had not only allowed the gospel to be preached and entered into the records, but he returned Paul unharmed to his cell. Paul was elated with praise for Christ. "Yes, and the Lord will always deliver me from all evil and will bring me into his heavenly Kingdom. To God be the glory forever and ever. Amen!"[29]

Paul was not the only apostle given to visionary experiences. John the Beloved is renowned for the insights given unto him through dreams and visions, the most notable being the book of Revelation. And Simon Peter, the common man's apostle, also had profound experiences with dreams and visions.

A Breath of Fresh Air

The trip to Joppa had taken longer than Peter expected. The interruptions by people recognizing him and asking him to tend to some desperate need had taken their toll. Now he was the one in need. Hadn't the Lord said, "Come apart and rest awhile," he reasoned? When the invitation came from Simon to spend some time at the beach, Peter *knew* it was the Lord's will. (Somebody say amen!)

Simon the Tanner — now there's an occupation for you. I once heard a preacher explain that in order to practice his trade, a tanner collected the feces of dogs throughout the town and stored them in special vats at his home. Apparently, the acidic properties of the decomposed waste were essential in tanning hides. One can imagine what it must have smelled like around Simon's house. Perhaps this is why Peter was on the rooftop! It might also explain why he was in a trance! (Of course I'm only teasing.)

The Bible tells us that while Peter was on the roof enjoying the view and waiting for lunch, he fell into a trance.[30] The Greek word is *ekstasis,* from which we get *ecstasy.* It literally means "to stand outside." The idea is one of displacement, especially with reference to the mind. In other words, a person's normal condition becomes so altered that they are thrown into a state of ecstasy, transported out of themselves into a revelation from God.[31] That's what happened to Peter.

"He saw the sky open and a great canvas sheet, suspended by its four corners, settle to the ground. In the sheet were all sorts of animals, snakes and birds [forbidden to the Jews for food]. Then a voice said to him, 'Go kill and eat any of them you wish.' 'Never, Lord,' Peter declared, 'I have never in all my life eaten such creatures, for they are forbidden by our Jewish laws.' The voice spoke again, 'Don't contradict God! If he says something is kosher, then it is.'"[32]

This was a real stretch for Peter. I believe the Lord spoke while he was in a trance (outside of himself) because he was about to be stretched beyond his prejudicial upbringing. God was literally taking Peter "outside himself"!

The vision happened three times. "Peter was very perplexed. What could the vision mean? What was he supposed to do? Just then the men sent by Cornelius had found the house and were standing outside at the gate, inquiring whether this was the place where Simon Peter lived!"[33]

Cornelius? That's Not a Jewish Name

Cornelius, a captain of an Italian regiment in the Roman army, lived in the city of Caesarea. He was a godly man, deeply reverent, as was his entire household. He gave generously to charity and was a man of prayer. While wide awake one afternoon he had a vision — it was about three o'clock — and in this vision he saw an angel of God coming toward him.

"Cornelius!" the angel said. Cornelius stared at him in terror. "What do you want, sir?" he asked the angel. And the angel replied, "Your prayers and charities have not gone unnoticed by God! Now send some men to Joppa to find a man named Simon Peter, who is staying with Simon, the tanner, down by the shore, and ask him to come and visit you."[34]

How interesting that Cornelius did not say, "Never, Lord!" He simply obeyed. Why is it that those who do not know the Lord seem sometimes more responsive to His will than those who have walked with Him for awhile? At what point do we become self-confident in spiritual matters? May the Lord give us as many visions as necessary to take us "outside ourselves."

Meanwhile, Back at the Ranch

"Meanwhile, as Peter was puzzling over the vision, the Holy Spirit said to him, 'Three men have come to see you. Go down and meet them and go with them. All is well, I have sent them.'[35] The old King James puts it, "Go with them; doubting nothing." The word is diakrino (from *dia,* "asunder;" *krino,* "to judge"). It means to separate oneself from another for the purpose of discrimination.[36]

The vision happened *three* times. While Peter was puzzling over it, *three* Gentiles knocked on the door. *Hmmm.* What do you think *that* means? Do you remember Peter's sermon on the day of Pentecost? He had stood and said to the people, "This is that..." (Acts 2:16). Do you think now that it might have occurred to Peter on the rooftop that the three Gentiles were connected to the threefold vision of the unclean things? "Do not call common and unclean what I have cleansed," the Lord had said to Peter. When the knock came on the door, Peter had to think, This is that!

This is proven by Peter's words to Cornelius when he arrived at his house. "You know it is against the Jewish laws for me to come into a Gentile home like this. But God has shown me in a vision that I should never think of anyone as inferior. So I came as soon as I was sent for. Now tell me what you want."[37]

The issue was not meat or drink, but rather the prejudice that the Jews had toward the Gentiles. The vision was God's way of confronting Peter's deep-seated religious bigotry. This had to be dealt with before he would go to the Gentiles and tell them of Christ's redeeming love.

Peter preached Christ to Cornelius and his household. Before he could even finish his sermon, the Holy Spirit came powerfully upon them, just as He had on the day of Pentecost.[38] Peter and his companions were astounded. They had just witnessed yet another turning point in history — the Gentiles are included in Christ's salvation! (Oh, somebody needs to shout "Glory!")

The Great Escape

Wicked King Herod arrested James, the apostle John's brother, and executed him with a sword. When he saw how this pleased the people, Herod then arrested Peter and placed him in a fortified dungeon. His plans were to bring him out and kill him after the Feast of Unleavened Bread. All the believers in Jerusalem set themselves to pray earnestly for Peter's safety.

"The night before he was to be executed, he was asleep, double-chained between two soldiers with others standing guard before the prison gate, when suddenly there was a light in the cell and an angel of the Lord stood beside Peter! The angel slapped him on the side to awaken him and said, 'Quick! Get up!' And the chains fell off his wrists! Then the angel told him, 'Get dressed and put on your shoes.' And he did. 'Now put on your coat and follow me!' the angel ordered.

"So Peter left the cell, following the angel. But all the time he thought it was a dream or vision and didn't believe it was really happening. They passed the first and second cell blocks and came to the iron gate to the street, and this opened to them of its own accord! So they passed through and walked along together for a block, and then the angel left him.

"Peter finally realized what had happened! 'It's really true!' he said to himself. 'The Lord has sent his angel and saved me from Herod and from what the Jews were hoping to do to me!'"[39]

Perhaps at this moment Peter called to mind one of the songs of ascent which he had sung countless times as a Jewish boy in pilgrimage to Jerusalem.

"When the Lord brought back the captives to Zion, we were like men who dreamed. Our mouths were filled with laughter, our tongues with songs of joy. Then it was said among the nations, "The Lord has done great things for them." The Lord has done great things for us, and we are filled with joy!"[40]

Like Them That Dream

Though the deliverance from prison was actually happening to

149

Peter, he thought it was a dream or a vision. I find that intriguing. It seems to imply that Peter had experienced dreams and visions enough to make the assessment that this encounter was like the others.

Dreams and visions do have definite surrealistic qualities. You can fly in dreams. Animals talk. Impossible things seem ordinary and unchallenged. Scenes change randomly, as do people with whom you are talking. You sometimes even see yourself doing something, as though you are watching yourself in a movie. A man is sometimes a woman; a woman, sometimes a man. A baby can be the size of a whale, and a whale can fit in a fish bowl.

Peter's Final Word

Peter indeed did dream, but he was no dreamer in the derogatory sense of the word. He was a man of proven character, having been lifted up by the resurrected Christ and reborn to a living hope. Like Jacob of old, Peter had wrestled an angel and limped thereafter the rest of his life. His name also was changed to *Rock Solid.* We can believe him when he tells us about Jesus Christ, for he was among His closest friends.

Peter wrote in his final letter, "We did not follow cleverly invented stories when we told you about the power and coming of our Lord Jesus Christ, but we were eyewitnesses of his majesty. For he received honor and glory from God the Father when the voice came to him from the Majestic Glory, saying, 'This is my Son, whom I love; with him I am well pleased'

"We ourselves heard this voice that came from heaven when we were with him on the sacred mountain. And we have the word of the prophets made more certain, and you will do well to pay attention to it, as to a light shining in a dark place, until the day dawns and the morning star rises in your hearts.

"Above all, you must understand that no prophecy of Scripture came about by the prophet's own interpretation. For prophecy never had its origin in the will of man, but men spoke from God as they were carried along by the Holy Spirit."[41]

We know, therefore, that what we hold in hand and call the Holy Bible is holy indeed. It is inspired by God and complete in itself, needing nothing added unto it, nor anything taken from it.

We also know that dreams and visions make up portions of that holy Word and therefore should be respected as a means whereby God communicates to mankind. Furthermore, we know that Jesus Christ, in whom God summed up all revelation, continued speaking to His apostles after He ascended into heaven.

The question we now ask is, did He continue speaking in dreams and visions after the apostolic period ended? The answer is yes.

TWO THOUSAND YEARS
OF DREAMS AND VISIONS

The crucifixion of Jesus of Nazareth had little more than a numbing effect upon the small region of Judea, and had there been no resurrection, nor any subsequent outpouring of the Holy Spirit upon the church, the story would have passed as little more than a footnote in Jewish history. But He did rise from the dead, and He did send forth the Holy Spirit to empower His followers as witnesses of the truth. Thus, the animosity that nailed Him to the cross soon began to target those who dared continue speaking in His name.

In the book of Acts we read how Peter and John were beaten by the council and threatened to no longer speak in the name of Jesus. It didn't work. The church mounted a spiritual offensive through prayer, asking God for even more boldness to preach the word of the Lord. They had no sooner sounded the "amen" when the place where they were assembled was shook by yet another outpouring of the Holy Spirit. God heard from heaven, answered their request and unleashed the church with a fiery zeal for preaching the name of Jesus.

The religious leaders were incensed by the boldness of those who followed Jesus. The tension finally reached its flash point when Stephen, one of the disciples, gave his masterful defense before the tribunal. His speech is one of the most comprehensive recitals of history found in the Scripture.

The Vision of Stephen (A.D. 35)

"Stephen, full of the Holy Spirit, looked up to heaven and saw the glory of God, and Jesus standing at the right hand of God. 'Look,' he said, 'I see heaven open and the Son of Man standing at the right hand of God.'"[1] Did not Peter say on the day of Pentecost that "young men would see visions"? How quickly did the Lord confirm that word with signs following!

Upon hearing Stephen's vision, the religious leaders screamed, covered their ears and rushed at him. They dragged him out of the city and stoned him. Stephen prayed, "Lord Jesus, receive my spirit." Then he fell on his knees and cried out, "Lord, do not hold this sin against them." When he had said this, he fell asleep [died].[2] On the day of Stephen's death a great persecution broke out against the church at Jerusalem. The believers were scattered throughout Judea and Samaria. Many died at the hands of those who persecuted them.

Years later Pionius, a disciple of Jesus and a close associate with Polycarp (who himself was martyred), venerated the wondrous manner in which Christian martyrs (beginning with Saint Stephen) had faced the moment of death:

> And truly, who can fail to admire their nobleness of mind, and their patience, and their love towards the Lord which they displayed? Who, when they were so torn with scourges, that the frame of their bodies, even to the very inward veins and arteries, was laid open, still patiently endured, while even those that stood by pitied and bewailed them. But they reached such a pitch of magnanimity, that not one of them let a sigh or a groan escape them; thus proving to us all that those holy martyrs of

Christ, at the very time when they suffered such tor-
ments, were absent from the body, or rather, *that the Lord
then stood by them, and communed with them.*[3]

Stephen's martyrdom not only ignited a fierce persecution
against the church, it also set faith aflame in the hearts of the believers — a faith that Christ did not disappoint. Inasmuch as Stephen
gives us biblical text to support the validity of visions being given
unto martyrs, who can doubt that many others also beheld the Lord
in their moment of agonizing departure? And who can fail to appreciate here the tender mercies of the Lord to provide such comfort in
so dark a moment?

Ignatius of Antioch (A.D. 40-107)

Ignatius was nicknamed *Theophorus* (one carried by God), in
keeping with the belief that he was in fact the child that Jesus took
in His arms and set before the disciples as a pattern of humility.[4]
There is credible support for the authenticity of this claim.[5]

Ignatius was personally discipled by the apostle John and
esteemed by all who knew him to be "a man in all respects of an
apostolic character." He governed the church at Antioch with great
care throughout the nightmarish persecution under Domitian. While
he rejoiced that the church had been restored to a season of peace,
his heart grieved within him that he had not attained to perfect rank
as a disciple.

He felt strongly that the confession which is made by martyrdom
would bring him into a yet more intimate relation to the Lord. At
length he attained the object of his desire. Sometime between the
years A.D. 107 to A.D. 116, Trajan arrested Ignatius for preaching the
gospel and, after a mock trial held in Antioch, issued the following
decree: "We command that Ignatius, who affirms that he carried
about within him Him that was crucified, be bound by soldiers, and
carried to the great city of Rome, there to be devoured by the beasts,
for the gratification of the people."[6]

Upon hearing this death sentence Ignatius cried out with joy, "I
thank Thee, O Lord, that Thou hast vouchsafed to honor me with a
perfect love towards Thee, and hast made me to be bound with iron
chains, like Thy Apostle Paul." Ignatius then with delight clasped

the chains about himself tightly and was led away to a martyr's death in Rome.

The ferocious nature of the lions left nothing but skeletal remains, which were wrapped in linen by disciples and carried back to Antioch. The account is reported by Philo and Agathopus, who are mentioned in the epistles written by Ignatius as having attended him on that journey to Rome which resulted in his martyrdom. They conclude their testimony with a most remarkable vision:

> Having ourselves been eye-witnesses to these things, and having spent the whole night in tears within the house, and having entreated the Lord, with bended knees and much prayer, that He would give us weak men full assurance respecting the things which were done, it came to pass, on our falling into a brief slumber, that some of us saw the blessed Ignatius suddenly standing by us and embracing us, while others beheld him again praying for us, and others still saw him dropping with sweat, as if he had just come from his great labor, and standing by the Lord. When, therefore, we had with great joy witnessed these things, and had compared our several visions together, we sang praise to God, the giver of all good things, and expressed our sense of the happiness of the holy martyr.[7]

Polycarp, Bishop of Smyrna (A.D. 69-155)

Persecution continued to be unleashed against the Christians. Polycarp, well advanced in years, was content to wait in the city, not fearing what should become of him. His close friends prevailed upon him to retreat to a small estate not far from the city. There he passed the time with a few companions, "wholly occupied night and day in prayer for all men and for the church throughout the whole world; as indeed was his habit. And while at prayer he fell into a trance three days before his arrest and saw his pillow set on fire. And he turned and said to his companions, 'I must needs be burned alive.'"[8]

Shortly thereafter, Polycarp was arrested and led into the city. The proconsul urged him, "Swear, and I will release thee; curse the Christ."

Polycarp answered, "Eighty-six years have I served him, and he hath done me no wrong; how can I blaspheme my King and my Savior? Since thou art vainly urgent that I should swear by the fortune of Caesar, and pretendest not to know who and what I am, hear me declare with boldness, I am a Christian."

The proconsul then threatened Polycarp, first with being thrown to wild beasts, and then with being consumed by fire.

Polycarp replied, "Thou threatenest me with fire which burneth for an hour, and after a little is extinguished, but art ignorant of the fire of the coming judgment and of eternal punishment, reserved for the ungodly. But why tarriest thou? Bring forth what thou wilt!"[9]

Polycarp was bound to a stake and the pile was thrown about him to be burned. He lifted his eyes to heaven and prayed. When he had pronounced the amen, those who were appointed for the purpose kindled the fire. Eyewitnesses tell what happened next:

> As the flame blazed forth in great fury, we, to whom it was given to witness it, beheld a great miracle, and have been preserved that we might report to others what then took place. For the fire, shaping itself into the form of an arch, like the sail of a ship when filled with the wind, encompassed as by a circle the body of the martyr. And he appeared within not like flesh which is burnt, but as bread that is baked, or as gold and silver glowing in a furnace. Moreover, we perceived such a sweet odor coming from the pile, as if frankincense or some precious spices had been smoking there.[10]

History tells us that a dagger had to be thrust into Polycarp's side in order to kill him. Thus, in keeping with his vision, he was assuredly "burned alive." Polycarp's faith and courage carried him to the point of death, and there can be little doubt that the *vision* carried him through it.

The Testimony of Tertullian (A.D. 160-230)

In *Treatise of the Soul* Tertullian wrote, "We are bound to expound what is the opinion of Christians respecting dreams, as incidents of sleep, and as no slight or trifling excitements of the soul." He described what took place in dreams as *ecstasy*. "In fact," he stated, "with what real feeling, and anxiety, and suffering do we experience joy, and sorrow and alarm in our dreams!"

But not everybody shared Tertullian's views. A chief opponent named Epicurus was very vocal and sarcastic in his ridicule of dreams and visions. Perhaps Tertullian's reply to Epicurus might now serve as a reasonable response to those who mock dreams and visions today.

> Epicurus has given it as his opinion that dreams are altogether vain things. Yet, who is such a stranger to human experience as not to sometimes have perceived some truth in dreams? I shall force a blush from Epicurus, if I only glance at but a few of the more remarkable instances.[11]

Tertullian, in some detail, listed numerous historical instances of how dreams have been highly valued.

- Astyages, King of the Medes, saw in a dream a flood which inundated Asia, issuing from his daughter's womb. He dreamed a second time and saw a vine growing from her womb, which overspread the whole of Asia. As it turned out, the son born to Astyages' daughter was Cyrus the Great, whom the Lord called "His anointed."[12]

- Philip of Macedon, before he became a father, saw upon the lower abdomen of Olympias, his consort, the imprint of a signet ring with a lion as the royal seal. Philip concluded that the dream meant that Olympias would bear him no children. He could not have been further from the truth, for the son she bore to Philip was none other than Alexander the Great.

- Cicero learned in a dream how that one who was yet a boy and of a plain and private station in life, by the name of Julius Octavius (a name personally unknown at the time to Cicero), was the destined Augustus, emperor of Rome. We today know him as Julius Caesar.

Tertullian concluded his discourse with the deliberate exaggeration, "The whole world is full of oracles of this description!" While he did not teach that all dreams were from God, Tertullian did say, "From God must all these visions be regarded as emanating, which may be compared to the actual grace of God, as being honest, holy, prophetic, inspired, instructive, and inviting to virtue."[13] My sentiments exactly!

Jerome's Startling Testimony (A.D. 345-420)

Jerome was a man of devout faith and superior intelligence. He is most known for the Vulgate, the first translation of the Bible into the language of the common people. He took great pride in his library, which he had accumulated at no small cost over several years. He frankly confessed to preferring the heady writings of Cicero and other prominent philosophers of his day over the simple words of the prophets, saying that "their style seemed rude and repellent. I failed to see the light with my blinded eyes."

While traveling to Jerusalem, Jerome became gravely ill and fell unconscious with a burning fever. After he recovered, he testified of having a life-changing experience through a vision.

> Suddenly I was caught up in the spirit and dragged before the judgment seat of the Judge; and here the light was so bright, and those who stood around me were so radiant, that I cast myself upon the ground and did not dare to look up. Asked who and what I was I replied: "I am a Christian." But He who presided said: "Thou liest, thou art a follower of Cicero and not of Christ. For where thy treasure is, there will thy heart be also."
>
> Instantly I became dumb, and amid the strokes of the lash — for He had ordered me to be scourged — I was tortured more severely still by the fire of conscience. I began to cry, "Have mercy upon me, O Lord; have mercy upon me." Amid the sound of the scourges this cry still made itself heard.
>
> At last the bystanders, falling down before the knees of Him who presided, prayed that He would have pity on my youth, and that He would grant me space to repent of

my error. He might still, they urged, inflict torture upon me should I ever again read the works of the heathen. Under the stress of that awful moment I should have been ready to make even still larger promises than these.

Accordingly I made an oath and called upon His name, saying: 'Lord, if ever again I possess worldly books, or if ever again I read such, I have denied Thee.' Dismissed, then, on taking this oath, I returned to the upper world, and, lo, to the surprise of all, I opened upon them eyes so drenched with tears that my distress served to convince even the incredulous.

Jerome concluded his testimony with understandable conviction.

And that this was no sleep or idle dream, such as those by which we are oftened mocked, I call to witness the tribunal before which I lay, and the terrible judgment which I feared. May it never, hereafter, be my lot to fall under such an inquisition! I profess that my shoulders were black and blue, that I felt the bruises long after I awoke from my sleep, and that thenceforth I read the books of God with a zeal greater than I had previously given to the books of men.[14]

Augustine of Hippo (A.D. 354-430)

Augustine stands out in history as one of the preeminent theologians of the Christian faith. He has been called "the greatest genius among the Latin fathers,"[15] and his writings have widespread acclaim throughout Christendom. While we thank God for such a man, we must be quick to add a special blessing for the man's mother. Had it not been for her faith in the Lord's word, a faith that was most wonderfully enkindled through a dream, history might have seen an altogether different man than the Augustine who followed Jesus. For before the dream came to his mother concerning his conversion, Augustine was in all manners a most calcified sinner.

The Dream of Augustine's Mother

In The Confessions, Augustine writes of the memorable dream

given to his mother. "For whence was that dream with which Thou consoledst her, so that she permitted me to live with her, and to have my meals at the same table in the house, which she had begun to avoid, hating and detesting the blasphemies of my error?"

In the dream she saw herself standing upon a ruler, which signified the rule of faith. An angel approached her and asked a reason for her sorrow, and she answered that it was the perdition of her son that she was lamenting. The angel then assured her in the dream, saying that where she was, there also would her son be (i.e., upon the rule of faith). The encouragement and hope which the dream gave her was unshakable.

Augustine wrote, "When she had narrated this vision to me, and I tried to put this construction on it, 'That she rather should not despair of being some day what I was,' she immediately replied, 'No; for it was not told me that where he is, there thou should be, but where thou art, there he shall be.'"

Upon hearing her reply Augustine later admitted to God, "I confess to Thee, O Lord, that, to the best of my remembrance (and I have oft spoken of this), Thy answer through my watchful mother — that she was not disquieted by the spaciousness of my false interpretation, and saw in a moment what was to be seen, and which I myself had not in truth perceived before she spake — even then moved me more than the dream itself."

Augustine blessed God for the dream, its interpretation and its fruit in his conversion to Christ. "Thou sendest Thine hand from above, and drewest my soul out of that profound darkness, when my mother, Thy faithful one, wept to Thee on by behalf more than mothers are wont to weep the bodily deaths of their children. For she saw that I was dead by that faith and spirit which she had from Thee, and Thou heardest her, O Lord."[16]

It would indeed seem that, for Augustine, knowing Jesus was a dream come true!

Mere Creations of Fancy?

Evodius, the Bishop of Uzala and a close friend of Augustine, was so disturbed by dreams and visions that he asked, "What are we after death?" Augustine replied with testimony of the personal visitations he himself experienced in sleep from those who had died and gone on to be with the Lord. His purpose was to convince Evodius that there must be life after death — otherwise, how could his friends have appeared unto him?

> I do not at this moment concern myself about the mere creations of fancy, which are formed by the emotions of the uneducated. No, I speak of visitations in sleep, such as the apparition to Joseph in a dream. In the same manner, our own friends also who have departed this life before us sometimes come and appear to us in dreams, and speak to us.
>
> I myself remember that Profuturus, and Privatus, and Servilius, holy men who within my recollection were removed by death from our monastery, spoke to me, and that all the events of which they spoke came to pass according to their words. Or if it be some higher spirit that assumes their form and visits our minds, I leave this to the all-seeing eye of Him before whom everything from the highest to the lowest is uncovered.[17]

To conclude the case Augustine told one more fascinating story, known as the Night Visitation of Gennadius.

> I will narrate briefly one fact which I commend to your meditation. You know our brother Gennadius, a physician, known to almost everyone, and very dear to us, who now lives at Carthage, and was in other years eminent as a medical practitioner at Rome. You know him as a man of religious character and of very great benevolence, actively compassionate and promptly liberal in his care of the poor.
>
> Nevertheless, even he, when still a young man, and most zealous in these charitable acts, had sometimes, as he himself told me, doubts as to whether there was any life after death. Inasmuch, therefore, as God would in no wise forsake a man so merciful in his disposition and conduct, there appeared to him in sleep a youth of remarkable appearance and commanding presence, who said to him: "Follow me."

Following him, he came to a city where he began to hear on the right hand sounds of a melody so exquisitely sweet as to surpass anything he had ever heard. When he inquired what it was, his guide said: "It is the hymn of the blessed and the holy." He awoke; the dream vanished, and he thought of it as only a dream.

On a second night, however, the same youth appeared to Gennadius, and asked whether he recognized him, to which he replied that he knew him well, without the slightest uncertainty. Thereupon he asked Gennadius where he had become acquainted with him. There also his memory failed him not as to the proper reply: he narrated the whole vision, and the hymns of the saints which, under his guidance, he had been taken to hear, with all the readiness natural to recollection of some very recent experience.

On this the youth inquired whether it was in sleep or when awake that he had seen what he had just narrated.

Gennadius answered: "In sleep."

The youth then said: "You remember it well; it is true that you saw these things in sleep, but I would have you know that even now you are seeing in sleep."

Hearing this, Gennadius was persuaded of its truth, and in his reply declared that he believed it. Then his teacher went on to say: "Where is your body now?"

He answered: "In my bed."

"Do you know," said the youth, "that the eyes in this body of yours are now bound and closed, and at rest, and that with these eyes you are seeing another?"

He answered: "I know it."

"What, then," said the youth, "are the eyes with which you see me?"

He, unable to discover what to answer to this, was silent.

While he hesitated, the youth unfolded to him what he was endeavoring to teach him by these questions, and forthwith said: "As while you are asleep and lying on your bed these eyes of your body are now unemployed and doing nothing, and yet you have eyes with which you behold me, and enjoy this vision, so, after your death, while your bodily eyes shall be wholly inactive, there shall be in you a life by which you shall still live, and a faculty of perception by which you shall still perceive. Beware, therefore, after this of harboring doubts as to whether the life of man shall continue after death." This believer says that by this means all doubts as to this matter were removed from him."

Then Augustine asked, "By whom was he taught this but by the merciful, providential care of God?"[18]

Augustine concluded his reply with this thoughtful summary:

Someone may say that by this narrative I have not solved but complicated the question. Nevertheless, while it is free to everyone to believe or disbelieve these statements, every man has his own consciousness at hand as a teacher by whose help he may apply himself to this most profound question."[19]

Indeed.

Saint Patrick's True Confessions (A.D. 389-461)

The Confessions of Saint Patrick relates several testimonies of God's miraculous care in the life of a young boy who had been captured by Irish pirates and carried away from Britain to live as a slave in Ireland. His captivity lasted a full six years and ended when God spoke to Patrick in a dream.

One night I heard a voice say to me in a dream, 'You have been right to fast because you will soon return to your country; Look, your ship is ready.' Being a full two hundred miles from shore, Patrick wasn't sure what to make of the dream. But moved by it, he took to flight and, as he tells it, "I came in the power of God who was guiding my way for a good purpose and I had no fear all the time until I reached the ship.[20]

Through God's intervention, which Patrick dramatically

explains, he boarded the ship and that night heard yet another message from the Lord. "You will be with them [on board the ship] for two months." It happened as the Lord said, even to the exact day.[21]

Patrick returned home to much rejoicing. His parents, who had grieved much over his loss, entreated him to swear that he would never leave them again. Patrick wrote,

> It was there that I saw in a vision of the night a man coming apparently from Ireland whose name was Victoricus, with an uncountable number of letters, and he gave me one of them and I read the heading of the letter which ran, "The Cry of the Irish."
>
> While I was reading aloud the heading of the letter I was imagining that at that very moment I heard the voice of those who were by the Wood of Volcut which is near the Western sea, and this is what they cried, as with one voice, "Holy boy, we are asking you to come and walk among us again." I was struck deeply to the heart and I was not able to read any further and at that I woke up. God be thanked that after several years the Lord granted them according to their cry.[22]

Patrick returned to Ireland and worked zealously for the rest of his life. His labors were so successful that he became known as one who "found Ireland all heathen and left it all Christian." It is estimated that Saint Patrick founded over 300 churches, and baptized more than 120,000 persons.[23]

There are several other accounts given by Patrick of the Lord visiting him in dreams and visions. He stands out as one of the more fluent dreamers in church history. At your convenience you should read Patrick's *True Confessions* about:

- The miraculous provision of food in answer to prayer[24]
- The stone thrown upon him by Satan[25]
- The exquisite voice of Jesus[26]
- The intercessory groaning of the Holy Spirit within him[27]
- The displeasure of God with those who slander His servants[28]

Patrick closes his *Confessions* with an unapologetic declaration:

Let anyone laugh and revile me who wants to. I will not keep silence nor will I conceal the signs and wonders which have been shown me by the Lord many years before they took place, for He it is who knows everything even before times eternal.[29]

Thomas Aquinas (A.D. 1225-1274)

An Italian Dominican monk, theologian and philosopher, Thomas is the outstanding representative of scholasticism. History tells us that Aquinas "was a large, shambling, taciturn, somewhat absent-minded man."[30] When his classmates at Cologne teased him about being a "dumb ox," the teacher, Albert Magnus, remarked that one day the lowing of this ox would fill the world.[31] Aquinas is most known for his ambitious work *Summa Theologica,* in which he applied Aristotelian methods to Christian theology.

Aristotle held that nothing was real that could not be experienced by the five senses. Once Aquinas imported this world view into Christianity, it left little room for direct spiritual encounters with God. Therefore, dreams and visions were played down, along with other supernatural aspects of our faith (angels, miracles, speaking in tongues and prophecy). Through the influence of Aquinas, knowledge about the things of God slowly began to take the place of actually knowing God Himself. This philosophical approach to the Bible pervades the Western church to this very day.

Aquinas was indeed a brilliant man. He was often ridiculed for his obesity, but he was never criticized for his mind. He would dictate three books at one time to separate scribes, never losing his train of thought on each book. It is understandable how a man of this mental stature could come to venerate intelligence and to inevitably spawn a pedigree of like-minded adherents. Understandable, but not excusable. We who contend for the faith are to embrace *all* aspects of it, the lovely as well as the ludicrous, and not just that which suits our own fancies.

As for Aquinas, his final words should carry a greater weight than himself. His life ended before completion of his *Summa Theologia.* It was not that he could not finish it, rather that he would not finish it. Though he had long taught against such things that could not be rationally comprehended, Aquinas in fact had a profound experience with God in a dream, after which he ceased to write and dictate.

When he was urged by his colleagues to resume, Aquinas answered, "I can do no more. Such things have been revealed to me that all I have written seems as straw. And now I await the end of my life."[32] Aquinas died three months later.

John Bunyan (A.D. 1628-1688)

As I walked through the wilderness of this world, I lighted on a certain place where was a den, and laid me down in that place to sleep; and as I slept, I dreamed a dream. I dreamed, and behold, I saw a man clothed with rags standing in a certain place, with his face from his own house, a book in his hand, and a great burden upon his back."[33]

The story that this dream inspired has become one of literature's all-time classics. It is none other than *Pilgrim's Progress,* which, until more recent years, was required reading in American classrooms. Bunyan wrote the book while in the contemplative quiet of the small prison on Bedford Bridge, away from the excitement of frequent preaching. It is the story of his own spiritual pilgrimage, illustrated by a fascinating dream.[34]

The book is a remarkable allegory of the Christian walk, from conversion unto heaven. To give a detailed account of a story so universally accessible, whose main features are so well known, is superfluous. Suffice it to say, therefore, that I heartily recommend it to you, for it serves as an excellent example of how God speaks to His beloved people through dreams and visions.

John Newton's Amazing Grace (A.D. 1725-1807)

Virtually every nation in the world has a national anthem, a song that rallies the people by recounting in lyric those noble themes that unite them. The Church, it would likewise seem, has an anthem. What Christian around the world has not stood at attention, stirred deeply in heart and soul, while joining in with other believers to sing *Amazing Grace?*

John Newton wrote it in reflection of God's mercy over his life. Little did he know his song would so captivate the hearts of millions throughout the ages. Little do we know today that the song had its origin in a dream! Newton writes in his autobiography of a "most remarkable warning" that came to him in a dream.

> The scene was the harbor of Venice. It was night, and my watch upon the dock. As I was walking to and fro by myself, someone brought me a ring, with an express charge to keep it carefully, assuring me that while I preserved that ring I should be happy and successful. But, if I lost or parted with it, I must expect nothing but trouble and misery. I accepted the present and the terms willingly, not in the least doubting my own care to preserve it, and highly satisfied to have my happiness in my own keeping.
>
> Then a second person came to me and, observing the ring on my finger, took occasion to ask some questions concerning it. I readily told him its virtues. He expressed surprise at my weakness in expecting such effects from a ring. He reasoned with me some time, and at length urged me to throw the ring away. At first I was shocked at the proposal, but his insinuations prevailed. I began to reason and doubt, and at last plucked it off my finger and dropped it over the ship's side into the water. At that same instant a terrible fire burst out from a range of the mountains, a part of the Alps which appeared at some distance behind the city of Venice. I saw the hills as distinctly as if awake, and they were all in flames.
>
> I perceived, too late, my folly. My tempter, with an air of insult, informed me that all the mercy of God in reserve for me was comprised in that ring, which I had willfully thrown away. I understood that I must now go with him to the burning mountains, and that all the flames I saw were kindled on my account. I trembled, and was in a great agony, but my dream continued.
>
> As I stood self-condemned, without plea or hope,

suddenly a third person, or the same who brought the ring at first (I am not certain which), came to me and demanded the cause of my grief. I told him plainly, confessing that I had ruined myself willfully and deserved no pity. He blamed me for my rashness, and asked if I should be wiser supposing I had my ring again. I could hardly answer for I thought it was gone beyond recall. Indeed, I had not time to answer before I saw this unexpected friend go down under the water, just in the spot where I had dropped the ring. He soon returned, bringing it up with him.

The moment he came on board, the flames in the mountains were extinguished, and my seducer left me. Then was the prey taken from the hand of the mighty, and the lawful captive delivered. My fears were at an end, and with joy and gratitude I approached my kind deliverer to receive my ring again. But he refused to return it, and spoke to me: "If you should be entrusted with this ring again, you would very soon bring yourself into the same distress. You are not able to keep it, but I will preserve it for you. Whenever it is needful, I will produce it on your behalf."

I awoke in a state of mind not easy to be described. I could hardly eat or sleep, or transact my necessary business for two or three days. But the impression soon wore off, and I totally forgot it. It hardly occurred to my mind again till several years afterward.

A time came when I found myself in circumstances very nearly resembling those suggested by this extraordinary dream, when I stood helpless and hopeless upon the brink of an awful eternity. Had the eyes of my mind been then opened, I should have seen my grand enemy who had seduced me willfully to renounce and cast away my religious professions, and to involve myself in complicated crimes. I should have probably seen him pleased with my agonies, and waiting for permission to seize and bear away my soul to his place of torment.

I should, perhaps, have seen likewise, that Jesus, whom I had persecuted and defiled, rebuking the adversary, challenging me for His own, and as a brand plucked out of the fire, and saying, "Deliver him from going down to the pit: I have found a ransom." However, though I saw not these things, I found the benefit; I obtained mercy. The Lord answered me in the day of my distress; and blessed be His name, He who restored the ring (or what was signified by it) vouchsafes to keep it. Oh, what an unspeakable comfort is this, that I am not in my own keeping! The Lord is my Shepherd.[35]

How right was the Psalmist to declare, "When the Lord brought back the captives to Zion, we were like men who dreamed. Our mouths were filled with laughter, our tongues with songs of joy" (Ps. 126:1-2, NIV). Next time you sing *Amazing Grace* you will have an even deeper appreciation for how the words came to burn within the heart of their author.

General William Booth (A.D. 1829-1912)

One of the most gripping visions I've come across in my research on the subject was told by General William Booth, founder of The Salvation Army. In the vision Booth saw millions of people tossed about in a dark and stormy ocean. There were intermittent flashes of lightening followed by loud peals of thunder. In the midst of the ocean a mighty rock rose up above the storm clouds. All around the base of this rock was a wooden platform upon which few exhausted souls had found safety.

Booth watched as others struggled to climb upon the platform. He was most intrigued by the fact that some already safe upon the platform would actually throw themselves back into the sea, trying to help those who were still adrift. Booth writes,

> I hardly know which gladdened me the most — the sight of the poor drowning people climbing onto the rocks, reaching the place of safety, or the devotion and self-sacrifice of those whose whole beings were wrapped up in the effort for their deliverance.[36]

As the vision continued, Booth observed a mixed company upon the platform. There were, of course, the few valiant souls engaged in the rescue of those still perishing in the sea. Then there was a greater multitude who occupied themselves with pleasure and employment in many things.

Booth admitted to being puzzled at how those who had been saved from danger could so soon forget it and go on with life as though they had never known the peril of the sea. He marveled that they could block out the sea all around them and go about their business as though no one was perishing. He tells also of the gatherings upon the Rock where the rescued would call out to the wonderful being who made the rock appear. "Come to us!" they would cry. "Help us!"

In General Booth's words,

> Some wanted Him to come and stay with them, and spend His time and strength in making them happier. Others wanted Him to come and take away various doubts and misgivings they had concerning the truth of some of the letters He had written them.
>
> Some wanted Him to come and make them feel more secure on the rock — so secure that they would be quite sure that they would never slip off again into the ocean. Numbers of others wanted Him to make them feel quite certain that they would really get off the rock and onto the mainland someday. For these, and sundry other reasons, the people would call out to the wonderful being over and over, "Come to us! Come and help us!"
>
> All the while the wonderful being was down [by His Spirit] among the poor struggling, drowning creatures in the angry deep, with His arms around them trying to drag them out, and looking up — oh! so longingly, but all in vain — to those on the rock, crying to them with his voice all hoarse from calling, "Come to *ME!* Come, and help *ME!*"

Booth concluded,

> And then I understood the vision.

This proved to be the driving force behind The Salvation Army's zeal to "rescue the perishing."[37]

Charles H. Spurgeon (A.D. 1834-1892)

On April 16, 1868, Charles Spurgeon ascended the steps to his pulpit with a word from the Lord burning within his heart. He had made this same climb to the celebrated pulpit of Metropolitan Tabernacle many times before. But this time was different. This time he not only had the Bible in his hand, he had a *dream* in his heart.

Spurgeon had prepared a sermon for his congregation because of a most stirring dream which had come to him in the night. He felt so certain of its truthfulness that he could not rest until he had shared it with the people. His scripture text, chosen to prepare the congregation for the sermon, was none other than Acts 2:17, "Your young men will see visions, your old men will dream dreams (NIV)."

Spurgeon uncharacteristically went to great length in his introduction so as to assure himself of a fair hearing. His opening statement set forth first the qualifier that not all dreams or visions are from God. He said, "Many visions have led to the most disastrous results," to which the people said, *Amen.*

Spurgeon continued:

> 'Many visions have been wretchedly delusive. Men have dreamed of finding the fairy pleasure in the dark forest of sin. Carnal joys have danced before their eyes as temptingly as the mirage in the desert, and they have pursued the phantom forms to their misery in this world, and to their eternal ruin in the next.' Again, the people said, *Amen.*
>
> 'Yet, for all this' Spurgeon declared, 'good and grand visions are not unknown — visions which came from the excellent glory; visions which, when young or old men have seen them, have filled them with wisdom, and grace, and holiness. Visions which have wrought with such effect upon their minds that they have been lifted up above the level of the sons of men, and made sons of God, co-workers with the Eternal.'

The congregation sat stunned by the lofty heights which Spurgeon had so quickly scaled!

As further preparation of his hearers seemed to be in order before he spent upon them the pearl of his dream, Spurgeon continued with his explanation of why God would speak to men in dreams and visions at all.

> 'All divine things,' he said, 'when they first come to men from the Lord, are as visions because man is so little prepared to believe God's thoughts and ways. We are so gross and carnal, even when most clarified and made fit to receive divine impressions, that God's spiritual messages and directions to us must unusually at the first float dimly before the sense, and only in after thoughts become solid and clear.'

To emphasize the importance of giving such things as dreams and visions their proper due, Spurgeon then stated, "We must take care that we do not neglect heavenly monitions through fear of being considered visionary; we must not be staggered even by the dread of being styled fanatical, or out of our minds. For to stifle a thought from God is no small sin."

To sum up his introduction, Spurgeon spoke highly of George Fox as "that most eminent of dreamers, who dreamed more, and more vividly, than any other man." The work for spiritual revival, the charitable ministries of benevolence, the establishing of peace within communities, the campaign for the abolition of slavery — "Where would these things be," Spurgeon asked his listeners, "if the wild Quaker had been content to let his impressions come and go and be forgotten?" Then, in further defense of Fox, Spurgeon said, "These things, which nowadays are ordinary Christian doctrines, were considered in his day to be but the prattle of fanatics."

Finally, Spurgeon gave a word of encouragement for all who dream, and his words reach into our hearts today.

> 'O young men, if you have received a thought which dashes ahead of your times, hold to it and work at it till it comes to something. If you have dreamed a dream from the Lord, turn it over and over again till you are quite sure it is not steam from a heated brain, or smoke from hell. When it is clear to your own heart that it is fire from off God's altar — then work, and pray, and wait your time!'

Feeling satisfied that he had opened a wide berth in the hearts of his beloved congregation for the potentially controversial topic of his sermon, Spurgeon then declared, "I will now confess that, after my own fashion, I, too, have seen a vision; and though you should say of me in days to some, 'Behold, this dreamer cometh,' yet, as he that hath a dream is bidden to tell his dream, so tell I mine."[38]

And what was Spurgeon's dream? He saw a great revival among the young of England, stirring them with a burning missionary zeal for the lost of that nation, as well as for the nations of the world. It appeared to him as "the great chariot of Christ" rolling onwards from one end of England to the other in rapid victories. Spurgeon dedicated himself and his preaching to the fulfillment of this dream.

He prayed thus:

> O God, send us the Holy Ghost! Give us both the breath of spiritual life and the fire of unconquerable zeal. O Thou art our God, answer us by fire, we pray Thee! Answer us both by wind and fire, and then we shall see Thee to be God indeed. The kingdom comes not, and the work is flagging. Oh, that Thou wouldst send the wind and the fire! Thou wilt do this when we are all of one accord, all believing, all expecting, all prepared by prayer.
>
> Lord, bring us to this waiting state! God, send us a season of glorious disorder. Oh, for a sweep of the wind that will set the seas in motion and make our ironclad brethren, now lying so quietly at anchor, to roll stem to stern!
>
> Oh for the fire to fall again — fire which shall affect the most stolid! Oh, that such fire might first sit upon disciples, and then fall on all around! O God, Thou art ready to work with us today even as Thou didst then. Stay not, we beseech Thee, but work at once. Break down every barrier that hinders the incoming of Thy might! Give us now both hearts of flame and tongues of fire to preach Thy reconciling word, for Jesus' sake! Amen.[39]

Conclusion

By now I feel like the writer of the book of Hebrews, "What more shall I say!" I have only touched upon a few of the many, *many* stories of dreams and visions that fill the pages of church history. In the words of Tertullian, "the whole world is full of oracles of this description!" Time and space dictate that I stop here. But, surely, this has been sufficient to my task. Surely, dear reader, you are persuaded by the power of these testimonies, along with the text of Scripture to accept that God most definitely speaks to His beloved sons and daughters through dreams and visions.

If not, then sleep well, my friend, and know that God loves you dearly. But, before you doze off, could I ask you to look at one more piece of evidence? I will now tell you of dreams and visions that are stirring in the lives of Christians *today!*

THE DREAM LIVES ON

It was Saturday, January 7, 1989. I awakened in the early morning hours with a disturbing dream vividly in my mind. In the dream I was standing in the hallway at our church as a woman whom I did not know came walking toward me. She was deeply troubled. She asked me if I knew a certain man who was attending our church at that time. When I acknowledged that I did, she said, "Well, he is having an affair with me and I want him to stop." I told her I would take care of it for her, and the dream ended.

As the day began I felt impressed to go to my office, something I ordinarily do not do on Saturday. While I was sitting at my desk wondering what I was doing there, I heard the door to the church open. I turned around and saw the very man I had dreamed about standing in the doorway of my office. I was so stunned that I could do nothing but tell him the dream and ask if it was true. He turned pale, hung his head and said, "I knew that God was going to tell you." I was speechless."1 (And as anyone who knows me will tell you — that is miraculous!)

I calmly collected my pastoral sense about me, sat the man down in my office, and helped him work through the issues that had brought him to the edge of ruin. He responded to the Lord's discipline in his life and continues walking in the fear of God. From time to time I'll see him around the church and I'll say, "Hey, I had a dream about you last night!" For some reason it makes him really nervous. Go figure.

That incident was amazing to me. Though the Lord had spoken to me in dreams many times before, none had ever been so specific and with such immediate fulfillment. That seemed to stir within me a deeper sense of expectancy for God to speak in dreams and visions. From that time until now there has indeed been an increase in the frequency, scope, accuracy and fulfillment of dreams and visions in my life. There also are prolonged seasons where there have been no dreams or visions whatsoever. (For some reason the Lord seems very interested in balance).

I am a dreamer. I certainly do not posture myself as an expert on the subject, nor do I declare myself to be a prophet. I merely affirm that the Lord has been pleased from time to time to speak to me through dreams and visions. It is a fact that I will not deny. Certainly not every dream I've had has proven itself to be a word from God, but a few most definitely have. Frankly, I am as amazed as anyone else when this happens.

Out of the overflow of this wonderful friendship with God, I discreetly offer some of the things that make up this chapter. The poet Yeats wrote, "But I, being poor, have only my dreams; I have spread my dreams under your feet. Tread softly, because you tread on my dreams."2 And if, in the final analysis, these dreams and visions I tell are nothing more than the results of a highly active imagination, or the clever contrivances of gifted wit — then at least agree with me in giving glory to God for any good that may come of them.

On the other hand, whatever they may do that proves harmful or irresponsible — I shall bear that alone in humble repentance. Nevertheless, I cannot but speak the things that I have seen and heard.

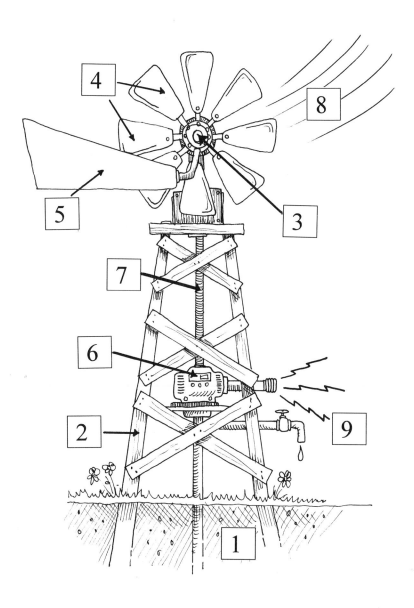

The Windmill

My associate pastor had no idea what was occurring as we knelt together in prayer one morning at the church. Nor was I at all expecting that God would visit our prayer time with anything out of the ordinary. Frankly, our prayers were rather perfunctory that morning. After all, praying is what pastors are supposed to do, along with studying the Scriptures, caring for the flock and printing up the Sunday bulletin. So we were doing our duty. Suddenly, however, the Lord visited us and turned duty into delight.

While my eyes were closed tight in prayer, I saw clearly before me a windmill in the midst of a field. The details of the vision were unmistakable and unforgettable. As I pondered what I had seen, the Holy Spirit said to me, "This is a parable showing the nine elements that are essential for the church to fulfill its purpose in the world."

Then, in a matter of moments, the understanding of the vision unfolded before me as I studied the various working parts of the windmill. Indeed, each part corresponded to some vital aspect of church life. I was fascinated by the accuracy and the simplicity of the vision. I was also blessed that the Lord would give me something so useful to the ministry of building up the church.

I have shared this vision with pastors and church leaders across the nation, and in every place the Lord has blessed His ministers with renewed confidence and joy in fulfilling their call. Here is what I saw.

Follow along with me as I briefly explain the nine different working parts of the windmill. I am confident that you will see it clearly, and that the Lord will use it to help you know what to specifically focus on in your church.

1. Love

The Windmill (i.e., church) is built upon a foundation that is rooted and grounded in love.[3] This is vital. If the foundation is insecure, then the entire structure will collapse when the wind blows upon it. This is why the Holy Spirit does not move powerfully in some churches. The lack of love would cause the church to collapse under the weight of God's presence.

Ask yourself a simple question, and try to give an honest answer. "What would happen this coming Sunday in my church if the Lord actually came to the service in His power and glory?" Would people cry? Would they shout for joy? Would they laugh, leap, dance and run? Would they fall on their faces and beg for mercy? Would they embrace one another in forgiveness and reconciliation? Yes, all of the above, and then some.

Now let me ask you a rather pointed question. If these things are not happening, does that mean the presence of the Lord is not there? Not necessarily; He may be present to accomplish something completely different. In quietness and rest shall be your strength. Be still and know that I am God.

You see the difficulty, don't you? For some of us the presence of the Lord brings peace, and stillness, a holy quiet suitable for reflective meditation that lifts us above the clamor of a carnal world. Yet, for others, His presence is atomic — yea, nuclear! There is an explosive chain reaction of power that blasts us to kingdom come! Now, who is right and who is wrong?

That is not the question we are to concern ourselves over. The question before us always is, "Do you love the Lord with all your heart, and your neighbor as yourself?" for according to Jesus, this is the sum of the Law and the prophets.[4] Love is patient and kind; it does not exalt itself, nor does it push its own preferences. It differs to another, and seeks to honor what is of value to the other. Love is a servant seeking to bless another, not a warrior seeking to conquer.

Denominations are at war with each other because they are not walking in love. Even within individual churches there are vicious spats that wound tender-hearted people indefinitely. Yet all the while we each call upon the Lord to come in power and move us onward to glory. He will, once we start loving one another. Love is the foundation. The church goes no higher than it first goes deeper into the rich soil of God's love — rooted and grounded in love. We must take root downward in order to bear fruit upward.[5] And as Paul said, "If the root is holy, so are the branches."[6]

2. Relationships

Like the windmill standing in the prairie, the church is to be "fitly framed together."[7] Each piece must be securely fixed in the place where it fits in order for the windmill to stand together under the strain of its service in the field. Likewise in the church, each member must be secure in their relationship with one another so that the church can stand together in the strain of the ministry. The church struggles when its members are "out of joint."

It is commonly held that people come to a church for many reasons, but they stay at a church for only one reason — *relationships*. They may come because the preacher is good, or the worship is excellent, or the children's ministry is exciting and godly, or because the prayer services are rich or the missions programs are strong — all good and noble and necessary. But if there is nothing within the church that builds strong relationships between its members, the people will not stay.

Relationships get us through whatever is to come. When we know and love one another, we are strengthened to stand tall with one another and do the greater works. We are also able to more readily recognize the unique talents and gifts that God has distributed among His people, and to encourage one another to employ their abilities for God's glory. We can actually help one another find out where we fit in the body of Christ.

Jesus is the head of the church. "Under His direction the whole body is fitted together perfectly, and each part in its own special way helps the other parts, so that the whole body is healthy and growing and full of love."[8]

3. Vision

"Where there is no vision, the people perish" (Prov. 29:18). The word *perish* means "to cast off restraints; to fly off in all directions." Imagine what would happen to the blades of the windmill if they were not fastened to the center hub that holds them together. Now think what would happen to a church if the believers had no vision to which they could be committed. Would they not "fly off in all directions?"

Vision is such a crucial part of the church. There are so many things that cannot happen until there is vision. For example, and perhaps most importantly, there can be no provision if there is not first a vision. The word *pro*vision means "toward the vision." Many pastors struggle each Sunday when the offering is dismal. Might I suggest that the vision may be dismal as well? If the pastor has a vision, and the people can see it clearly enough to become committed — there will be *pro*vision!

A church must be united in its vision in order to fulfill the purpose of God in its community. In the proverbs and songs of Solomon he tells us that our *eyes* (vision) and our *words* (testimony) are to be so well-fitted to our situation, that we stand out like apples of gold in settings of silver.[9] Just as we are to be fitly framed together in fellowship, so also are we to stand united in our vision and our testimony, so that "with one heart and mouth you may glorify the God and Father of our Lord Jesus Christ."[10]

4. Believers

The blades of the windmill are a truly remarkable example of the kind of members a church must have in order to be effective. First, they are bolted to the hub, totally committed to the vision.[11] Second, they are yielded to the wind, each facing the same direction so as to receive the full benefit of the wind's power moving upon them.[12]

What pastor doesn't long for such a congregation? There are so many people who pass through the doors of our churches and never commit themselves to the church — even when the vision is clear and noble. Then there are some who say they are committed, but it turns out that their own agenda supersedes the mission of the church. They are in fact committed only unto themselves.

And then there are those who are indeed bolted, in a manner of speaking, and nothing is going to move them. "We were here before you came, and we will be here long after you are gone!" If a blade is facing the wrong direction when the wind blows, the entire mechanism suffers undue stress. The windmill becomes dysfunctional and is likely to shake itself apart.

Believers who are committed to the vision and yielded to the Holy Spirit are vital to the Church's mission.

5. Leadership

A predominant feature of the windmill is the rudder. It seems almost to stand apart from the rest of the structure. Leadership is like that. But notice this — the purpose of the rudder is to discern which way the wind is blowing, and to turn the entire upper assembly into the most suitable position for receiving the full benefit of the wind. The rudder accomplishes this by literally placing itself in servanthood to the blades! "He that would be the greatest among you, let him become your servant," Jesus said to His disciples.[13]

Of course, another way to look at it is that the rudder illustrates how leaders have to "stick their necks out" in order to turn the blades in the proper position. May I make an appeal on behalf of my brothers in the pastorate? Let me give but two scriptures for you to consider.

"Let the elders who rule well be counted worthy of double honor, especially those who labor in the word and doctrine;"[14] and "Obey your leaders and submit to their authority. They keep watch over you as men who must give an account. Obey them so that their work will be a joy, not a burden, for that would be of no advantage to you."[15]

For my colleagues who often labor unrewarded, I offer the following thought: "God is not unjust; he will not forget your work and the love you have shown him as you have helped his people and continue to help them."[16] Stay with it, brother; the wind's a-comin'!

Leadership is vital to the mission of the church. Can you imagine what would happen to the windmill if there was no rudder? Why, the silly thing would spin around in circles and finally break itself apart. The same thing happens when people try to do anything without someone who has the gift and calling of leadership. The leader must rise up and provide direction, and the people must follow.

6. Motivation

When you look at a windmill cranking away out on the prairie, there is one question that always arises: "What's it *doing?*" Obviously, it's not there simply to entertain the cows. There has to be some purpose for it being there. Located at the heart of the rigging one will find the answer. A generator produces power, and a pump draws up water. Light and life — that's the motivation of the windmill's machinery.

What a coincidence that the church stands alone on the prairies of the world doing the same thing! We exist to bring the light of Jesus to those who are in the darkness, and the life of Jesus to those who are dead in trespasses and sins.

Jesus said, "Let your light so shine before men that they may see your good works, and glorify your Father which is in heaven."[17] Paul taught us that God, who was in Christ reconciling the world unto Himself, has now committed unto us the ministry of reconciliation.[18] We therefore stand as a beacon of hope to those who are hopeless and a tower of life to those who are lifeless.

This must be at the heart of all we do. It is the motivation that gives the church its mission — all, of course, for the glory of God. In keeping with this, dear reader, may I extend to you even now the appeal which is at the very heart of this book? May I be so bold as to say that I am working together with God in urging you to be reconciled unto God through faith in Jesus Christ?

Surely by now the Holy Spirit has captured your heart with the reality of God's love and faithfulness. Surely the stories that have come down through the ages of how God has revealed Himself to men and women just like you have by now stirred something within your own heart — a longing for Him to also reveal Himself to you?

Know this to be the truth — God longs for you far more! If you will turn from trusting in yourself and yield the control of your life to Jesus Christ as your Lord, the Holy Spirit will flood your soul with the cleansing power provided for you by Jesus' blood. Your sins will be forgiven, and you will be born again into the family of God. The nightmare will be over, and Jesus will be your dream come true!

Pray this: "Dear God, I am a sinner, and that is the heart of all my troubles. I try to do right but fail. Even my best efforts at being good fall short. No matter how much I want to be better, I cannot change my own heart; only You can. Forgive me for all my sins, and cleanse me from every wrong. Change my heart, O God, and make me the person You want me to be. I confess that Jesus Christ is Lord, and I accept Him alone as my Savior. Fill me, Holy Spirit, and give me the power to live for the honor of God and the good of my fellow man. Amen."

If you prayed that with all your heart, now ask God to show you a church you can commit yourself unto. Go and tell the pastor, "I'm a blade! Bolt me in, turn me right, and let's get this thing spinnin' for Jesus!"

7. Wisdom

The power drive that connects the movement of the upper assembly to the generator is of utmost importance. It is the means whereby all the activity is harnessed and applied most effectively. Without the power drive, the windmill would make a lot of racket but never get anything done.

In the same way, the church must have godly wisdom supplied by men and women of proven character. This is the power drive of any dynamic congregation. Call them elders and deacons, the presbytery, board of directors, advisory council or whatever — just *call* them! They work together with the leaders to see that the church is actually doing something about its vision.

The Bible not only says that people perish where there is no vision, but also "where there is no counsel, the people fall"[19] Many a church has come to ruin through lack of godly wisdom. They had great potential, but were never able to harness it to a practical purpose. Perhaps they exalted the charismatic above the pragmatic, and failed to realize that the two must operate together in balance.

On the other hand, in some locations, there are those who have gone to the other extreme. It would appear that they have actually built the windmill to serve the power drive (so to speak), and have no blades spinning in the wind at all. This is equally wrong.

A church, to be effective in fulfilling its mission from God, must have solid Bible preaching and practical guidance, along with believers who move in the power of the Spirit.

8. The Wind

It goes without saying that all is vain if the wind doesn't blow. Imagine how silly it would be if a farmer built a windmill inside his barn. Somebody ought to tell him that it 'aint gonna work! "Why not?" he may ask.

"Well, Dufus, the wind doesn't blow inside the barn!"

Let me ask you a probing question, dear pastor. Is your windmill built inside a barn? Are you bound within a structure that blocks the movement of the Holy Spirit upon your people? Aren't you tired of standing on the hay loft blowing on the blades with your sermons, trying to get them to finally start turning around?

My advice to you is to blow the doors off instead! Let the Holy Spirit in, and He will get the believers turning so fast you won't be able to keep up with them. "And suddenly there came a sound from heaven as of a rushing mighty wind, and it filled all the house where they were sitting."[20] They didn't *sit* any longer!

The power of God launched the church out of the temple into the streets, resulting in a massive ingathering of souls. This happened not once, nor even twice, but many times. It is God's will that it happen today — in *your* church. Jesus said to Nicodemus, "Just as you can hear the wind but can't tell where it comes from or where it will go next, so it is with the Spirit. We do not know on whom he will next bestow this life from heaven."[21]

Come, wind of God, and blow!

9. Results

The windmill, in the final analysis, must accomplish something of worth, or else it becomes a pointless curiosity occupying needed real estate. If it serves no appreciable purpose other than standing as a relic of the past, a museum piece for future generations to muse over, then it will be taken down and set aside to that end.

Children will walk by it and hear their teachers say, "This was helpful in the early days of our nation, children, for it provided the settlers with power and water. But, we today no longer need these old relics. We have come up with something much better."

I wonder as I write these words, how many guided tours go by *your* windmill? Do the people of your community see your church as an old relic, a tribute to an archaic way of life? Or, do they feel the love of God each time they draw near? Do they hear the hum of blades turning in unison, and see the light of the glory of God shining from your labors?[22] Do they thirst for the living water, and can they get a drink when they come in?[23]

Overview

Each of these nine elements is vital, and the church cannot operate if any one of them is missing. Take away love, and the entire structure collapses. Take away relationships, and the believers never rise to the occasion of God's visitation. Take away vision, and everybody flies off in several directions.

Take away committed, yielded believers, and there is never any movement within the church. Take away leadership, and the believers spin around in circles. Take away motivation, and there is no service to the surrounding community. Take away wisdom, and there is no practical outworking of the charismatic activity.

Take away the wind, and nothing happens at all. The entire thing just sits there rusting. Take away results, and no one will ever utilize the ministry of the church in any area of their lives.

Some Assembly Necessary

After presenting this teaching to a group of pastors, I opened the meeting for questions and answers. Things were going along fine until one man said, "What about prayer? You didn't list it anywhere on the windmill. Don't you think prayer is vital to the church?" Little did he realize just how vital I thought it was, for I began praying earnestly right then!

Just when I thought a great teaching was about to be reduced to a nice try, the Holy Spirit spoke to me. "This was revealed to you while you were in prayer," He said. "And *that* is the only way it can be assembled!"

Here is what to do. Go before the Lord in prayer, and ask Him which piece is missing from your church. Once you discern the area of need, take the matter before your congregation and "pray it through." Lead your church in prayer over each area until the windmill is up and running. Then, let there be light as you bring God's life to a dark and dying world!

The Master Illustrator

Jesus is the master illustrator. He can take *anything* and turn it into a lesson about the kingdom of heaven. I'll never be able to look at windmills the same, since the Lord gave me this illustration. Every time I see one, I think of Jesus and the church. I bet you will also, having read this descriptive account of my vision. That's the power of a parable from the Lord.

During the days of His life on earth, Jesus taught the people with parables. Often His disciples would ask Him afterward, "What in the world are you talking about?" The Lord would then explain the parable unto them. Mark tells us, "He did not say anything to them without using a parable. But when he was alone with his own disciples, he explained everything."[24]

Did you know that Jesus is still at it today? Now, instead of walking the shores of Galilee telling parables, He communes with us in our hearts through dreams and visions, giving us contemporary parables that illustrate some truth of God's Holy Word, endearing it even more to our hearts and lives. And if, like His disciples, we will get alone with Him — He will explain everything!

Preachers are always looking for great stories to illustrate their sermons. And it's a good thing for the congregation when they find one! Far too often the preaching of the Word is rather dry and distant. The right illustration can make all the difference in how effectively the message impacts the lives of our listeners.

How merciful and gracious that the Lord, from time to time, would grant such illustrations unto His servants through dreams and visions.

The Old Gray Mule Ain't What She Used to Be

Pastor Wally was a good man. He loved his church and labored tirelessly to build them up in the faith, and to care for their needs in times of distress. He would rise early in the morning for personal devotions, and then arrive at the church to spend his morning in endless counseling appointments. He would grab a burger at the drive-thru on his way to the afternoon visitations — first to the hospitals, and then to the shut-ins who needed his pastoral attention.

His nights were often spent at board meetings, special services or emergency calls (which seldom were real emergencies). Often, he would not get to bed until midnight. Most of the time, he kept himself going by saying, "It's all for the glory of God." But late at night when the lights were out, and silence set in, Pastor Wally discovered a haunting sense of personal despair. He was losing his love for the church. He was on the edge of burnout.

Exhausted one night after a marathon of ministry, Pastor Wally dreamed that he was hitched to a covered wagon like an old gray mule. He laboriously pulled the wagon along the rugged road. Finally, he reached a place in the road where the mud was so deep that his efforts to move the wagon even an inch were all but futile.

He thought it rather peculiar that there was no momentum, for the last time he had looked, the entire congregation was behind the wagon, pushing it along as he pulled it forward. Since he could go no further, he looked to see what was happening behind him. All the church members had quit pushing and were sitting in the wagon, criticizing the pastor for not being able to move it along any faster. The dream ended there, and Pastor Wally woke up.

Dreams often reveal the preoccupation of the dreamer with his or her work or profession, hobbies and goals, and the political, social and environmental milieu in which the dreamer lives. Thus, a pastor would understandably dream such a thing as pulling a wagon by himself while everybody onboard complained — it's a common dilemma faced by pastors everywhere.

It is likely that Pastor Wally's dream was brought on by the stress of his endless labors. However, this does not diminish the impact of the dream. On the contrary, because it *was* a dream, the message often can have even greater force than if the pastor simply made up a story to get his point across.

He himself has more conviction to stand before the congregation and tell them the truth because he feels that the Lord showed him the problem through a dream. And, if the dream indeed came from the Lord, then the congregation will feel the conviction of the Holy Spirit when the pastor uses the illustration which God supplied to him through the dream.

The pastor slept; God gave him a clue in a dream; and, it helped him solve his problem.

A New Job Description

Pastor Wally woke up from his dream and prayed for wisdom from the Lord. "How do I get the people out of the wagon?" he asked. The Lord directed him to the book of Ephesians, and Wally read familiar words that now seemed to come alive: "He gave pastors...for the equipping of the saints to do the work of the ministry."[25] That's when it hit him. "I'm not supposed to do all the work myself," Wally exclaimed. "I'm supposed to equip the people to do it with me!"

The dream had served its purpose. It brought Pastor Wally to the Word of God where he found the answer to his predicament. He shared the incident with his church (dream and all), and because God had spoken so clearly to him in the Word, there was joy instead of condemnation among the people. They became excited about being equipped to minister. In a manner of speaking, they got out of the wagon and starting doing their part. And now, the old gray mule, she ain't what she used to be! The church has become healthy, growing and is full of love.

The Cranky Old Priest

In a dream, I stood outside a great, imposing cathedral. Its

188

towering ramparts and massive arches were spectacular, but also very confusing. No one could tell where the door was! If it had not been for my sheer determination, I would have never found my way inside.

Once inside the cathedral, I found it even more perplexing. There were hallways that led nowhere, doors that opened into walls, stairs that went up into the ceiling and other architectural anomalies. Somehow I knew that the only way to get anywhere inside the cathedral was to take every opportunity for going upward. Never go down, always move upward.

I followed each step or ledge that would take me higher and higher. At length I came into a spacious, luxurious office suite. Sitting behind an intimidating, gold-plated desk was a cranky old priest. His face was as wrinkled as a prune. He looked up and saw me staring at him, and snapped, "What do you want?"

I took him by the hand with uncanny boldness and replied, "Follow me." He rose from his chair and walked with me as I began to take him down to the first floor. As we descended the steps, the old priest began to turn young again. The lower we went, the more youthful and radiant he became. He started whistling, and finally began singing aloud of his love for Jesus.

As we arrived on the first floor I heard a voice say, "The secret of happiness is servanthood. Your youth will be renewed like the eagle as you humble yourself and return to your first love, serving the Lord Jesus with gladness." The dream ended.

First Floor Christianity

The church that no one can find the way into, the confusing corridors that bewilder you once you are inside, climbing to the top as the only way to get anywhere, sitting in the lap of luxury filled with more misery than those who don't even know the Lord — this dream almost interprets itself. The Lord is calling His leaders at the top to get back to first floor Christianity. The secret of happiness is servanthood.

Less than a week after I had this dream, I was with a national leader of a major denomination. While we were together, I remembered the dream and felt impressed to share it with my friend. The man listened respectfully and responded, "That's me you're talking ᴀᴜᴏᴜᴛ. I have been just like that cranky old priest, and the Lord has been telling me to return to my first love." When I inquired specifically what that was, he replied, "Serving the Lord by serving others — that's what I loved most in the early days of my ministry."

Go for it, brother!

The Devil's Hat

One night I dreamed that a seductive woman was standing before me, seeking to lure me into her embrace. I was enchanted by her beauty, and tormented by the thought that I might actually surrender to her passions. Yet, somehow I was able withstand her, and I indignantly said, "No! I will not come to you!"

The moment I said those words, the woman literally vanished right before my eyes. There, standing in her place, was the devil himself. He appeared like the classic Hollywood characterization of a dapper, old gentleman with sparkling eyes. He looked at me with the most contemptuous glare, huffed in scornful disdain, spun about on his heels and began walking away.

I was glad to see him go. As he left, it appeared that he was descending a stairway in the floor, but there was none there. He simply vanished through the floor. However, his hat remained on the floor after he was gone. I thought, "Oh, no! He's got to come back for his hat." That's when I woke up.

The proverbs of Solomon teach about the dangers of falling into the embrace of a seductive woman. While this obviously applies in the literal sense, it also has a much broader application. The "woman" is the world that seeks to lure us away from faithfulness to God. Proverbs contrasts two women — the street walker and the virtuous lady. These two represent the world and the church.

In my dream the Lord was showing me how powerful the lure of the world is to servants of God. If I almost yielded when faced with her painted charms, then how much more so do those who have not the Spirit! I said "No!" and incurred the contempt of the devil.

Let's talk about the hat on the floor. As I pondered that image, the Holy Spirit said, "The devil's hat is on the floor because you said no. He wants to put it on your head, so that you will be under his way of thinking. Never say 'Yes' to the devil. Keep the devil's hat on the floor, under your feet."

A Rowdy Response

I shared a message with my congregation discussing the various ways that Satan tries to thwart the work of God in our lives and in our church. At the conclusion of the sermon, I told the above dream and asked, "Is there anybody here who would let the devil put his hat on your head?"

Of course everybody yelled, "No!" I decided to have a little fun with that, so I said, "Well, I just happen to have that hat with me today," as I pulled a hat out from under the pulpit. The people went along with me and said, "Boooo! Hissss! Get thee behind us!" (It was one of our more noble moments as a church!)

I said, "There is really only one thing to do with this hat, and that's to step on it." I tossed it on the floor at the front of our sanctuary, and said, "If you feel that the devil has been trying to put his hat on your head in any area of your life, the invitation today is for you. Rise up, come to the front and stomp on the devil's hat!"

In all my years of ministry I have never witnessed such an explosive response from the people. They leapt to their feet and literally ran down the aisle in the church. Hundreds pressed forward taking their turn on the devil's hat. By the time they were finished the hat was in fifteen tattered pieces, and the people were whole!

What Is Your Vision?

In a dream I saw the letter *Y* suspended before me. As I watched, it took on the likeness of an old-fashioned slingshot, the kind you might have played with when you were a kid. I then saw a man's hand firmly take hold of the *Y* at the bottom, making it now look like a *V* sitting atop a closed fist. He placed a solid rock in the leather pouch, and drew the bands back to his cheek, holding his arm straight in front of him as he prepared to fire the slingshot.

In the dream, I was looking over the man's shoulder from behind him. As he let the rock go, it soared across the room, straight as an arrow, and hit the target with such force that the whole room shook. Then a most peculiar thing happened.

Another man came and took the slingshot out of the hands of the first man. He looked it over, and scornfully said, "No, no, *no*! This is all wrong. It's entirely too big!" He then squeezed the *V* until only

191

a very small opening appeared. "There, that's much better," he said as he prepared to shoot it. However, he had closed it so tight that no rock would pass through the small opening.

He tried a few times, and became frustrated and embarrassed. Rather than put it back the way it was, the second man threw the slingshot down on the ground and stomped out of the room. Then a third man appeared. He was a shadowy figure. Picking the thing up he said, "Here is what it needs," and with that he closed it shut completely. Now, what first looked like the letter *Y* appeared instead as the letter *I*.

The dream ended, and I woke up.

Say Yes to Jesus

The Holy Spirit spoke to me, "The *Y* stands for yes. When a man says yes to Jesus, the Lord takes his life in His strong hands and gives vision to the man — that's what the *V* signified. Then, He puts the solid rock of His Word within his heart, draws the man to seek His face and then sends him forth on his life's mission.

"As you beheld in the dream, when a man is thus sent by Christ — he will stay true in flight. He will go the distance, and his life will have lasting impact.

"But the man who appeared and took the sling out of the Lord's hands, represents those who think their idea of living is better than God's. As you saw, the vision which the man had for himself was puny and ineffective. The man limited himself to something small and meaningless, and finally threw his life away as having no value.

"The shadowy man is the devil. He takes up the discarded life of the unrepentant and tightly closes it to the letter *I*. This shows that the smallest vision a man can have is when he is totally focused upon himself."

The Golden Cloud of God's Glory

I dreamed I was looking at North America from a perspective high in the sky, far enough removed that I could virtually see the entire continent. Just as you would see on a weather map, a high pressure system was moving toward the United States from the north Pacific. My eye was riveted upon the massive front as it slowly approached the nation, because the clouds were gold and glorious. I knew I was seeing a manifestation of the glory of God, and I was awestruck that it was about to move upon America.

Just as the cloud touched the northwestern edge of the nation, a word appeared written across the face of the country: *"Abortion."* The letters were made of ashes, as if they had been poured out of an urn onto the ground. I watched with dreadful anxiety as the cloud of God's approaching glory shuddered and stopped from advancing any further. I knew that the glory would come no further.

I cried out in great anguish of heart, "No! Don't turn away! Have mercy, O God! It is true we are a nation of abortionists! We have aborted not only our children, but also our faith, our love, our honor, our courage, our vision and our heritage. O Lord, please stop us — do not let us now also abort the offer of Your glory! Come and cleanse our land, forgive us and heal our nation!"

The dream continued. I watched from the heavenlies as the hand of a man came up from the ground in the heart of the nation, and reached across the country to lay hold of the glory cloud. Seizing it firmly, the hand then pulled the cloud into the center of America. At that instant, a golden hue permeated the country and a great awakening swept the entire continent. The dream ended and I woke up.

The images in this dream have gripped my heart to this day. If, to borrow the words of Spurgeon, this is simply the "steam of an overheated brain," then forgive me. But, what if it is a promise from heaven? What if the Lord is indeed offering to America a sweeping move of His Holy Spirit — to forgive us, cleanse us and heal us; and, to flood our land with His glory?

Could it be that *Promise Keepers* is the "hand of the man" that rose from the ground to seize the moment of God's visitation? It seems possible that it is. The movement certainly reflects a ground swell of men who are seeking to repent before God, be reconciled to one another and redeem their broken promises. This, joined together with the many ministries that have labored in prayer and faithfulness over the years, could result in God's glory sweeping across the nation and around the world!

Get Real, Man!

"These are the voyages of the Starship Enterprise." So begins a popular television show, which, of course, we know is make believe. Sometimes a dreamer can seem to people like someone from outer space. There have been times when, judging from the looks on people's faces, perhaps I should preface my testimony of dreams with a similar log entry — "These are the voyages of the dreamer James." This is not to suggest that what I am saying is contrived. Though the dreams and visions I tell are fantastic, they are not fantasies.

Yet, I am appreciative of the fact that some may read dream stories (such as I have told), and wonder first if they are really true, and then, if so, why something like this never happens to *them*. It is my belief that it happens more than you may realize.

Let's get practical.

Let's Get Practical

The enthusiastic student arrived early to class so as to be first in line when the moment would come. He had signed up months earlier merely as a favor to his sister, but during the training he himself had become infected with the bug. Oh, I didn't tell you — today was the day they would jump out of the plane! He was an aspiring parachutist.

In the first weeks of the class, they talked about parachutes, the FAA Regulation Handbook, altimeters, flaps, drop zones, cables, rip cords and *safety*. Always the talk would turn to safety. No matter what the class topic was on any particular day, they would wrap up with yet another pep talk about safety. The instructor would often say, "You never get a second chance to make a first impression — in the ground!"

After months of preparation, the day of the jump had finally come. Steve was thirty-four, but on this day he felt as if he was only ten. He had tossed and turned all night, like a kid going to the fair the next day. And now the moment had arrived. In a few minutes the plane would take them up, and the rest would be up to Steve.

When Do We Jump?

Imagine how Steve would feel if the instructor had only talked about jumping, but never actually did it. There are few people in life who would settle for merely talking about anything. We are creatures of action; we want to *do* it.

It occurs to me that the bulk of this book has been devoted to talking about dreams and visions, giving several stirring examples of how others (myself included) have had dreams that have significantly influenced their lives. We have examined both the biblical and historical perspectives on this topic, and have undoubtedly stimulated the hearts of many to new heights of holy imagination. Great. Now, when do we jump?

"I want to dream," someone may be saying. "How do I do it?" Well, frankly, I can tell you many things about dreams and visions, but I cannot tell you *how* to dream; nobody can. I can only provide some navigation to prepare you *should* you dream. There is no formula (thank God), apart from having a heart that is open to the Lord should He decide to speak to you in this manner.

There are no simple answers to the mysteries surrounding dreams and visions. John Wesley, founder of Methodism, posed the question, "What is a dream?" Then he followed his question with an observation:

> You will say, "Who does not know this?" Might you not rather say, "Who *does* know?" Is there anything more mysterious in nature? Who is there that has not experienced it, that has not dreamed a thousand times? Yet he is no more able to explain the nature of it, than he is to grasp the skies.[1]

Though dreaming is a difficult thing to grasp, like chasing a shadow, there are, nonetheless, a few practical guidelines that provide some sense of definition to an otherwise indefinable phenomenon.

Eight Practical Steps for Would Be Dreamers

Practically speaking, there are a few things you can do that will prepare you for God to speak to you in a dream — but these in no way guarantee that He will. It ultimately rests with Him alone. Nevertheless, following these steps will produce tremendous personal benefits, whether you ever have a dream or not. Therefore, do these things:

1. Set your heart upon the Lord.

God told Jeremiah the prophet, "If you return, then I will restore you — before Me you will stand; And if you extract the precious from the worthless, you will become My spokesman."[2] The object is not to have dreams just for the sake of seeming novel or holy. The goal is to know God through a personal relationship with Jesus Christ. He is the Dream come true!

As we seek to know Him more and more, He renews our minds and restores our souls, enabling us to discern what is precious from that which is vile. This, in turn, empowers us to speak His word as He has made it known to us.

"The secret of the Lord is with them that fear him; and he will show them his covenant."[3] How awesome is this privilege given to us by grace! We may stand in the chambers of the King and hear His private deliberations. Jesus said, "My sheep hear my voice."[4] The word means to listen, to hear and to recognize.

This applies to every means the Lord uses to speak to us — from the preaching of the Word on Sunday mornings, to the meditations of dreams and visions in the night watches. If our hearts are set on the Lord, we will be able to listen, hear and recognize when He speaks to us.

2. Repent of wrong attitudes.

This has a broader application than our immediate subject, but for the sake of focus I want to fix it specifically to the matter of dreams and visions. In order for you to receive a dream from the Lord, you must first repent if you have had an attitude that despised such things in the past.

We have been specifically admonished in Scripture to despise not the chastening of the Lord, the parental authority of our fathers and mothers, the innocence of children and the mysterious wonder of inspired prophesying.[5] Dreams and visions are within the boundaries of the prophetic gift. We are not to despise them.

The word Paul used in the Greek means "to consider unworthy of your consideration; to deem beneath your dignity to notice; to set at naught without a second thought."[6] This is a common attitude among many evangelicals today regarding dreams and visions. This needs to change.

Your prejudice against dreams and visions can be a substantial block to ever receiving any from the Lord. Gregory of Nyssa called dreams "the fantastic nonsense which occurs to us in sleep." He taught that dreaming consisted of "wandering among confused and inconsequential delusions." He was forced, however, by the evidence of Scripture and experience, to admit that *some* dreams have proven to be from God.

He wrote, "Some men are deemed worthy of evident divine communication; so, while the imagination of sleep naturally occurs in a like and equivalent manner for all, some, *not all,* share by means of their dreams in some more divine manifestation."[7]

Hopefully this book has helped you see that there is more to dreams and visions than perhaps you previously thought. Go to the Lord in prayer and acknowledge that you haven't regarded these things with the merit they deserve.

The story is told of a farmer who went to visit his son who had left the farm to study science at the university. When he arrived, his son gave him the customary tour, including a stop at the campus science lab. "Dad, look at this," the son said. Peering into a microscope, the father gasped in amazement at the sight before him. "What in tar'nation is it?" he asked. His son replied, "It's a dandelion, Dad."

The farmer paused in silence as he took another long and studied gaze through the lens, and then said, "God, forgive me; I've stepped on thousands."

3. Study the Bible faithfully.

The Bible is the Word of God. You must pour your heart into it, so that your thoughts, opinions, inclinations, preferences and conclusions are formed and guided by its superior revelation. Paul instructed Timothy, "Do your best to present yourself to God as one approved, a workman who does not need to be ashamed and who correctly handles the word of truth."[8]

I cannot emphasize this strongly enough. Dreams and visions are not given by God to take us away from the Scripture, nor to add something more to the Scripture. They are given to draw us deeper into the Word of God that we might know and love the Lord more and more. St. Benedict wrote, "Diligent examination of dreams produces a most fitting knowledge of them, very fine in itself, and serves immensely to illuminate several obscure passages in the holy Scripture."[9]

The more comprehensive your grasp of biblical truth, the more likely you are to discern when the Lord is speaking to you through a dream or vision. And, the more adept you will be in arriving at a sound and sensible interpretation.

4. Be committed to your church and pastor.

It is within the community of believers that the Lord publicly confirms the words He speaks to us in private. Paul said that "we have the mind of Christ."[10] Note that little word — *we*. You, by yourself, do not have the mind of Christ, nor do I. It is only as we come together that *we* have the mind of Christ. The Bible says that "we know in part, and we prophesy in part."[11] (This, undoubtedly, is one reason the devil works so deliberately at keeping us apart. Can you imagine the horror that would seize his wicked heart if we ever put all our parts *together?*)

The Lord has provided us with perspective, wisdom and understanding in our relationships with one another within the church. It is our responsibility to be teachable, faithful and accountable to each other. Sadly, not everybody plays by the rules. Some feel they have the inside track with God, and therefore need no one else calling them into account.

Dreamers and visionaries (not all) are notorious for their temperamental immaturity and self-assured proclamations of the latest word from God. It only makes matters worse when you come across one who refuses to listen, hear or recognize the true word of the Lord through their pastor or church leader.

Let me implore anyone who dreams or sees visions — please get in right relationship with your pastor and trust the Lord to use him to keep you from going whack-o. Your gifts are needed in the church, don't let the devil rip off you and the church by pride and independence. Humble yourself, and the Lord will lift you up.

5. Ask in faith.

If you believe God speaks in dreams and visions, and your heart longs for Him to speak to you — ask Him to do so! Jesus said, "Ask and it will be given to you; seek and you will find; knock and the door will be opened to you." Jesus made it very clear, "Which of you fathers, if your son asks for a fish, will give him a snake instead? Or if he asks for an egg, will give him a scorpion?

"If you then, though you are evil, know how to give good gifts to your children, how much more will your Father in heaven give the Holy Spirit to those who ask him!"[12] Perhaps you have asked and nothing happened. Might it be that you asked amiss, with wrong motives?

Some ask for dreams because it makes them appear more spiritual than others. Some ask because they are looking for a shortcut to sanctification. Others want God to speak to them so they can know things others don't know. And there are those who want to have dreams so as to give them the upper hand in the lives of other people. God will not accommodate these wishes. But the devil will. Get your heart right or your dreams will be wrong!

6. Be alert in your sleep.

The lover in Solomon's Song said, "I slept but my heart was awake." You can go to sleep, yet your heart can be awake. What a fascinating concept, especially in light of the fact that we see dreams with the eyes of our heart. The singer continues, "Listen! My lover is knocking, 'Open to me, my sister, my darling, my dove, my flawless one. My head is drenched with dew, my hair with the dampness of the night.'"[13]

Love the voice of the Lord more than you love sleep. Leave the lights on in your heart, with the door slightly ajar. Cultivate a value system that alerts you to the presence of the Lord — even in your sleep! Sometimes we are most awake toward God when we are asleep toward the world.

Jesus Himself said, "I stand at the door and knock. If anyone hears My voice and opens the door — I will come in and sup with them, and they with Me."[14] Many nights my final prayer of the day has been, "Lord, I now sleep, but my heart is awake listening for Your voice. Come and sup with me, and I with You, if it be according to Your will. Amen." Sometimes He comes.

7. Wake up and write down the dream.

I can't recall how many times I have awakened in the middle of the night from a vivid dream, thinking I would surely remember it when the morning came. But, alas, I never do! I've learned two things in this regard.

First, if you wake in the middle of the night from a dream, take a moment and write the dream down. "In the first year of Belshazzar king of Babylon, Daniel had a dream, and visions passed through his mind as he was lying on his bed. He wrote down the substance of his dream."[15]

Be prepared to do this by keeping a pad and pen at your bedside. Also have a night light readily available. These very acts of preparation can help your mind stay focused enough to capture the illusive bird called dream.

Second, if you write it down and go back to sleep — be prepared for the Lord to give you more! There have been a few nights where I have dreamed up to five or more separate dreams, each holding some bit of insight that proved itself helpful in the days that followed.

8. Apply your heart to wisdom.

What do you do when you've written a dream in the night and wake up to read it in your pad the following morning? You take it to the Lord in prayer. Get your Bible, and pick the dream apart with the tools of truth. Separate the precious from the worthless. Ask God to give you a date with wisdom!

Solomon pictured wisdom as a beautiful lady standing on the side of the busy street, saying, "To you, O men, I call out; I raise my voice to all mankind. You who are simple, gain prudence; you who are foolish, gain understanding. Listen, for I have worthy things to say; I open my lips to speak what is right."[16]

This is not a hollow invitation. Wisdom has much to offer to anyone who will allow her influence in their lives. Here are some of the gains you will have if you seek wisdom:

- Understand proverbs, parables, and riddles (Prov. 1:5-6)
- Personal relationship with God (2:5)
- Discretion, preservation and deliverance from evil (2:11)
- Length of days filled with happiness and peace (3:16-17)
- Public safety and private security (3:23-24)
- Counsel, strength, authority and justice (8:14-15)
- Riches, honor and righteousness (8:18-21)
- Life and favor from the Lord (8:34-36)

Looking this list over, it's hard to imagine why anybody would spurn wisdom. Yet, people do it all the time.

Tips for Interpretation of Dreams

"Doesn't the Bible command us not to interpret dreams?" a seminar attendee once asked me, citing Deuteronomy 18:10: "Let there not be found among you him who observes dreams [omens]." I knew the brother had a bias against dreams and was trying to trap me with his question.

"If we apply your argument," I answered, "then we will have to say that both Joseph and Daniel sinned against God when they interpreted the dreams of Pharaoh and Nebuchadnezzar." In a follow-up question, another asked: "What then are we to make of the verse from Deuteronomy?"

On this most important question, I cite the writings of St. Thomas Aquinas.

> It is irrational to deny as real that which men experience in common. Specifically speaking, it is the experience of all men that a dream sometimes contains some indication of the future. The holy Scripture states that God instructs men through dreams. And we read of holy men such as Joseph and Daniel interpreting dreams. Therefore, to make use of divination by dreams is not unlawful.

But the contrary is written in Deuteronomy 18:10, "Let there not be found among you him who observes dreams." My answer to that is, as I have said before, that divination based on *false* opinion is superstitious and unlawful. Consequently one must consider what is *true* in the foreknowledge of the future, through dreams.

One must observe that the cause of dreams is sometimes within and sometimes without. The inward cause may be the things with which a man was occupied with while he was awake. The outward cause of dreams is sometimes from God, who by the ministry of angels reveals something to men. But sometimes it is by the operation of demons that certain images appear to sleepers.

Accordingly, one must say that if anyone uses dreams for predicting the future, provided the dreams proceed from divine revelation, or from a natural cause, it will not be unlawful divination.

But if divination arises from revelation by *demons* with whom there is an unlawful agreement either openly because they have been invoked to this end, or implicitly because a divination of this kind is extended beyond what it can possibly reach, the divination will be unlawful and superstitious."[17]

In other words, Aquinas argued that the commandment of Moses was given to stop the practice of *false* divination, not the true interpretation of dreams from God. Therefore, the issue of interpretation is right or wrong exclusively on the basis of whether the dream is from God or satanic sources.

Consider the Source

Practically speaking, the first step towards making sense out of your dreams is to consider the source. Why the dream happened is as important as looking into what the dream may reveal. Wesley, though uncertain about the mystery of dreams, suggested with confidence some of their causes.

We do know the origin of dreams, and that with some

degree of certainty. There can be no doubt, but some of them arise from the present constitution of the body, while others of them are probably occasioned by the passions of the mind. Again, we are clearly informed in the Scripture, that some are caused by the operation of good angels, as others undoubtedly are owing to the power of malice of evil angels.

From the same divine treasury of knowledge we learn, that on some extraordinary occasions, the Great Father of Spirits has manifested himself to human spirits, 'in dreams and visions of the night.' But which of all these arise from natural, which from supernatural influence, we are many times not able to determine."[18]

St. Benedict offered a similar perspective as Wesley:

There is no one class of dreams nor one explanation for them. Therefore, the cause of all of them is not the same, so that they should not all be either confirmed or rejected on the same grounds.

Indeed, sacred works deride many dreams and even condemn them; but certain dreams they praise and highly respect. For the majority of them are groundless; and more than a few are natural, arising from definite causes in nature. Others, moreover, are thrust upon mortals by the cunning and malice of the devil. Finally, some are given to men by divine inspiration.[19]

Some Common Causes for Dreams Today

1. Diet

Though it is often used as a topic of humor, and therefore might not seem credible, what one eats can in fact affect the mind during sleep. As one man asked after a weird dream, "Was that God or was it pizza?"

Our bodies are a complex composition of chemicals. If we introduce something into our system that interacts in an abnormal manner, it is likely to show up in our dreams. One author wrote, "Bad dreams and nightmares frequently occur to hypoglycemic sufferers after eating sugar or some allergen-bearing food at night. When the blood sugar is maintained at a normal level, dreams are good."[20]

2. Activity

John Calvin wrote, "Even profane writers very correctly consider dreams connected with divine agency. Yet, it would be foolish to extend this to all dreams. Indeed, we know dreams to arise from different causes; as, for instance, from our daily thoughts."[21]

The things one experiences during the course of a day can activate the mind to dream, especially if the events were out of the ordinary course of daily activities. For example, a person from the city could spend a day on a dude ranch, riding horses and roping cows. That night he could possibly dream that he was John Wayne, leading the troops to Fort Apache.

It would be my humble suggestion to the man that he *not* pay a psychologist several hundred dollars to solve the mystery of his dream. Unless, of course in the dream he was wearing a pink tutu and acting strangely affectionate toward the horse!

3. Memory

Each of us are curators of what I call the "Museum of Memories." Throughout our lives we collect a variety of pictures reflecting our perception of what we have experienced. We frame each painting and hang it upon the corridors of our memories. From time to time we take a walk down Memory Lane and relive the emotion that we have attached to the picture.

Occasionally, the Lord Himself will tour our museum! In a dream He will walk our hallways and view our collections. His purpose is always singular — to make us whole. When He sees a "painting" that needs His critique, He will say to us, "That memory is all wrong."

"What do you mean?" we quickly protest, "that's what happened to me. I remember it well."

"Of course you do," the Lord responds. "But the problem is that you forgot something in your picture?"

"What?" we earnestly ask.

"You forgot ME! I was *there* when that happened to you; didn't you see Me? Shouldn't you now change this picture to include Me in the scene?"

Once we update our paintings (so to speak) and view them from the *Lord's* perspective — everything looks completely different to us. What a wonderful difference His presence makes in our Museum of Memories. If He keeps it up, we will be able to open the doors for public tours, so all can view the works of the Master! "Come behold the works of the Lord!"

While the Lord often uses the dreams that arise from our memories to effect a change in our lives, calling such dreams a word from the Lord would be stretching the point a bit. It is more accurately a *work* of the Lord through a resurfaced significant memory.

4. Emotions

Solomon noted, "As a dream comes when there are many cares, so the speech of a fool when there are many words."[22] When the heart is burdened with cares and filled with strong emotion, whether it be good or bad, the mind can be stimulated to dream accordingly.

Gregory said,

> Most men's dreams are conformed to the state of their character. The brave man's fancies are of one kind, the coward's of another; the wanton man's dreams of one kind, the continent man's of another; the liberal man and the avaricious man are subject to different fancies; while these fancies are nowhere framed by the intellect, but by the less rationale disposition of the soul, which forms even in dreams the semblances of those things to which each is accustomed by the practice of his waking hours.[23]

5. Physiological Causes

A lady fell asleep in a tanning booth and dreamed she was lying on a sunny beach (I can't imagine why!). A man dreamed he was falling off a cliff, and was awakened when he tumbled to the floor out of his bed. A young boy had tossed and turned through the night so as to become entangled in his bed sheets. He dreamed a monster snake had him in its mouth.

These kinds of dreams are common. They are a marvelous witness to the integration of our mind and bodies. Even when we are asleep, the information processors of our brains are on active duty, alerting us to physiological developments within and about us.

✓

6. Secret Sins

Sometimes the Lord will use a dream to specifically purge some area of our personality or life that is buried too deep for us to readily see on our own. After I had finished speaking to a large group of men at a retreat, one of the fellows came to me with a testimony of a very graphic dream. In the dream, the man saw himself as a visitor at a prison. From where he was standing he could see inside the cell block. There were several prisoners loitering about the prison completely naked, each fondling himself sexually.

It was an appalling sight, so disgusting and shocking that it woke the man up. He told me that he awoke from the dream with these words ringing in his ears, "Don't go back into the prison!" He shared with me that the Lord used this dream to help him overcome an excessive, lifelong habit of masturbation.

Some might take a superficial offense that I would dare put something like this in print, but there are those who struggle with shame and sorrow in their private battles against sexual compromises. This brother's dream experience could be used by the Lord to help others overcome, just as it helped him.

7. Training Film

Sometimes you may experience a run of unrelated, non-sensical images and ideas in a dream which seem like they should mean something because of their clarity and symbolism. Yet try as you might, you will never find any palatable interpretation. And if you press the issue, you will appear to others quite foolish.

Calvin commented about this very thing: "Indeed, we see some persons never passing by a single dream without a conjecture, and thus make themselves ridiculous." My suggestion is to regard such encounters merely as "training films." Look at them as God's way of keeping your sense of sight and discernment sharpened while you are asleep.

8. Satanic Dreams

False teachings, evil premonitions, terrors and nightmares! These types of dreams reflect the perversion of Satan and provide us with clues to his intentions against ourselves and others. A wife is vexed by a disturbing dream in which she sees her husband horribly killed;

a child is tormented by the sight of a ghoulish head floating in his room; a business man away on a trip dreams that his home explodes and his family perishes.

Each of these instances requires some deliberate action on the part of the dreamer to assure that these things are not true, in order to be restored to peace of mind. Dreams like this distract you by preoccupying your mind with fear and dismay. During the time your heart is seized with grim thoughts, the wicked thief celebrates his diabolical mischief.

I have found that the best recourse for this type of satanic interference is to stand firm in faith and annul his strategies with a resolute *No!* — in the name of Jesus Christ!

Remember, the devil is like an alley cat. When the porch light goes on, and the homeowner says, *"Scat!"* — he is out of there! Or, to put it in more Biblical tones, "Resist the devil, and he will flee from you!"[24]

9. Dreams That Come From God

The purpose of this book is to verify that God speaks to us through dreams, and I have gone to great length to show this. I need not elaborate the point at this time. Suffice it to say that God does indeed cause some of the dreams that we experience.

Categories of Dreams

In order to properly assess any dream that you may have, first determine the source of the dream. Secondly, you must develop some sense of category.

David Lyle Jeffery wrote a scholarly review of the Christian view of dreams which developed during the Middle Ages. He said:

A fivefold classification of dreams helped establish our terms of reference: the *visum,* or apparition, in which the dreamer thinks himself awake while imaging specters, and the *insomnium,* or nightmare related to evident physical or mental stress, required little or no interpretation.

But the enigmatic *somnium* conceals with strange shapes, and veils with ambiguity the true meaning of the information being offered, and requires an interpretation for its understanding. More declaratively, the prophetic *visio* is a dream which comes true, and the *oraculum* is a dream in which a parent or other revered figure reveals the future and gives advice.

Augustine further divides this last category into *visio corporale* (a sensory and realistic presentation of natural images), *visio spirituale* (resulting from spiritual powers shaping the imagination by use of sensory images), and *visio intellectuale* (a revelation of divine mysteries without the mediation of images, appealing directly to the intellect).

By the twelfth century the various classifications of authentic dreams and visions were reduced to a single class, generically called *revelation*. Revelatory dreams were seen to be influenced, however, by malignant as well as holy angelic influence. The *spiritus malus,* such as troubled Saul, produces not revelation but illusion, so that discerning the spirits becomes a pivotal question in dream interpretation.[25]

These categorical references are helpful, but let's put it in a practical framework. Here are some of the basic questions I ask when I approach a dream for interpretation.

- Is it personal — a word from God to the dreamer?
- Is it prophetic — a word from God through the dreamer?
- Is it pathetic — not a word from God at all!
- Is it pizza — merely the results of spicy food?
- Is it literal — something that is actual and real?
- Is it symbolic — like a parable that is not to be taken literally?
- Is it futuristic — something which is going to happen?
- Is it reflective — something that has already happened?
- Is it revealing — insight on things past, present or future?

These categories often "mix and match." A dream can be personal and symbolic, or prophetic and literal, and so on. The point is that "interpretation belongs to God." We must humble ourselves and ask Him what He is trying to show us in these things — if indeed the dream is from the Lord.

Four Pitfalls to Avoid

The dreamscape has deep pits that must be avoided at all cost. Some have fallen off into these treacherous chasms never to be seen or heard from again!

1. Pride

When Pharaoh asked Joseph to interpret his perplexing dreams, Joseph replied, "I cannot do it, but God will give Pharaoh the answer he desires."[26] This exact sentiment was echoed by Daniel centuries later. "As for me," Daniel said, "this mystery has been revealed to me, not because I have greater wisdom than other living men, but so that you, O king, may know the interpretation and that you may understand what went through your mind."[27]

In both instances humility was the crucial virtue. God resists the proud, but gives grace to the humble. In the matter of dreams and their interpretations, there is no place for pride. Dreams belong to God, as do their interpretations and their fulfillment. The pure in heart see, and the humble of heart understand.

2. Irresponsibility

"Here is a dream from the Lord that I am supposed to give to you. I have no idea what it means. I just receive the message and deliver the mail." That's a mild form of irresponsibility, but its better than some abuses I've witnessed.

A pastor called me for advice, after a young man in his church, who promoted himself as a prophet, told a lady suffering from a life-long paralysis: "The Lord showed me in a dream that you are demon-possessed, and that's why your body is twisted and torment-ed. Repent of your sin of bitterness and God will heal you!"

The dear lady was devastated. The pastor wanted support in con-fronting the irresponsible brother, and so he called me. We worked together trying to bring healing to the situation. The arrogant young man left the church, shaking the dust from his feet as a sign against them. Thankfully, we were able to restore our sister to peace of mind and fruitful devotion to Christ.

3. Presumption

"This dream means what I say it means! After all, I'm the one who had the dream; not you!" This is a common mistake that immature dreamers often make. It is true, sometimes, that we dream and also have the interpretation — but not always. God wants us to relate well with others, and will often wrap the interpretation within a relationship we are to pursue. Remember, "we prophesy in part."

4. Anxiety

Dreams and visions come and go. It's important, therefore, that one not be so caught up with them that anxiety sets in when they stop. Sometimes I have dreamed as many as eight distinct dreams in one night. But there have also been prolonged periods of time when I have not dreamed at all — or at least not remembered any dreams I may have had. This is normal and should not cause us to become filled with anxiety. If God wants to get through to you in a dream — He will.

Paul wrote, "Do not be anxious about anything, but in everything, by prayer and petition, with thanksgiving, present your requests to God. And the peace of God, which transcends all understanding, will guard your hearts and your minds in Christ Jesus."[28] Remember, dreams and visions come and go, but the Lord's Word abides forever. Don't fret if you aren't dreaming; turn to the Bible and God will speak to you every day.

Here are a few examples of dreams and their interpretations. Several have already been provided throughout the book, so I think only a couple are necessary at this point.

Rachel's Revelation

My fourteen-year-old daughter Rachel dreamed one night she was riding in the car with Mom (Belinda) in a most unlikely place — the church building. As they drove around, Rachel noticed that Belinda was not looking ahead, but was instead reading a book that rested upon the stirring wheel of the car.

Rachel looked up and saw a huge pig run in front of the car. Belinda, not seeing the pig, ran over it without any damage to the car. However, there was no trace of the pig left. Then, oddly enough,

Belinda said, "The walls will now come down."

The dream then changed scenes, and Rachel found herself in the youth room of our church building. She saw a large python snapping at the water fountain, and several smaller rattlesnakes coiled and hissing about the floor. She quickly ran and told our church custodian about the snakes, and he returned with her to remove them. As they entered back into the room they saw a large bear killing all the snakes. The dream ended.

What in the World Does That Mean?

The amazing thing I've discovered about interpretations of dreams, is that they are usually rather instant — like being in a foreign country and suddenly hearing someone speaking your native language. You don't *try* to understand, you simply know what is being said.

The second thing I've found is that you never have to force or contrive an interpretation. It is usually so simple and clear that people readily comprehend the meaning of the dream. Now, then, is there any meaning to Rachel's dream? Yes, I believe there is.

My wife Belinda drives a car with specialized tags, *GRACE2U.* In the dream, she symbolized the ministry of our church — bringing the grace of Jesus Christ to our community and the world beyond us. This is the driving motive of our church; one would not be stretching the point to say it is our *auto*-motive! It is why we do what we do.

Belinda was not looking ahead (i.e., taking no thought for tomorrow), but was reading a book that rested on the stirring wheel. This symbolizes walking by faith, and not by sight — being guided by the Word of God, which holds the controls of our lives.

Rachel represents the youthful heart that longs for a better tomorrow. She was the one who saw the huge pig dash in front of the car. This represents the potential obstacles that seek to cut us off from fulfilling God's purposes for our lives; the unclean things that try to stop our progress; distractions that try to detour us from the destiny that God has ordained for our lives.

Anybody would naturally brake for an animal, but Belinda didn't see it and so she ran over it. This speaks of having our eyes fixed upon Jesus, and laying aside every weight and the sin that so easily entangles us. The power of Belinda's transportation was sufficient to overcome the pig, without damage to the ministry of the church.

The walls came down as soon as the pig was overrun, symboliz-ing the removal of barriers and restrictions which keep us from being everything God wants us to be once we turn from distractions. The changing scene in itself is also instructive. The message is clear: If we will not let big distractions detour us from God's pur-pose, we will see the walls come down that separate us from the youth of today. I believe that is what the youth room symbolizes.

The python symbolizes an evil spirit that seeks to choke the life out of the church. Notice, however, that it was not constricting the fountain, it was merely biting at it. That is not what pythons do. This means that the evil spirit is itself constricted by God! The fountain symbolizes the pastors and leaders of the church who provide the living water by preaching the Word of God. The devil attacks the leaders with biting words of intimidation and criticism, so as to cut off the supply of living water. If he succeeds, the church will become stagnant and tepid.

The coiled rattlesnakes represent the hidden agendas of the devil, hissing along the paths we walk. He seeks to inject his poison into our feet and legs, to destroy our strength and cripple our walk of faith.

The custodian represents the ministry of the Holy Spirit. He has come as the Caretaker of the church. He provides cleansing, makes sure all the lights are working and keeps all the facilities ready for use. He holds the keys that open every door, and oversees the lost and found department.

When Rachel ran to get the custodian, she symbolized the act of importunate intercession. When she returned from prayer with the Holy Spirit, a bear was killing the snakes. The bear symbolizes the power of God that validates the word of the Lord, like when Elisha prophesied and a bear came out of the woods and fulfilled the word he spoke![29]

So What?

Now having gone through all of that, one question must be asked — So what? So my daughter had a weird dream, and I can cleverly read into it some rather interesting meanings that seem to symbol-ize things about the Lord, the church and our walk as Christians — So what?

That is precisely the attitude I hope to change by writing this book. Many of us would hear a dream like that and think it was complete foolishness to look for any meaning in it whatsoever. But, it is just that kind of thinking that robs us of so many wonderful gifts the Lord has for us.

This dream, if we accept it as a gift from the Lord, accomplishes a variety of redemptive objectives. First, it has stirred the heart of my daughter with more love and wonder toward the Lord, and drawn her closer to Him in devotion to His word. Also, it provided a golden opportunity for her mother and me to share a special moment together with her in talking about the Lord, thereby strengthening our family bond — and her personal faith. How thrilled she was to think that God showed her this.

Second, it gives specific insights for our church to pray over on behalf of the pastors, youth and our ministry to the community. Third, it cautions us as a church against distractions and detours caused by uncleanness, and it alerts us to the diabolic attack of the enemy against the preaching of the Word, the fountain of life. Finally, it accomplished what Paul said prophecy would do — edify, exhort and comfort.

Behind Enemy Lines

I dreamed that a squad of soldiers, who were separated from their regiment, came under heavy fire behind enemy lines and were captured by the adversary. I followed them into captivity and found that they were left alone in a city that was covered with ashes. They were not chained, nor in any other way detained. Their legs were broken, but they were left free to move about the forsaken city as best they could.

As soldiers, they were puzzled by the apparent carelessness of their captors until it became clear to them why things were this way. The report back home was that these soldiers had been killed in action. Nobody knew they were still alive and in captivity, so no one would bother searching for them. There would be no rescue. They would be abandoned behind enemy lines. At that moment, an overwhelming sense of hopelessness came upon the men. The dream ended.

As I pondered this particular dream, I felt it was a picture showing the condition of many people who, through division and strife, have been separated from the church. Isolated from fellowship, the devil attacked them fiercely and led them off as captives.

Their walk of faith has been crippled and they are left among the ashes (which could signify *burnout*). Now, these captive soldiers are haunted behind enemy lines, realizing that no one is going to bother searching for them to bring them back to the Lord's side.

What are the enemy lines?

The *lies* of the devil are the only enemy lines that a Christian can be held captive behind. Here are some of Satan's most effective lies:

- The pastor doesn't care about you.

- No one at that church knows what has happened to you, and besides, they don't care what happens in your life.

- You are all alone.

- God has forsaken you.

- The Bible isn't true; it doesn't work; it's all a lie.

- The church is filled with hypocrites.

- All they want is your money.

- They don't even love each other, what makes you think they will love you?

These are some of the lines the enemy uses to hold POW's in captivity. God is looking for a few virtuous commandos filled with uncommon valor, who will break through the enemy lines with the sword of truth, and rescue those who are crippled and captive among the ashes. Any volunteers?

Maybe you know someone who is behind enemy lines. Pray for them that "God will grant them repentance leading them to a knowledge of the truth, and that they will come to their senses and escape from the trap of the devil, who has taken them captive to do his will."[30] It is a prayer that God will answer.

O.K., now it's *your* turn! It's time to jump out of the plane! Apply the principles provided in this chapter and interpret the following dream.

The Three Dishes

I saw three empty dishes before me in a dream. The first bowl was labeled "Salvation." The second was "Instruction," and the third, "Persecution." Then the hand of the Lord appeared holding a vase from which water was being poured into the first dish. The water was murky and undesirable. The Lord took a cloth rag and used it to sop up the dirty water from the bowl of salvation and squeeze it into the next bowl of instruction.

The water appeared cleaner in the second bowl, but was still cloudy and gray. The Lord then took the same cloth and sopped the water up once more, this time squeezing it into the final bowl of persecution. In this third bowl the water was crystal clear and very pure. The dream ended.

Questions

- Is this a dream from the Lord?

- What kind of dream is it?

- What do the three empty dishes mean?

- What does the vase symbolize?

- What does the dirty water represent?

- Why does the Lord use a cloth rag to sop up the dirty water?

- What does the rag symbolize?

- Why does the water get purer each time it is squeezed from one bowl to the next?

- What is the "moral of the story?"

Jump, trooper! And let me know if you land safely.[31] It's late, and I'm going to bed!

NOW I LAY ME DOWN
TO SLEEP

here was nothing I could do. Standing there alone in the brightly lit vestibule of a large European castle, with my hands stuck inside two crystal jars, made me feel like an idiot. I thought about breaking the jars by smashing them together but was afraid I would cut my hands to shreds in the process. I tried to pull my hands free from the jars but it was hopeless, the rims were too tight about my wrists.

I was perplexed and frustrated. The strangest part is that I don't even know how my hands got inside the jars in the first place, nor what I was doing in such an unusual predicament. Not knowing what to do, I just stood there — very much bewildered and more than a little exasperated.

Looking around I saw an old-fashioned, upright washing machine. You know, the kind with the wooden rollers on top to squeeze the water out of the clothes. It seemed out of place in the classy surroundings of the castle. Curious, I walked over to it to get a closer look.

As I stood by the washer, my hands seemed to thrust themselves into the water. Before I could react and pull my hands free, the agitator in the washer began to swirl about at great speed — so violently that it made the washing machine vibrate as though it would fall apart. I thought for sure that the jars would be shattered and that I would be cut by all the broken glass.

However, my hands abruptly jerked upward out of the water without any injury to them at all. Somehow the commotion of the washing machine had freed my hands from the crystal jars. "How strange," I mused to myself. Little did I know that the bizarre experience was far from over.

I quickly checked my hands closely to make sure everything was all right. I noticed that my skin felt tough like leather, and yet it was still supple like flesh. "Strong and yet gentle; gentle and still strong." That's the thought that entered my mind at the time.

While I pondered this, an enormous purple curtain fell unexpectedly on top of me! I collapsed to the floor buried under its weight and reacted as though someone was playing a trick on me. "What's going on here?" I blurted out. "What's the big idea?"

That's when I heard the Voice. It was the kind of voice that stops you in your tracks and makes your hair stand on end.

It came from above me and had an unmistakable air of authority about it. The Voice simply said, "This is the mantle of Zechariah!" My agitation suddenly faded and I was filled with wonder and awe. I stood there quietly waiting for what would happen next.

Knock, Knock! Who's There?

Three thundering knocks came from a towering castle door to my left and echoed throughout the large room. The Voice spoke once again, this time calling my name, saying, "James, it is the Lord!" I then realized Jesus was standing at the castle door.

I turned and walked toward the great door, but was interrupted by a man entering the vestibule from a side room. He was anxious and very demanding. Taking one look at me, he said, "Put that silly cloak down and get into these work clothes! I need help right away with all these whining children!" In deference to his sense of urgency, I looked in the side room from which he had come. It was a church sanctuary filled with boys and girls. They were playing with toys, coloring the pictures in books and making plaster figurines. The scene was disorderly and fraught with carelessness. No wonder the man was so disturbed.

Yet, I knew the Lord was waiting, so I graciously excused myself from the frustrated man and continued toward the door. My heart raced with a strange mix of exhilaration and fear; a glorious rapture and a holy dread. I held the vast purple mantle firmly about my shoulders and walked slowly toward the great door to open it, knowing that I was about to see the Lord face-to-face. Just as I reached for the door handle, I woke up and realized that I had been *dreaming!*

Have you ever tried to go back to sleep and finish a dream? It just doesn't work. I wanted so much to close my eyes and "open that door" so that I could see the Lord — but I just couldn't get back to sleep.

It was about three o'clock in the morning. I remained in my bed for a little while thinking about what I had just dreamed. It was too fascinating to forget, and too *real* to dismiss. I quietly got up and went into my study to read the book of Zechariah. I figured that was the best place for me to start the process of understanding what the Voice meant when it said in my dream, "This is the mantle of Zechariah."

Reading the book of Zechariah, one discovers almost immediately that the man was a dreaming prophet. In the truest sense of the word, he was a seer. His book opens with no less than eight distinct visions shown to him by the angel of the Lord.

One would not be wrong in saying that the "mantle of Zechariah," if it means anything at all, has something to do with dreams and visions. This is an understandable conclusion in light of how frequently and clearly God spoke to Zechariah through dreams and visions.

Could it be that He still speaks this way today? As one has said, we are never more awake to God than when we are asleep to the world. Is it possible that my dream, strange as it is, contains a message for us from the Lord; some godly insight that illustrates the Truth of His holy Word? Let's take a look and see.

Wait Upon the Lord

The castle vestibule represents the place of waiting in the house of the Lord. My hands symbolize service, but they were inside the jars. This illustrates how God sets us apart in order to preserve us and prepare us for ministry. During the process you often are alone, and sometimes feel quite foolish.

Your hands are not free to do as you wish, you are held back from things that others seem able to do without any consequence. "Others may; you may not." Why? Because the Lord has marked you as His Own; He has set you apart unto Himself. The Bible says, "It is good for a man to bear the yoke while he is young. Let him sit alone in silence, for the Lord has laid it on him."[1]

One could break the jars to free himself, but by so doing would disfigure his hands and quite possibly even disavow his call to the ministry. How many times have we seen young and impatient individuals rebel under the yoke of the Lord, and are now useless in serving Him?

There is not much one can do in a vestibule — you simply have to *wait*. But, this does not mean you are passive. God uses this time to teach you, correct you, mature you and draw you closer unto Himself. David prayed, "Show me Your ways, O Lord; teach me Your paths. Lead me in Your truth and teach me. For You are the God of my salvation; on You I *wait* all the day."[2] The word *wait* means "to bind together."[3] God *binds* your heart unto Himself, and His heart unto you, during those first trusting moments in the castle vestibule. It is a bond that will never be broken.

Therefore, do not think it strange, nor seek to quickly cast aside, the indefinite season of waiting — for the rewards are eternal. To this Isaiah bears witness, "But they that wait upon the Lord shall renew their strength; they shall mount up with wings as eagles; they shall run, and not be weary; and they shall walk, and not faint."[4] A glorious conversion is taking place in the vestibule. You in Christ, and Christ in you — the exchanged life — the key to effective living and fruitful service.

The Soul-Cleansing Power

The old-fashioned, upright washing machine with the roller on top, could symbolize the time-proven process God uses to bring us into serving the Lord. The process is two-fold. First, there is *surrender* — the hands must go into the water. Then there is the *stirring* — the Holy Spirit must move in our lives in cleansing power, shaking everything that can be shaken so that only the unshakable things of God remain.[5]

There is a label affixed to many jars in your local grocery store. It says simply, "Shake well before using." I think maybe the Lord has stuck that label on all of His servants! Job speaks for many, when he said, "I was at ease....but He has shaken me to pieces!"[6]

Someone might wonder why the Lord would do such a thing. The purpose is, that, having survived the *shaking* of God, we can withstand the puny tempests of trials and tribulations![7] The shaking of the Lord humbles us by showing our weakness; and, yet, it also solidifies us in the soul-cleansing power of God's love. We are thereby softened and strengthened. Thus the riddle in my dream: "Strong and yet gentle; Gentle and still strong."

The wooden roller on top the washer is a further witness to the pressures that we must go through in becoming trusted servants of the Lord. Have you been through the wringer lately? The wringer has a way of twisting and squeezing out all of the selfish ambitions and hidden agendas we each carry within the folds of our personalities. We are to be without spot and wrinkle — the wringer takes care of this in a most accommodating manner!

The Man God Chooses

When God wants to drill a man, and
thrill a man, and skill a man;
When God wants to mold a man
to play the noblest part;
When He yearns with all His heart
to create so great and bold a man
that all the world shall be amazed —
Watch His methods, watch His way!
How He ruthlessly perfects
whom He royally elects!
How He hammers him and hurts him,
and with mighty blows converts him

Into trial shapes of clay which
Only God understands —
While his tortured heart is crying
And he lifts beseeching hands!
How God bends but never breaks
When man's good He undertakes;
How He uses whom He chooses
And with every purpose fuses him,
By every act induces him
To try His splendor out!
God knows what He's about!
— Anonymous

The apostle Paul summed it up this way: "We speak as men approved by God to be entrusted with the gospel. We are not trying to please men, but God, who tests our hearts."[8] In other words — God tests us, then He trusts us, then He entrusts us with the Gospel.

Five Keys to Hearing God's Voice

The Voice that spoke in my dream was in keeping with the promise of Jesus, "But when He, the Spirit of truth, comes, he will guide you into all truth. He will not speak on his own; he will speak only what he hears, and he will tell you what is yet to come. He will bring glory to me by taking from what is mine and making it known to you."[9]

Hearing the voice of God is the heritage of the holy; the reward of the redeemed; the birthright of the born again. Jesus said, "My sheep hear my voice, and I know them, and they follow me: And I give unto them eternal life; and they shall never perish, neither shall any man pluck them out of my hand."[10]

As Christians we are not orphans left without the voice of our Father. God speaks to us daily, personally — *really!*[11] Perhaps the most celebrated promise in this regard are the words which the Lord Jesus spoke through John the Beloved, saying, "Behold, I stand at the door and knock: if any man hear my voice and open the door, I will come in to him, and will sup with him, and he with me."[12]

Let me offer five practical keys to unlock the door of your heart so you can hear God's voice. They are found in the words of the prophet Habakkuk, who said, "I will stand at my watch and station myself on the ramparts; I will look to see what he will say to me, and what answer I am to give to this complaint."

Then the Lord replied: "Write down the revelation and make it plain on tablets so that a herald may run with it. For the revelation awaits an appointed time; it speaks of the end and will not prove false. Though it linger, wait for it; it will certainly come and will not delay."[13] The five keys we see in God's answer are:

1. Meet with the Lord regularly in a special place of prayer: "I will stand on my guard post."

2. Look for God to speak to you in dreams and visions: "I will keep watch to see."

3. Listen for the word of the Lord: "He will speak to me."

4. Keep a journal of things that God says: "Record the vision."

5. Wait for God to bring it to pass: "It will surely come."

Your devotion will not be idle, your time will not be spent in vain. You have to your credit the promise of the Great Promise Keeper — "Blessed is the man who listens to me, watching daily at my doors, waiting at my doorway. For whoever finds me finds life and receives favor from the Lord."[14]

The Means and the Mission

The "mantle of Zechariah" not only refers to the means of how God spoke to the prophet (dreams and visions), but also to the mission God sent Zechariah to accomplish — that of encouraging the post-exile Jews as they rebuilt the ruined Temple of the Lord.

"So the elders of the Jews continued to build and prosper under the preaching of Haggai the prophet and Zechariah, a descendant of Iddo. They finished building the temple according to the command of God."[15]

This is rich in meaning for us today. It could be argued quite convincingly that just as the Jews had broken God's covenant and were exiled in Babylonian captivity, so also has the church of today undergone a similar displacement from our high calling, and has suffered shame in a prolonged season of confusion and captivity.

Jesus said we were the light of the world, but our history is not exactly stellar. In fact, the period of history in which the church supposedly held the greatest position of power and influence is ironically called the Dark Ages.

In more recent years the church in the West has suffered a significant crisis of credibility as some of our more visible and vocal emissaries have fallen into glaring disrepute. Never mind that they do not represent the whole of Christendom — we understand that, but the world makes no such distinction. We each bear our brother's guilt. A measure of shame has fallen upon all.

Our problems have been further compounded by the unspeakable horrors of bizarre cults like the People's Temple of Jonestown and the Branch Davidians of Waco — insanity parading in the name of the Lord. Such illegitimate behavior has now cast disrepute upon that which is quite legitimate. True prophets are judged side-by-side with the false, and the eyes of Issachar are shut for Balaam's transgression.

Add to this the murdering of abortion doctors, the hateful debates with homosexuals and feminists, the implacable animosity between differing denominations and the disdainful, self-righteous arrogance of so-called Christian research institutions as they slander other Christians — and you can see that we desperately need help.

Like the Jews of old, we today are mocked by our opponents as we try to rebuild the walls of our faith. We are taunted by their jeers as we seek to resettle our communities with hope and love. We are spurned by their rejection as we try to offer them forgiveness of sin in Jesus' name — for they see that we do not walk in forgiveness ourselves.

Just as back then, so today the ruins are great and our resources small. We need a Haggai and a Zechariah to step forth with dreams and visions from God — inspiring us with their anointed preaching to stay the course of faith with courage as we recover from the ruins of our fall.

This Is More Than One Man Can Handle!

The mantle that fell upon me in the dream was enormous and

very heavy. Clearly, it was more than any one person could handle alone. Paul asked, "Who is sufficient for such things?" And then he gave the answer, "Our sufficiency is from God." The Living Bible puts it this way, "Not because we think we can do anything of lasting value by ourselves. Our only power and success comes from God."[16]

The "mantle of Zechariah" must be carried by many. It is not for one man or woman, rather, it is for *all* who wait upon the Lord — young and old, male and female, bond and free alike. On a personal note, I want to make it clear that I in no way believe that God has called *me* to be "the prophet Zechariah in the last days." I believe He is calling this generation to receive the empowering of the Holy Spirit so as to speak the Word of the living God with inspiring relevance unto a desperate world in need of hope.

To those who respond let me offer this counsel. Steer clear from the side rooms of superficial activity. I want to be kind while I am honest in saying that some spend their time in the church playing childish games, coloring within the lines of pictures others have drawn for them, and making plaster statues to decorate their homes. As for you, don't be distracted by the frenzied zeal of anxious people who have lost their focus upon the Lord, and have in effect turned the church into a kindergarten for children.

The tyranny of the urgent has been the delay, if not the downfall, of many noble callings. Do not discard your mantle for the work clothes of another man's anxious activity, for *that* work is not profitable. Hold firm to the purple mantle and press onward toward the Lord!

The Color Purple

I have given some thought to the fact that the mantle was *purple.* Sometimes colors are a significant key to the meaning of a dream or a vision. James Sexton wrote:

> Color designations in the Bible have general symbolic significance. Color symbolism became for the writers of apocalyptic literature an appropriate tool for expressing various truths in hidden language. In their writings one may find white representative of conquest or victory,

black representative of famine or pestilence, red representative of wartime bloodshed, paleness representative of death, and purple representative of royalty.

Though the majority of color references in the Bible are of a descriptive nature, the possibility of a symbolic use of color necessitates a careful study on the part of the Bible student. Only by careful study can the student discern the writer's intent and so interpret correctly the biblical text. While the use of color imagery was not the foremost interest of the writers of biblical literature, it proved an aid to their writing purposes.[17]

Allowing that the color purple may symbolize royalty, and knowing the mantle to represent an anointing similar to the one to whom the mantle belongs,[18] the *purple* mantle of *Zechariah* might very well represent a spiritual blessing from the Lord upon this generation to see dreams and visions in a more nobler fashion than our forebears.

This is certainly in keeping with the express will of God. "In the last days," God said, "I will pour out my Holy Spirit upon all mankind, and your sons and daughters shall prophesy, and your young men shall see visions, and your old men dream dreams. Yes, the Holy Spirit shall come upon all my servants, men and women alike, and they shall prophesy."[19]

Moreover, it is most befitting to the ever-increasing glory of Jesus Christ that we who are nearer the end should excel in all virtues those who were first to walk the pilgrim way in ages past. So say the prophets, "The glory of the latter house shall be greater than that of the former."[20] Indeed, was it not said of our Lord, "You have saved the best till now!"[21] It would stand to reason, therefore, that *our* vision would be clearer as the Lord's return draws nearer.

Five Practical Steps to Spiritual Vision

The Lord says, "You who are far away, hear what I have done; you who are near, acknowledge my power! The sinners in Zion are terrified; trembling grips the godless: 'Who of us can dwell with the consuming fire? Who of us can dwell with everlasting burning?'

"He who walks righteously and speaks what is right, who rejects gain from extortion and keeps his hand from accepting bribes, who stops his ears against plots of murder and shuts his eyes against contemplating evil — this is the man who will dwell on the heights, whose refuge will be the mountain fortress. His bread will be supplied, and water will not fail him. Your eyes will see the king in his beauty and view a land that stretches afar."[22]

In the above passage of scripture, the prophet Isaiah lists for us the five critical issues which must be faced before our eyes can "see the King in His beauty." They are:

1. Conviction of Sin: "the sinners in Zion are terrified."

2. Repentance toward God: "dwell with the consuming fire."

3. Faithfulness in Obedience: "he who walks righteously."

4. Confession of Truth: "speaks what is right."

5. Purity of Life: "rejects dishonest gains, turns his ear away from violence, and shuts his eyes against evil."

To carry the outline a step further, let me say that any person who will pursue the Lord by diligently following the above five steps, will undoubtedly find themselves:

*   Seated in the heavenlies: "he will dwell in the heights."

*   Secure in Christ: "his refuge is the mountain fortress."

*   Supplied with the Word of God and the power of the Holy Spirit: "his bread shall be supplied, and his water shall not fail."

Now, put all these things together and they add up to the single, most sought after grace of all — *vision.* We will have a vision of Christ Jesus and the glories of heaven! "Your eyes will see the King in His beauty, and view the land that stretches afar!"

Your Eyes Shall See the King

The Greeks of old approached the disciples and said, "Sir, we would see Jesus."[23] It is a request that has been echoed throughout the ages by all who hunger and thirst for righteousness: "O God, give me a vision of Jesus!" Our prayer does not fall on deaf ears. The Lord longs to make Himself known to each of us! But we must look with eyes that can see.

Jesus said, "The one who obeys me is the one who loves me; and because he loves me, my Father will love him; and I will too, and I will reveal myself to him."[24] Obedience opens our eyes to see the King. Isaiah's prophecy tells us that those who shut their eyes against contemplating evil are the ones who will see the King in His beauty.

God has given each one of us what I call *vision hunger* — an appetite for revelation from God, an inner need for visual soul stimulation. Too often we pull up to the table of entertainment and "pig out on junk food," filling our eyes with the visions of the world and spoiling our appetite for visions from heaven. Let me encourage you to "make a covenant with your eyes."[25] Turn away from the things that turn you away from seeking the Lord. He will satisfy your hunger and quench your every thirst.

The Lord Is at the Door!

The thunderous knock on the door in my dream might very well signify the nearness of the Lord's return. "The Judge is standing at the door!"[26] The fact that I woke up before I could open the door speaks volumes. "The hour has come for you to wake up from your slumber, because our salvation is nearer now than when we first believed. The night is nearly over; the day is almost here. So let us put aside the deeds of darkness and put on the armor of light."[27]

It is time for Christians to wake up and be about our Father's business. Jesus came to seek and to save that which was lost. He has called us to be His co-workers in the harvest.

Our hands have been prepared for service and we have been covered with the seamless garment of His mighty Word. And why? It is that we might be light to those in darkness, and give life to those who are dying.

It is time to rise and shine. Seize the moment. Stand up for Jesus. Join the fellowship of the unashamed. Be bold. Be strong. For the Lord our God is with us! Run through the camp and tell everybody the good news of Jesus Christ — a Dream come true! Tell of His excellent greatness, praise Him in the streets and shout His Word from the housetops. In this you can stand with unshakable faith: "It shall come to pass that whoever calls upon the name of the Lord shall be saved!"[28]

Conclusion

I believe that God is raising up a people in these last days who will receive profound insight into the Scriptures in dreams and visions. Their personal faithfulness and ceaseless devotion to the study of the sacred text will ignite anew with the fire of revelation. The sanctity of God's holy Word will stand inviolate as its redeeming power and ageless relevance are brought fully to bear upon this blind world by God's assembled army of seers.

They are a people of faith, vision and courageous compassion. A people who will proclaim on the housetop that which the Lord has whispered in the ear. A people who will let their light shine before men. A people who will awake to righteousness, and sin not. A people who will walk with resolve unto the Lord, no longer charmed by the world's delight. A people who confess openly of the sweeter, nobler things that have allured their sights — the King and His Kingdom.

Perhaps, dear reader, you are one of them. If so, then let me leave you this final prayer that you may make your own:

O God of Dreams

O God of dreams invade our sleep
and wake us to Thy grace.
Our spirits tend, our souls do keep
as we behold Thy face.
Let naught of ill bestir our hearts
while we compose in dreams
The vision which Thy love imparts
to us in sweeter themes.

And glory to Thy Son's great Name
shall evermore increase,
With rising flood of earthly fame
for wondrous gifts as these.
And we who see in vision sweet
whatever comes of You
Will bow in love at Jesus' feet —
He is our Dream come true![29]

Goodnight, dear friend,
and pleasant dreams.

Dedication

1. *The Wind Beneath My Wings,* by Jeff Silbar and Larry Henky, ©
1982 WB Gold Music Corp. (ASCAP) and Warner House of Music
(BMI). All rights reserved. Used by permission, Warner Bros.
Publications Inc.: Miami, FL 33014.

Preface

1. Acts 2:17, NKJV
2. D. D. Whedon, *Commentary on the New Testament, Acts–Romans*
(Salem, Ohio: Schmul Publishers, Rare Reprint Specialists, 1979), p. 34.
3. Matthew Henry, *Acts to Revelation,* vol. 6 of *Matthew Henry's
Commentary on the Whole Bible* (New York: Fleming H. Revell
Company, 1986), p. 20.
4. Simon J. Kistemaker, *Exposition of the Acts of the Apostles*
(Grand Rapids, Mich.: Baker Book House, 1990), p. 89.
5. John Peter Lange, *The Gospel According to John* (New York:
Charles Scribner's Sons, 1884), p. 48.
6. Ibid.
7. Everett Ferguson, ed., *Encyclopedia of Early Christianity,* (Garland
Publishers Inc., 1992), pp. 280-281.
8. Morton T. Kelsey, *God, Dreams and Revelation* (Minneapolis,
Minn.: Augsburg Fortress Publishers, 1991), p. 7 (italics added).

Chapter 1
Midnight in a Carpenter's Shop

1. Matthew 1:20-21, NIV
2. 1 Peter 1:10-12
3. Matthew 2:12
4. J. M. Lower, ed., *The Zondervan Pictoral Encyclopedia of the
Bible* (Grand Rapids, Mich.: Zondervan Publishing House, 1975),
vol. 2, p. 890.

5. James Hastings, *A Dictionary of Christ and the Gospels* (New York: T & T Clark, 1906), vol. 1, p. 494.

6. Job 20:8, NIV

7. Psalm 73:20, TLB

8. Ecclesiastes 5:7, TLB

9. See Isaiah 29:8

10. *Apocrypha;* Ecclesiasticus 34:2

11. William Wordsworth, "Intimatinos of Immortality," an ode from *Recollections of Early Childhood* (1807), stanza 4.

12. Luke 1:19, TLB

13. Luke 1:35, NIV

14. Luke 2:10-12

15. Alfred Edersheim, *The Life and Times of Jesus the Messiah* (McLean, Va.: MacDonald Publishing Co., 1883), book 2, p. 155.

16. *The Confessions of St. Augustine,* vol. 1 of *Nicene and Post-Nicene Fathers* (Peabody, Maine: Hendrickson Publishers, 1994), Letter 9.2.

17. Charles Spurgeon, *Metropolitan Tabernacle Pulpit* (Carlisle, Pa.: The Banner of Truth, 1991), vol. 14, sermon #806.

18. Morton T. Kelsey, *God, Dreams and Revelation* (Minneapolis, Minn.: Augsburg Fortress Publishers, 1991), p. 17.

19. Charles Spurgeon, *Metropolitan Tabernacle Pulpit* (Carlisle, Pa.: The Banner of Truth, 1991), vol. 14, sermon #806.

20. James Hastings, *A Dictionary of Christ and the Gospels* (New York: T & T Clark, 1906), vol. 1, pp. 496-497.

21. The taped message of Carl's testimony is available by writing the Boulder Valley Vineyard, 7845 Lookout Road, Longmont, CO 80503. Ask for Carl Menderas' message, "The Mission to the Muslims."

22. Bill Bright, *The Adventure of a Lifetime,* Strategy for Evangelism Conference, Campus Crusade for Christ International, Green Lake, Wisconsin, 1967.

23. The unsuspecting young believer was the Honorable Richard Halverson, who has served the Lord faithfully for many years. Most recently he has completed fourteen years of service as the chaplain for the United States Senate.

24. This was transcribed from a taped interview with Dr. Bill Bright in January 1995.

25. Dr. Bill Bright also spoke of this in his book *The Coming Revival* (Orlando, Fla.: New Life Publication, 1995), p. 29.

26. Walter G. Clippinger, *The International Standard Bible Encyclopedia* (Grand Rapids, Mich.: Wm. B. Eerdman's Publishing Co., 1939), vol. 2, p. 875.

27. John Farrar, *Biblical and Theological Dictionary* (1889), p. 195.

28. James Hastings, ed., *A Dictionary of the Bible* (New York: Charles Scribner's Sons, 1908), vol. 1, p. 622. See the article by F. B. Jevons on dreams.

29. Psalm 8:4

30. Henry Wadsworth Longfellow, *A Psalm of Life* (1839), stanza 1.

31. *Cyclopedia of Biblical Literature,* 3rd ed. (Edinburgh, Scotland: Adam and Charles Block, 1862), vol. 1, p. 699.

Chapter 2
Why Bother With Dreams and Visions?

1. This is a true story, told to me by Jack Taylor, president of Dimensions in Christian Living, headquartered in Melbourne, Florida. He was the young evangelist who had the dream!

2. Job 1:1-22

3. Job 2:1-8

4. Job 2:9, TLB

5. Job 2:11-13

6. Job 4:12-17, NIV

7. See Genesis 15:1; Judges 6:23; Daniel 10:12-19; Luke 2:10, 5:10; Acts 27:24; and Revelation 1:17

8. Job 6:2-3, NIV

9. Job 6:14-17, TLB

10. Job 7:13-14, NIV

11. Job 8:1-2, author's paraphrase

12. Job 11:1-6, TLB

13. Job 32:1-5

14. Job 33:12-18, NIV

15. Judges 7:9-11, NIV

16. Judges 7:13-15, NIV

17. 1 Samuel 28:15, NIV

18. Jack Taylor, *The Hallelujah Factor* (Nashville, Tenn.: Broadman Press, 1983). You may find this booklet worth your reading.

19. Matthew 1:20-21

20. See Job 33:16

21. 2 Chronicles 29:5, NIV
22. 1 Timothy 1:20
23. 1 Corinthians 5:5, TLB
24. Matthew 2:12, NIV
25. Matthew 2:13, NIV
26. Matthew 2:23
27. See Genesis 29–31
28. Genesis 31:24, NIV
29. Genesis 20:3, NIV
30. Genesis 20:7-8, NIV
31. Genesis 20:9, NIV
32. Matthew 27:19, NIV
33. Matthew 27:24, NIV
34. *Ante-Nicene Fathers* (Peabody, Maine: Hendrickson Publishers, 1994), vol. 8, pp. 459-467.
35. Paul Lee Tan, ed., *Encyclopedia of 7700 Illustrations* (Rockville, Md.: Assurance Publishers, 1979), article 4775.
36. Daniel 4:5, NIV
37. Daniel 4:19, TLB
38. Daniel 4:34, TLB
39. Daniel 4:37, NIV
40. Proverbs 13:10
41. Ezekiel 1:1
42. Psalm 126:1-3, NIV
43. Psalm 127:2, NAS

Chapter 3
Sleep-Fancies and Other Vain Imaginations

1. *Nicene and Post-Nicene Fathers* (Peabody, Maine: Hendrickson Publishers, 1994), vol. 2, 2nd series, p. 251.
2. Isaiah 8:19-20, TLB
3. Matthew 24:35
4. Matthew 7:24-27
5. John 6:63-64, NIV
6. Hebrews 4:12, TLB
7. Jeremiah 17:9, NIV
8. Jeremiah 17:9-10, NIV
9. 2 Peter 2:1-3, NIV

10. Deuteronomy 13:1-3, NIV
11. Deuteronomy 13:5, NIV
12. Jeremiah 23:16, NIV
13. Jeremiah 23:25-27, NIV
14. Jeremiah 29:8-9, TLB
15. John 3:20-21, NIV
16. 1 John 1:5-7, NKJV
17. Psalm 36:9
18. Charles Spurgeon, *The Treasury of David* (Peabody, Maine: Hendrickson Publishers, 1988), vol. 2, p. 178.
19. Psalm 119:105
20. Matthew 7:15-16, NIV
21. John 14:6
22. Galatians 1:6-9, NIV
23. Revelation 22:18-19, NIV
24. Romans 10:1-3, NAS
25. Proverbs 6:16-19, NIV
26. See James 3:15-18, TLB
27. Jeremiah 23:16, NIV
28. Leviticus 19:31
29. Jeremiah 23:17, NIV
30. Zechariah 10:2, NIV
31. Jeremiah 23:22, NIV
32. Jeremiah 23:28, NIV
33. Jeremiah 23:32, NIV
34. 2 Peter 2:1, NIV
35. Jeremiah 15:19, NAS

Chapter 4
Pillows of Stone

1. Hebrews 1:1, TLB
2. Genesis 12:1-3, NIV
3. Acts 7:2-3, NIV
4. Genesis 12:7-8, NIV
5. Genesis 13:14-17, NIV
6. Genesis 15:1-2, NIV
7. Genesis 15:3, NIV
8. Genesis 15:4, NIV

9. James Strong, *The New Strong's Exhaustive Concordance of the Bible* (Nashville, Tenn.: Thomas Nelson Publishers, 1984), s.v. "machazeh," #4235, a vision. From "chazah," #2372, a prim. root; to gaze at; mentally to perceive, contemplate (with pleasure); spec. to have a vision of: — behold, look, prophesy, provide, see.

10. Genesis 15:5-6, NIV

11. Genesis 15:7-8, NIV

12. Genesis 15:13-14, NIV

13. James Strong, *The New Strong's Exhaustive Concordance of the Bible* (Nashville, Tenn.: Thomas Nelson Publishers, 1984), s.v. "tardemah," #8639: a lethargy or trance. From "radam," #7290: a prim. root; to stun, i.e. stupefy (with sleep or death):— (be fast a —, be in a deep, cast into a dead, that) sleep.

14. Genesis 15:15, NIV

15. Genesis 15:16, NIV

16. Genesis 17:1-2, NIV

17. Genesis 17:4-5, NIV

18. Genesis 18:1-2, NIV

19. Genesis 21:1-4, NIV

20. John 1:49-51, NIV

21. Genesis 28:13-15, NIV

22. Acts 4:12, NIV

23. Genesis 28:20-22, NIV

24. Genesis 30:25-43, NIV

25. Genesis 31:10-13, NIV

26. Genesis 32:1, NIV

27. Genesis 25:26; 27:36, NIV

28. Genesis 32:28, NIV

29. Matthew 16:24-25

30. Genesis 32:30, NIV

31. Genesis 46:2-4, NIV

32. Genesis 37:5, NKJV

33. James Strong, *The New Strong's Exhaustive Concordance of the Bible* (Nashville, Tenn.: Thomas Nelson Publishers, 1984), s.v. "chalam," #2492, to bind firmly.

34. From Morton T. Kelsey, *Dreams: The Dark Speech of the Spirit,* as quoted by A. J. Gordon in *How Christ Came to Church: The Pastor's Dream* (Garden City, NY: Doubleday & Co., 1968), pp. 187-189.

35. Genesis 37:5-8 (TLB, italics added)
36. Genesis 37:9-11, (italics added)
37. Genesis 37:19-20, NIV
38. Genesis 42:21, NIV
39. Genesis 39:2, NIV
40. Genesis 40:8, NIV
41. Proverbs 25:2, NIV
42. Genesis 40:9-11, NIV
43. Genesis 40:12-13, NIV
44. Genesis 40:14-15, NIV
45. Genesis 40:16-17, NIV
46. Genesis 40:18, NIV
47. Psalm 105:18-19, NIV
48. See Genesis 41:17-24
49. Genesis 41:12-13, NIV
50. Genesis 41:15, NIV
51. Genesis 41:16, NIV
52. Genesis 41:16, NIV
53. Genesis 41:32
54. Genesis 41:37, NIV
55. Genesis 41:37-41, NIV
56. Genesis 41:42,45, NIV
57. I heartily recommend you read the story. You will find it in Genesis 42–50. It is filled with emotion and drama that will stir you deeply.

Chapter 5
The All-Seeing Eye

1. Numbers 12:1-9, NIV
2. Hosea 12:10
3. Hosea 9:7, NIV
4. James Strong, *The New Strong's Exhaustive Concordance of the Bible* (Nashville, Tenn.: Thomas Nelson Publishers, 1984), s.v. "dabar," #1696, to arrange; to speak; answer, appoint, command, commune, declare, give, name, promise, pronounce, teach, tell, think.
5. Exodus 33:20
6. Numbers 12:8

7. Exodus 3:2-4, author's paraphrase
8. 1 Samuel 9:9, NIV
9. Samuel (1 Sam. 9:11); Zadok the priest (2 Sam. 15:27); Gad (2 Sam. 24:11); Heman (1 Chron. 25:5); Iddo (2 Chron. 9:29); Hanani (2 Chron. 16:7); Asaph (2 Chron. 29:30); Jeduthan (2 Chron. 35:15); and Amos (Amos 7:12).
10. Proverbs 14:12; 16:25
11. Judges 17:6; 18:1; 21:25; Ruth 1:1
12. Amos 8:11-12, NIV
13. 1 Samuel 3:1, NIV
14. 1 Samuel 3:2-4, NIV
15. 1 Samuel 3:7
16. 1 Samuel 3:9, NIV
17. 1 Samuel 3:19-21, NIV
18. Isaiah 6:1-3, NIV
19. Isaiah 6:8
20. Isaiah 1:1
21. "Introduction to Isaiah" in *The Spirit-Filled Life Bible,* (Nashville, Tenn.: Thomas Nelson Publishers, 1991), p. 959.
22. Jeremiah 1:4-10, TLB
23. Jeremiah 1:11, NIV
24. Jeremiah 1:12, NIV
25. Jeremiah 33:3, NKJV
26. Psalm 145:18
27. Psalm 86:5
28. Psalm 50:15
29. See Exodus 3:3
30. Matthew 7:7
31. Ezekiel 1:1, NIV
32. Ezekiel 1:28
33. S. Sidlow Baxter, *Explore the Book* (Grand Rapids, Mich.: Zondervan Publishing House, 1960), vol. 4, p. 13.
34. Daniel 1:17
35. Daniel 1:20, NIV
36. Amos 7:14-15, TLB
37. S. Sidlow Baxter, *Explore the Book* (Grand Rapids, Mich.: Zondervan Publishing House, 1960), vol. 4, p. 129.
38. Amos 4:1, TLB
39. Proverbs 29:18

40. To illustrate, see *Leadership Magazine,* Spring 1993, vol. 14, p. 48.
41. Zechariah 1:7-17
42. Zechariah 1:18-21
43. Zechariah 2:1-5
44. Revelation 21:1-3
45. Zechariah 3:1-10
46. Zechariah 4:1-11
47. See Zechariah 4:6
48. Zechariah 5:1-4
49. Zechariah 5:5-11
50. Zechariah 6:1-8
51. Zechariah 1:18-21, TLB
52. Zechariah 3:5, NIV
53. "The burden of the word of the Lord" is a phrase that is used at least fifteen times to convey a word from God. The term is used by Hosea (8:10), Nahum (1:1), Zechariah (9:1; 12:1) and Malachi (1:1). Isaiah used it when he prophesied concerning Babylon (13:1), Moab (15:1), Damascus (17:1), Egypt (19:1), the Desert Sea (21:1), Dumah (21:11), the Valley of Vision (22:1), Tyre (23:1) and the Beasts of the South (30:6). Jeremiah rebuked the false prophets for using the term to validate their deceitful visions (Jer. 23:33-38). The word *burden* means "vision, prophecy, utterance," (Strong's #4853). Information obtained from Quickverse for Windows Version 3.od, (© 1992–1994, Rankin & Parson Technology, Inc. All rights reserved.)

Chapter 6
The Confession of Kings

1. Daniel 2:47, NIV
2. Daniel 2:19, NIV
3. Daniel 2:27-28, NKJV
4. Daniel 5:12
5. Here, on behalf of our nation, the questions must be asked, "Is there no Daniel in the palace of Babylon today?" Oh, sure, there are plenty of "spiritual advisors" tickling the ears of our leaders, but has God a prophet in the palace? Is there a doctor in the house? Evidently not. May God have mercy and forgive us for having a form of godliness but denying its power. Forgive us, Lord, for being

of such petty thought and of such passive spirit that the leaders of our nation see no cause to summon us for counsel in their time of need. Forgive us for stripping the church of its prophetic mantle for our nation, thereby pushing our presidents away from Jesus Christ and into the parlors of palm readers and stargazers! God grant us repentance and renewal in the things of Your Spirit that we may be like Daniel in wisdom and power, and thus surpass with excellence all the wizards of our day. Lord, do it again.

6. See Daniel 2:31-33

7. S. Sidlow Baxter, *Explore the Book* (Grand Rapids, Mich.: Zondervan Publishing House, 1960), vol. 4, p. 79

8. Joshua 1:2, NIV

9. Joshua 3:7, NIV

10. Joshua 5:13-15, NIV

11. "Joshua lifted up his eyes and looked." The word *looked* means "to see a vision." "Ra'ah" — a prim. root; to see, literally or figuratively. Its uses include to advise self, appear, behold, consider, discern, have experience, gaze, perceive, regard, see visions. See James Strong, *The New Strong's Exhaustive Concordance of the Bible* (Nashville, Tenn.: Thomas Nelson Publishers, 1984).

12. See 1 Samuel 16:6-13

13. Psalm 89:19-24, TLB

14. Psalm 139:17-18, NIV

15. George Gilfillan, "The Bards of the Bible," as quoted by Charles Spurgeon in *The Treasury of David: On the Psalms* (Pasadena, Tex.: Pilgrim Publications, 1983), vol. 7, pp. 230-231.

16. Charles Spurgeon, *The Treasury of David: On the Psalms* (Pasadena, Tex.: Pilgrim Publications, 1983), vol. 7, s.v. "Psalm 139," p. 228.

17. Each prophet in David's life had a specific role to play. Here's a listing of those roles. Gad's prophetic role: Guided David away from Saul's persecution (1 Sam. 22:1-5); gave David the choice of three judgments (2 Sam. 24:11-19). Nathan's prophetic role: The house of David will stand forever (2 Sam. 7:1-17); confronted David's sin with Bathsheba (2 Sam. 12:1-7); brought Solomon to the throne (1 Kings 1:11-14). Zadok's prophetic role: Confirmed David when Absalom rebelled (2 Sam. 15:27-28); present at Solomon's anointing as king (1 Kings 1:39).

18. Psalm 16:7, TLB

19. Psalm 17:3, TLB

20. Psalm 63:6, NIV

21. Psalm 119:148, NAS

22. Psalm 17:15, TLB

23. See 1 Chronicles 21:1—22:1

24. 1 Chronicles 21:16

25. 1 Chronicles 22:1, NIV

26. 1 Chronicles 28:11-12, TLB

27. See 1 Kings 3:5

28. 1 Kings 3:6-9, TLB

29. 1 Kings 3:10-13, NIV

30. 1 Kings 3:15, NIV

31. Zechariah 4:1-7, TLB

32. Ralph L. Woods and Herbert Greenhouse, *The New World of Dreams* (New York: MacMillan Publishing Co., 1974), p. 41.

33. Ralph L. Woods, *The World of Dreams* (New York: Random House, 1947), p. 362.

34. *The Concise Columbia Encyclopedia* (Microsoft Bookshelf CD, 1994, licensed from Columbia University Press, © 1989, 1991. All rights reserved.), s.v. "Constantine."

35. The Emperor Galarius, brought to the brink of death by a devastating disease, repented before God and issued an Edict of Toleration for the persecuted Christians. This was the firstfruit of a change in the Roman government toward the church. See *Ante-Nicene Fathers* (Peabody, Maine: Hendrickson Publishers, 1994), vol. 7, p. 314.

36. Morton T. Kelsey, *Dreams: The Dark Speech of the Spirit* (Garden City, New York: Doubleday & Co. Inc., 1968), p. 123 .

37. Quoted by Dr. Mark Rutland in a sermon series entitled "The Middle Ages," presented to the adult Bible class at Calvary Assembly in Orlando, Florida.

38. 1 Corinthians 11:27, NIV

39. Nicene and Post-Nicene Fathers (Peabody, Maine: Hendrickson Publishers, Inc., 1994), vol. 10, 2nd series, pp. 440-455.

40. A paraphrase adapted from Maymie Krythe, *All About Christmas* (New York: Harper & Brothers, 1954).

41. Ralph Woods, *The World of Dreams* (New York: Random House, 1947), pp. 83-86.

42. Ibid.

Chapter 7
Long Time No See

1. See Malachi 4:6
2. Thomas Paine, "The Age of Reason," as quoted in Ralph Woods, *The World of Dreams* (New York: Random House, 1947), p. 160.
3. 1 Thessalonians 5:19, NIV
4. *Ante-Nicene Fathers* (Peabody, Maine: Hendrickson Publishers, 1994), vol. 7, p. 73.
5. Hebrews 1:1-2, NIV
6. See Acts 7:54-60, NKJV, *The Spirit-Filled Life Bible*
7. See Acts 9:1-6, NKJV, *The Spirit-Filled Life Bible*
8. See Acts 9:10-16, NKJV, *The Spirit-Filled Life Bible*
9. Acts 9:17, paraphrase
10. Ephesians 1:18-19, NIV
11. Acts 26:19
12. The following scriptures give documentation of Paul's various experiences with dreams and visions: Acts 7:56 – 8:1; 9:1-16; 14:19; 16:9-10; 18:9-11; 22:18; 27:22-25; 2 Corinthians 12:1-4; Galatians 1:11-12; Ephesians 3:1-5; 2 Timothy 4:16-18.
13. Acts 22:18, NAS
14. Galatians 1:11-12, NIV
15. Ephesians 3:2-5, NIV
16. Acts 13:2, TLB
17. Galatians 2:2, NIV
18. James Strong, *The New Strong's Exhaustive Concordance of the Bible* (Nashville, Tenn.: Thomas Nelson Publishers, 1984), s.v. #602.
19. Luke 2:32, NAS
20. 1 Corinthians 14:6
21. Romans 10:14-15, TLB
22. See Acts 16:6
23. Acts 16:9-10, NIV
24. Acts 18:9-11, NIV
25. Acts 14:19
26. 2 Corinthians 12:1-4, TLB
27. Acts 23:11, NIV
28. Acts 27:22-25, TLB
29. 2 Timothy 4:16-18, TLB

30. Acts 10:10
31. W. E. Vine, Merrill F. Unger and William White, *Vine's Expository Dictionary of Biblical Words* (Nashville, Tenn.: Thomas Nelson Publishers, 1984), s.v. "amaze" and "trance," p. 148.
32. Acts 10:11-15, TLB
33. Acts 10:17-18
34. Acts 10:1-6, TLB
35. Acts 10:19-20, TLB
36. W. E. Vine, Merrill F. Unger and William White, *Vine's Expository Dictionary of Biblical Words* (Nashville, Tenn.: Thomas Nelson Publishers, 1984), s.v. "contend."
37. Acts 10:28-29, TLB
38. Acts 10:44-47
39. Acts 12:6-11, TLB
40. Psalm 126:1-3, NIV
41. 2 Peter 1:16-21

Chapter 8
Two Thousand Years of Dreams and Visions

1. Acts 7:55-56, NIV
2.. Acts 7:57-60, NIV
3. *Ante-Nicene Fathers* (Peabody, Maine: Hendrickson Publishers, 1994), vol. 1, p. 39 (italics added).
4. Matthew 18:2
5. *Ante-Nicene Fathers* (Peabody, Maine: Hendrickson Publishers, 1994), vol. 1, p. 127.
6. Ibid., p. 130.
7. Ibid., p. 131.
8. Ibid., p. 40.
9. Ibid., p. 41.
10. Ibid., p. 42.
11. Ibid., vol. 3, p. 224.
12. Isaiah 45:1-6
13. *Ante-Nicene Fathers* (Peabody, Maine: Hendrickson Publishers, 1994), vol. 3, p. 225.
14. *The Confessions of St. Augustine,* vol. 1 of *Nicene and Post-Nicene Fathers* (Peabody, Maine: Hendrickson Publishers, 1994), 2nd series, vol. 6, pp. 35-36.
15. Ibid., vol. 2, p. V.

16. Ibid., vol. 1, pp. 504-505.
17. Ibid., Letter 159.9.
18. Ibid., Letter 150.3, 4.
19. Ibid., Letter 159.5.
20. R. P. C. Hanson, *The Life and Writings of the Historical Saint Patrick* (New York: Seabury Press, 1983), p. 86, Confession 17.
21. Ibid., p. 92, Confession 21.
22. Ibid., p. 92, Confession 23.
23. Fulton J. Sheen, *The World Book Encyclopedia* (Chicago, Ill.: World Book Publishers, 1969), vol. 15, p. 174
24. R. P. C. Hanson, *The Life and Writings of the Historical Saint Patrick* (New York: Seabury Press, 1983), p. 86, Confession 19.
25. Ibid., Confession 20.
26. Ibid., Confession 24.
27. Ibid., Confession 25.
28. Ibid., Confession 29.
29. Ibid., Confession 45.
30. Earle E. Cairns, *Christianity Through the Centuries* (Grand Rapids, Mich: Academic Books, 1981), p. 237.
31. Ibid.
32. *Great Books of the Western World,* vol. 19 of *Encyclopedia Britannica* (Chicago, Ill.: William Benton Publisher, 1952), p. 5, see Thomas Aquinas.
33. Harold E. B. Speight, *The Author's Apology for His Book From the Life and Writings of John Bunyan* (New York: Harper & Bros., 1928), p. 98.
34. Bunyan's title page of the first edition reads, "The Pilgrim's Progress From This World, to That Which Is to Come: Delivered Under the Similitude of a Dream Wherein Is Discovered, the Manner of His Fretting Out, His Dangerous Journey and Safe Arrival at the Desired Country. 'I have used similitudes' (Hosea 12:10), by John Bunyan."
35. John Newton, *An Autobiography* (Chicago, Ill.: Moody Press, 1983), pp. 27-30.
36. The Wise Tracks gospel pamphlet for Last Days' Ministries, written by Keith Green (1982). He adapted it into modern English from "Who Cares?" by General William Booth.
37. Richard Collier, *The General Next to God* (London, England: Fontana/Collins, 1965).

38. Charles Spurgeon, *Metropolitan Tabernacle Pulpit* (Carlisle, Pa.: The Banner of Truth, 1991), vol. 14, pp. 217-228.
39. As read by David Bryant at a Concert of Prayer for the Promise Keeper's National Pastors' Summit held at Glen Erie, Colorado, February 1995.

Chapter 9
The Dream Lives On

1. James Ryle, *Hippo in the Garden* (Lake Mary, Fla.: Creation House, 1993), p. 12.
2. W. B. Yeats, "He Wishes for the Cloths of Heaven," from *The Collected Poems of W. B. Yeats* (New York: MacMillan Publishers, 1956).
3. See Ephesians 3:16-19
4. Matthew 22:37-40
5. 2 Kings 19:30 and Isaiah 37:31
6. Romans 11:16, NIV
7. Ephesians 2:21
8. Ephesians 4:16, TLB
9. Proverbs 25:11 and Song of Solomon 5:12
10. Romans 15:6, NIV
11. Philippians 1:27-28
12. Romans 6:13-19
13. See Matthew 20:26
14. 1 Timothy 5:17, NAS
15. Hebrews 13:17, NIV
16. Hebrews 6:10, NIV
17. Matthew 5:16
18. See 2 Corinthians 5:17-21
19. Proverbs 11:14
20. Acts 2:2
21. John 3:8, TLB
22. Matthew 5:13-16
23. Isaiah 55:1-2; John 7:37-39; Revelation 22:17
24. Mark 4:34, NIV

Chapter 10
Let's Get Practical

1. John Wesley, "The Resemblance Between Dream and Life," as quoted by Ralph Woods in *The World of Dreams* (New York: Random House, 1947), p. 157.

2. Jeremiah 15:19, NAS

3. Psalm 25:14, KJV

4. John 10:27

5. See Hebrews 12:5; Proverbs 23:22; Matthew 18:10; 1 Thessalonians 5:20

6. W. E. Vine, Merrill F. Unger and William White, *Vine's Expository Dictionary of Biblical Words* (Nashville, Tenn.: Thomas Nelson Publishers, 1984), s.v. "despise." "Exoutheneo" means to make of no account, to regard as nothing, to treat with contempt.

7. *Ante-Nicene Fathers* (Peabody, Maine: Hendrickson Publishers, 1994), vol. 5, pp. 400-402.

8. 2 Timothy 2:15

9. Benedict Pererius in *De Magia — Concerning the Investigation of Dreams,* book 2.

10. 1 Corinthians 2:16

11. 1 Corinthians 13:9

12. Luke 11:9-13, NIV

13. Song of Solomon 5:2, NIV

14. Revelation 3:20, author's paraphrase

15. Daniel 7:1, NIV

16. Proverbs 8:4-6, NIV

17. Thomas Aquinas, "Is Divination Unlawful?," translated by Holt Graham, as quoted by Ralph L. Woods, *The World of Dreams* (New York: Random House, 1947), p. 143.

18. John Wesley, "The Resemblance Between Dream and Life," as quoted by Ralph Woods in *The World of Dreams* (New York: Random House, 1947), p. 157.

19. Benedict Pererius in *De Magia — Concerning the Investigation of Dreams,* book 2.

20. Elizabeth and Dr. Elton Baker, *The UNmedical Book* (Drelwood Publications), p. 68. It should be noted that this bit of information came from a book with a disclaimer for its title: *The UNmedical Book.*

21. John Calvin, "The Operation of a Divine Agency in Dreams," translated by Thomas Myers, as quoted by Ralph Woods in *The World of Dreams* (New York: Random House, 1947), p. 149.
22. Ecclesiastes 5:3, NIV
23. *Ante-Nicene Fathers* (Peabody, Maine: Hendrickson Publishers, 1994), vol. 5, pp. 400-402.
24. James 4:7
25. David Lyle Jeffery, ed., *A Dictionary of Biblical Tradition in English Literature, Dreams and Visions* (Grand Rapids, Mich.: Wm. B. Eerdmans Publishing Company, 1992), pp. 213-216.
26. Genesis 41:16, NIV
27. Daniel 2:30, NIV
28. Philippians 4:6-7, NIV
29. 2 Kings 2:23-25
30. 2 Timothy 2:25-26
31. If you would like, you may send the results of your interpretation to me at the Boulder Valley Vineyard, 7845 Lookout Road, Longmont, CO 80503.

Chapter 11
Now I Lay Me Down to Sleep

1. Lamentations 3:27-28, NIV
2. Psalm 25:4-5, NKJV
3. James Strong, *The New Strong's Exhaustive Concordance of the Bible* (Nashville, Tenn.: Thomas Nelson Publishers, 1984), s.v. "qavah," #6960; a prim. root; to bind together (perh. by twisting), i.e. collect; (fig.) to expect: — gather (together), look, patiently, tarry, wait (for, on, upon).
4. Isaiah 40:31
5. Hebrews 12:27-29
6. Job 16:12
7. Luke 6:47-49
8. 1 Thessalonians 2:4, NIV
9. John 16:13-14, NIV
10. John 10:27-28
11. May I suggest you read my first book, *The Hippo in the Garden* (Lake Mary, FL: Creation House, 1993). It is filled with biblical and practical guidelines for hearing God's voice today.

12. Revelation 3:20
13. Habakkuk 2:1-3, NIV
14. Proverbs 8:34-35, NIV
15. Ezra 6:14, NIV
16. See 2 Corinthians 2:16; 3:5-6
17. James Sexton, "Colors," from an article in *Holman Bible Dictionary for Windows, Version 1.0d* (Parson Technology, 1994).
18. For an example, see when Elijah gave his mantle to Elisha (1 Kings 19:19, 2 Kings 2:14).
19. Acts 2:17-18, TLB
20. Haggai 2:9
21. John 2:10, NIV
22. Isaiah 33:13-17, NIV
23. John 12:21
24. John 14:21, TLB
25. See Job. 31:1
26. James 5:9, NIV
27. Romans 13:11-12, NIV
28. See Acts 2:21
29. "O God of Dreams," by James Ryle, copyright © 1995.

WE'D LIKE TO HEAR FROM YOU.

If you have had a significant dream that has come true
and would like others to know about it,
please send a typed copy with your complete
name and address to:

DREAM

**c/o Boulder Valley Vineyard
Christian Fellowship
7845 Lookout Road
Longmont, CO 80503**

Phone: (303) 449-3330

Fax: (303) 652-3237

You may also contact the church office
for information about other books and tapes
by James Ryle or speaking engagements.

ps. 208   1 visum
2. insomnium
3. somnium
4. visio
5. oraculum — counselor, wisdom, guidance

IF YOU ENJOYED *A DREAM COME TRUE,*
YOU WILL ALSO ENJOY ANOTHER GREAT BOOK
BY JAMES RYLE:

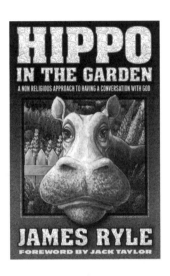

"God can speak to us at unusual times in unexpected places,"
says author James Ryle. Through his humorous
personal anecdotes and Scripture, you will discover
that every circumstance of life becomes
an opportunity to converse with God.

Available at your local Christian bookstore or from:

Creation House
600 Rinehart Road
Lake Mary, FL 32746
1-800-283-8494

Dreams   Brent Lively

1989 vision that I was called to Pastor → and woken from sleep met Satan - tried to choke me + I rebuked him.

1987 — JESUS standing by Shore with back to the North waving hand to follow him

1991 Dream fulfilled trip to Israel - while ill and alone on S side of Galilee - Jesus appeared in a vision behind me and said, You are exactly where I called you and gave me a vision of dream I had in 1987 where I was standing in exact place. This was a time of confirmation for me that I had been obedient and was exactly where Christ wanted me to be.

1985 Sitting in a church late evening outside of Florence, Italy, God spoke to me through the vision.

1995 November

Charda dreams that a foot falls
out of my Bible with a name tag — Laura Wilson
we were baffled a couple of days until the
Lord gave me the interpretation — that we
were to pray for this person — one month
later Friends traveling from west Texas visited
and we told them story — and it was their
Sister - she was walking away from the church.

— a ~~couple of weeks~~ week after Charda's dream I had
a dream and God spoke to me audibly and said
Ezekiel 13:5 — Several times. I awoke and
went straight to the Bible — it was Intercession —
This came after a long search as to how I would serve
God during a 1 yr. sabbatical.

Once I dreamed that I met a famous violinist
In my high school years.   Eugene FodoR!

'95 - October - ~~I was~~ dreamed that Chanda was
pregnant and had twins - And I missed
Seeing them born.